THEATRE of WAR in EUROPE

WINSTON CHURCHILL:
THE VALIANT YEARS

WINSTON CHURCHILL: THE VALIANT YEARS

By Jack Le Vien and John Lord

MAPS BY LIAM DUNNE

PUBLISHED BY
BERNARD GEIS ASSOCIATES
DISTRIBUTED BY RANDOM HOUSE

Manufactured in the United States of America

ACKNOWLEDGMENTS

Our deepest appreciation is expressed to Winston S. Churchill, who inspired this history of The Second World War. Without his leadership at a time of great crisis for mankind, it would have been impossible to publish this book or any other expression of free opinion.

The authors wish to acknowledge the editorial assistance of Len Giovannitti, as well as the cooperation of Solomon Granett, Burton Litwin, Jonathan Stern, and Caroline Cole Harloff. We also acknowledge the kind cooperation of Houghton Mifflin Company in granting permission for the use of excerpts from *The Second World War* by Winston S. Churchill.

—JACK LE VIEN and JOHN LORD

Grateful acknowledgment is hereby made to the following publishers for their kind permission to reprint the materials specified:

George Allen & Unwin, Ltd.: selection from *Voices from Britain*, edited by Henning Krabbe.

Chatto & Windus: selection from *Wing Leader* by J. E. Johnson (published in the United States by Ballantine Books, Inc.).

William Collins Sons & Co., Ltd.: selections from *The Turn of the Tide, 1939-1943: A Study Based on the Diaries and Autobiographical Notes of Field Marshal the Viscount Alanbrooke* by Sir Arthur Bryant (published in the United States by Doubleday & Company, Inc.); selections from *Triumph in the West, 1943-1946: Based on the Diaries and Autobiographical Notes of Field Marshal the Viscount Alanbrooke* by Sir Arthur Bryant (published in the United States by Doubleday & Company, Inc.); selection from *Bomber Offensive* by Marshal of the R.A.F. Sir Arthur Harris; selections from *So Few Got Through* by Martin Lindsay; and selections from *The Memoirs of Field Marshal the Viscount Montgomery of Alamein* by Bernard Law Montgomery (published in the United States by The World Publishing Company).

The Cresset Press: selection from *The Fuel of the Fire* by Douglas Grant.

Doubleday & Company, Inc. and The Fireside Press: selection from *The Goebbels Diaries: 1942-1943*, edited by Louis P. Lochner.

Harper & Brothers: selections from *Soldier: The Memoirs of Matthew B. Ridgway* by Matthew B. Ridgway and H. H. Martin, and selection from *The Time for Decision* by Sumner Welles (published in Great Britain by Hamish Hamilton Ltd.).

Houghton Mifflin Company: selections from *War As I Knew It* by George S. Patton, Jr. (published in Great Britain by W. H. Allen & Company).

Hutchinson & Company (Publishers) Ltd.: selection from *Daedalus Returned: Crete 1941* by Baron von der Heydte, translated by W. Stanley Moss; and selection from *The Only Way Out* by R. M. Wingfield.

William Kimber & Co., Ltd.: selection from *Convoy Commodore* by Admiral Sir K. Creighton; selection from *Escort* by Commander D. A. Rayner; and selection from *The Desert Generals* by Correlli Barnett (published in the United States by The Viking Press, Inc.).

Methuen & Co., Ltd.: selections from *The First and the Last* by Adolf Galland (published in the United States by Holt, Rinehart & Winston, Inc.).

Odhams Press, Ltd.: selection from *Hausfrau at War: A German Woman's Account of Life in Hitler's Reich* by Else Wendel with Eileen Winncroft.

To the Valiant Men,
Living and Dead,
Who Earned the Victory

CONTENTS

8]   CONTENTS

LIST OF MAPS

WINSTON CHURCHILL:
THE VALIANT YEARS

A PRETEXT
FOR WAR

I canna see the target
I canna see the target
I canna see the target,
It's o'er far away.
SONG OF THE HIGHLAND DIVISION

As THE cool luminous dawn of autumn rises over the eastern frontier of Germany it picks out the stark steel sinews of a radio mast, barely inside the German boundary. A few cows ramble heavily about the pastures, their breath steaming as they bend to crop the dewy grass. A faint mist outlines the shape of hedgerows and trees. Over all there is a pastoral stillness, but a stillness that carries a sinister air.

At the foot of the mast, grouped haphazardly and sprawling awkwardly as if caught up and scattered by some sudden appalling gale, lie twelve bodies. Their uniforms are cold with morning damp, their limbs stiffened. Each has died of multiple wounds. Each is dressed like a Polish infantryman. They provide a pretext for war.

Soon the exultant Gestapo will shepherd a party of foreign

newspapermen to the site, allow them to gaze, offer them facilities for sending off cables, return them to Berlin. If the newspapermen were given time they would quickly see that things are not as they appear. None of the weapons beside the bodies is loaded. Each man has been shot in the back. The whole thing is an inhuman fraud.

The previous afternoon twelve criminals have been taken in closed vans from a concentration camp, dressed in captured uniforms and driven to this quiet field near Gleiwitz. Blinking at the light as they tumble out they are surprised to see the lane blocked at both ends by SS troops squatting behind medium machine guns. Weapons are thrust into their hands and they are told to line up facing the steel mast. It is all a propaganda matter, the smiling Gestapo explain. They are to pretend to attack the radio station while a film is made. See—there are the cameras! Puzzled, docile, they lumber across the grass. A sudden clamor scythes them down. They are known, with a perverted appropriateness, by the code name CANNED GOODS.

Beyond them to the east, four German armies are systematically annihilating everything in their path. In the ears of every soldier ring the parting words of the Fuehrer: "I expect every soldier to be conscious of the high tradition of the eternal German soldierly qualities and to do his duty to the last. Remember always and in any circumstances that you are the representatives of National Socialist Greater Germany." It is 1 September 1939 and *Fall Weiss* is going according to plan, as Hitler felt confident it would when with a fat red pencil he added to his Directive Number 1 for the Conduct of the War "Time of attack—0445 hours." The glorious representatives of National Socialist Greater Germany storm eastward, conscious of their high calling. In their wake, villages smolder, Polish children scream beside the black-

The WAR BEGINS

At dawn on September 1, 1939, motorized armies of Nazi Germany launch "Fall Weiss," the long-planned invasion of Poland. September 3, Great Britain and France declare war on Germany. Poland is easily conquered. For six months there is a "twilight war" as both sides prepare their positions. On April 9, 1940, Germany invades Denmark and Norway. The Allies quickly engage the Germans by sea at Narvik, on land at Namsos and Trondheim.

ened bodies of their mothers. Theirs is a bitter and a brutal ambassadorship.

Striking for the heart, the *Luftwaffe's* heavy bombers swarm over Warsaw. Without fighters, without artillery, the city is spread-eagled like a sacrificial victim. Her destruction is a mere academic exercise, a mathematical question only of how quickly the requisite number of bombs can be carried from airfield to target and unloaded. For Warsaw, where the gentle heart of Chopin lies enshrined, there is only the appalling music of death.

Easily, efficiently, the Germans harrow Poland with fire and steel. Not yet fully mobilized, their armies caught off balance, their obsolete planes smashed on their airfields, the Poles fight with suicidal gallantry. Their cavalrymen charge with lance and saber against the tempered steel of panzers: the chivalry of the Middle Ages meets the mechanization of the twentieth century and gallantry alone proves futile.

Oblivious of the carnage, the English are enjoying an English weekend. The most famous fortuneteller in the land has read the stars and their welcome message is "No War This Year." Across England on this sparkling morning comfortable families digest their fat Sunday newspapers and their toast and marmalade and hope for the best. It is such a beautiful day for the time of year.

They are enjoying the last few moments of a world they will never see again. At ten o'clock the wireless says, "Stand by for an announcement of national importance." Every fifteen minutes people are warned that the Prime Minister will speak to the nation at eleven-fifteen. In the meantime there is light but decorous music. At eleven-fourteen a lady with a highly educated voice is giving a talk on "How to Make the

Most of Tinned Foods: Some Useful Recipes" when the air goes dead.

She is replaced by a thin, pedantic voice that sounds unutterably sad, mortally tired. It is Neville Chamberlain. Patiently he explains that his diplomacy has failed, that the country is already at war. "The situation in which no word given by Germany's ruler could be trusted, and no people or country could feel themselves safe, has become intolerable. And now that we have resolved to finish it, I know that you will all play your part with calmness and courage. At such a moment as this the assurances of support that we have received from the Empire are a source of profound encouragement to us. Now may God bless you all. May He defend the right. It is the evil things that we shall be fighting against—brute force, bad faith, injustice, oppression, and persecution—and against them I am certain that the right will prevail."

One man among his audience is not a bit surprised. For years Winston Spencer Churchill has been a prophet without honor in his own country, and now he has been proved right. He switches off the radio, and at that moment is dramatically vindicated. Wailing with a hideous urgency the air-raid sirens start up all over London. With all the panache of a seasoned warrior Churchill ushers his wife up to the flat roof of their town house. Fat silver barrage balloons are rising like ghostly whales all around them. They survey the miles of rooftops, the bustling target of a vast metropolis.

After a while, heeding their duty, they make their way down to a shelter, "armed with a bottle of brandy and other appropriate medical comforts." Below there broods a frightened stillness. *As I gazed from the doorway along the empty street*, Churchill remembers, *my imagination drew pictures of ruin and carnage and vast explosions shaking the ground, of buildings clattering down in dust and rubble, of fire*

*brigades and ambulances scurrying through the smoke, be-
neath the drone of hostile airplanes.* Despite his premoni-
tion, however, no hostile airplanes appear and Churchill goes
over to the House of Commons and sits quietly in his place,
filled with a strange exhilaration. The benches about him
have for years been deaf to his voice; now, at last, they will
hear him. Now they will acknowledge that he was right all
the time.

For Churchill the middle decade of his life has been the
years that the locusts have eaten. A firebrand, unorthodox,
unpopular for his favorite themes of India and Germany, he
is spurned by his Party and feared by the people. He exists
in a political wilderness: *I earned my livelihood by dictating
articles which had a wide circulation, not only in Great Britain and the United States, but also, before Hitler's shadow
fell upon them, in the most famous newspapers of sixteen
European countries. I lived in fact from mouth to hand . . .
I meditated constantly upon the European situation and the
rearming of Germany. I lived mainly at Chartwell, where I
had much to amuse me. I built with my own hands a large
part of two cottages and extensive kitchen-garden walls, and
made all kinds of rockeries and waterworks and a large
swimming-pool which was filtered to limpidity and could be
heated to supplement our fickle sunshine. Thus I never had
a dull or idle moment from morning till midnight, and with
my happy family around me dwelt at peace within my hab-
itation.*

But as he writes in his neat, small hand, standing at his
desk in the mullioned study of Chartwell, or as he relaxes
in the comfortable sun of a Kentish spring, when the blossoms cream and froth in every orchard, Churchill stays constantly on guard, with his eyes on Europe. He has been one

of the first to read the Nazi gospel, penned in Landsberg jail, the odious *Mein Kampf.* Its aggressive, unbalanced philosophy spells only one thing. When Hitler, triumphant after his years of struggle, speaks to the first meeting of the Reichstag of the Third Reich on 21 March 1933 Churchill can predict the outcome: *Adolf Hitler had at last arrived; but he was not alone. He had called from the depths of defeat the dark and savage furies latent in the most numerous, most serviceable, ruthless, contradictory, and ill-starred race in Europe. He had conjured up the fearful idol of an all-devouring Moloch, of which he was the priest and incarnation.*

No one will listen. The people of Britain have graver problems than a German fanatic, and those problems are closer to home. Like the rest of the world she is suffering a depression that is sending her unemployed by the hundreds of thousands to the pitiful lines that wait for charity outside drab offices in every town in the land. Poverty and want lay waste men's souls.

Some have been out of work for months, idling their empty days away standing on street corners. They do not talk, for there is nothing to discuss but unemployment. A few have not worked for years, and these men are as good as dead. Even those who still have worked stand at their lathes and presses with aching hearts, for who knows when the factory will close and throw them, too, on the rubbish heap?

Thus directed inwardly, the vision of the British does not distinguish the ominous movements in Europe. Hitler's National Socialist Party has been raised to power by funds from German industrialists, but it has won its security with its own strong right arm. By the spring of 1934 this force—the brown-shirted *Sturmabteilung,* the SA—has reached a total of almost three million men. Hitler has now gained the confidence of the Army, and with Himmler has built up an even deadlier security force, the black SS. He no longer needs the

SA, and is growing apprehensive of its strength. On the night
of 30 June 1934 he strikes. All that "Night of the Long
Knives" his SS execution squads kill and torture until every
possible threat to the Fuehrer has been extinguished in a
welter of blood.

This massacre, Churchill observes, *however explicable by
the hideous forces at work, showed that the new Master of
Germany would stop at nothing, and that conditions in Germany bore no resemblance to those of a civilized state.*

Sadly Churchill stands on the sidelines of history while
his country is betrayed, waiting for the next maneuver from
the Fuehrer. By now Hitler has broken the power of that
military caste whom once he wooed. He uses a personal
scandal to dispose of the clique of generals ruling the
Reichswehr and himself assumes supreme command and sets
up the *Oberkommando der Wehrmacht,* the OKW, an instrument with which he will later control the armed forces
of Germany in war. Every member of those forces must
swear an oath of loyalty not to Germany, but to Adolf Hitler.
He must solemnly declare, "I swear before God to give my
unconditional obedience to Adolf Hitler, Fuehrer of the
Reich of the German People, Supreme Commander of the
Wehrmacht, and I pledge my word as a brave soldier to
observe this oath always, even at peril of my life."

The gray troops of a resurgent Germany crumble frontier
after frontier, without let or hindrance. In the fall of 1938
the pathetic history of appeasement reaches its tawdry climax at Munich, where Hitler gives shameful audience to
Prime Minister Neville Chamberlain.

On his return to Horton aerodrome, Chamberlain waves
a joint declaration he and Hitler have signed that expresses
their common desire never to go to war. He waves it again
from the windows of 10 Downing Street as crowds below him
weep with relief. In his precise way he assures them, "This

is the second time there has come back from Germany to
Downing Street peace with honor. I believe it is peace in
our time." Next day Czechoslovakia disappears into the German maw.

In the House of Commons Churchill speaks her epitaph.
*All is over. Silent, mournful, abandoned, broken, Czecho-
slovakia recedes into the darkness.* He goes on with yet
another warning. *And do not suppose that this is the end.
This is only the beginning of the reckoning. This is only the
first sip, the first foretaste of a bitter cup which will be
proffered to us year by year unless, by a supreme recovery
of moral health and martial vigour, we arise again and take
our stand for freedom as in the olden time.*

When Hitler turns to the East, concludes a cynical pact
with Russia, and picks a quarrel over the free port of Danzig
with the Poles, Churchill knows that the crisis is almost at
hand. *If you will not fight for the right when you can easily
win without bloodshed; if you will not fight when your victory will be sure and not too costly, you may come to the
moment when you will have to fight with all the odds against
you and only a precarious chance of survival. There may
even be a worse case. You may have to fight when there is
no hope of victory, because it is better to perish than to live
as slaves.*

Now that time has come, ironically enough in a season of
warmth and gentle weather. For on this first day of War
London is flooded with the softness of an Indian Summer.
In the decent gloom of the debating chamber Churchill
savors the echoes of his many warnings that now—perhaps
too late—may be recognized as truth. Now Chance is king
and all rests upon the hazard. Now the testing time is come.
Of all men present in that ancient hall Churchill knows him-

self the one most fitted to endure the fire. That night he is
made First Lord of the Admiralty.

He goes to work at once. Captain Pim, an officer of
the Naval Reserve, is one of the first to meet him: "I was
ordered to report to the First Sea Lord, Admiral Sir Dudley
Pound. Sir Dudley told me three things. 'First,' he said, 'Mr.
Churchill is back with us. Secondly, he wants the War Room
as he had it in the First World War established in Admiralty
House. Thirdly,' he said, 'you've been selected to run this
War Room. Better go along and look at Admiralty House!'
So I went along to Admiralty House, to the library, a very
lovely room looking out onto the Horse Guards Parade, and
there I saw Mr. Churchill standing. He said, 'Who are you?'
I told him who I was. 'I've been ordered to look after your
War Room.' He said, 'Right! Get to the other end of this
carpet and we'll roll it up together.'"

Across the cold northern waters of Scapa Flow where the
massive battle squadrons of the Home Fleet ride at their war
stations the Aldis lamps and semaphores flash the message
WINSTON'S BACK! In the new impregnable harbor of Singapore, on the choppy tide-races of the Channel where lean
destroyers prowl day and night, from the barren rocks of
Aden to the icy cliffs of Newfoundland the signal flags flutter
and the sailors grin. The old war horse is back.

In his wood-paneled office Churchill fondly draws out
the great charts of the North Sea and the Western Approaches that have lain in the same drawer since he was
First Lord in another war, a quarter of a century before. All
the old problems, all the old fears and dangers flood back to
him. His old chair creaks under his weight as, settling back
in it, he remembers the past, probes the future. Already he
is immersed in the war at sea.

Already things have begun to go wrong. Off the Irish
coast, bound for the United States, the liner *Athenia* is am-

bushed by a U-boat. One hundred and twelve of her passengers are drowned, among them twenty-eight Americans. One of the survivors, a woman, sobs out her story to her rescuers. "The torpedo struck . . . everything went in darkness and nearly choked me with the fumes from it. I screamed for my husband and stayed where I was so he could find me. He found me and took me up to the deck and found me a boat to get in, and the last I saw of him he was standing on the rail watching me go down. I didn't know whether he was dead or alive for two days until just recently I found he was picked up in Ireland. It was a horrible tragedy . . . everybody getting killed . . . and the boats capsizing . . . I can't go on."

A worse blow is imminent. Caught in the tumultuous currents of the Pentland Firth, another U-boat is swept helplessly westward and into a staggering discovery. There is a way to penetrate the defenses of the Home Fleet! In Wilhelmshaven the German U-boat captains perfect a plan. Shortly after midnight, 13 October 1939, Leutnant Gunther Prien notes in the log of U-47, "We are in Scapa Flow!"

Cautiously he seeks out his target by the light of the moon. "Two battleships are lying there at anchor, and further inshore, destroyers. Cruisers not visible; therefore attack on the big fellows." Almost surfaced, Prien closes to three thousand yards. There is the hiss of compressed air from his forward tubes, and three faintly luminous streaks cut through the water. U-47 wheels, fires her stern tubes. Riding softly at anchor the battleship *Royal Oak* is obscured by a wall of white spray. Ripped open from stem to stern, she sinks in two minutes. Quietly Prien steals away, noting thoughtfully, "The torpedo misses I explain as due to faults of course, speed and drift. In tube 4, a misfire. The crew behaved splendidly throughout the operation."

When the news is flashed to the Admiralty, Churchill

suffers a moment of blind despair. First *Athenia,* then the aircraft carrier *Courageous,* now *Royal Oak.* What next? He looks at the craggy face of the First Sea Lord and turns back to his plans. Nothing is to be gained by giving way to doubt; what counts is foresight, resolution, calculation. He glances at the dispositions in the Atlantic.

The German pocket battleship *Admiral Graf Spee* was already at sea when war was declared. Heavily gunned, fast, designed as a commerce raider, she has been roaming the sea lanes of the Atlantic, picking off fat merchant vessels with ridiculous ease. Kapitan zur See Hans Langsdorff claims 50,089 tons of shipping sunk without cost.

But he has taken his last prize. On 13 December he is caught off the River Plate by three light cruisers. Outranged and outgunned, they cling to him like bulldogs, and after three days of a running fight he is glad to claw his way into Montevideo Harbor. The Government of Uruguay allows him seventy-two hours to bury his dead, put his wounded ashore and make his ship seaworthy. It is not enough.

Still faced by the battered cruisers prowling across his escape route, believing that British heavy ships have come up within range, Langsdorff limps out into the Montevideo roads. The British ships clear for action. But, as the shadow of a spotting aircraft crosses her bridge, the center of the *Graf Spee* dissolves in smoke and a huge tongue of flame leaps high above her mast. The cruisers on the horizon see a great yellow flash as her magazine explodes. The *Graf Spee* had committed suicide. Later, when Langsdorff learned how he had been tricked into scuttling his ship by faked reports of superior forces, he took his own life.

A small matter remains. Where are the merchant seamen taken by the *Graf Spee?* They have been committed to the prison ship *Altmark.* She is still at sea and the word goes out that she must be found.

Weeks later she is discovered in Josing Fjord in neutral Norway. A force of destroyers under Captain Vian of the *Cossack* blocks her escape. Churchill orders: "Board *Altmark*, liberate the prisoners, take possession of the vessel. . . ." Disregarding Norway's tender neutrality, Vian sails in. "*Cossack* forced her way past the torpedo boats and ran alongside the *Altmark*, which was under weigh, and attempting to ram, ran aground. In doing so the boarding party jumped across. Four Germans were killed, five wounded. The remainder of the crew surrendered, except for a few who decamped across the ice. Then came the cry, 'The Navy's here!' In battened-down storage and oil tanks 299 British prisoners were found." The Germans later erect a plaque on the spot. It reads: "Here, on 16 February 1940, the *Altmark* was overcome by British sea-pirates."

That night Churchill is dining in state at the Guildhall with the Lord Mayor of London. Beaming above the gold plate he rises to answer a toast with an exuberant speech hailing the victory. *This brilliant sea fight takes its place in our naval annals and I may add that in our dark, cold winter it warms the cockles of the British heart.*

But it is a small ray of warmth indeed. Churchill's sea captains are aggressive enough, but elsewhere the story is one of delay, hesitation, inadequacy. British bombers are forbidden to attack targets on land for fear of reprisals. *Good, decent, civilized people,* it appears to the frustrated Churchill, *must never strike themselves until after they have been struck dead. On the one side, "Don't be unkind to the enemy, you will only make him angry." On the other, doom preparing. . . .*

The RAF can only take on warships, and only by day. This proves so costly that they are finally limited, as Air Vice

Marshal Harris laments, "to the questionable employment of dropping pamphlets all over Europe, a game in which we never had the slightest faith. My personal view is that the only thing achieved was largely to supply the Continent's requirements of toilet paper for the five long years of war." On land the British Expeditionary Force digs in along the northeastern frontier of France and sings, unconscious of its irony, "We're Gonna Hang Out the Washing on the Siegfried Line" through the tedious winter of the phony war.

For the Allies: illusion, sloth, incompetence. For Hitler: an unholy crusade, conceived in hatred and executed with fanaticism. He tells Sumner Welles: "The German people today are united as one man . . . I can see no hope for the establishment of any lasting peace until the will of England and France to destroy Germany is itself destroyed. I feel that there is no way by which the will to destroy Germany can itself be destroyed except through a complete German victory. I believe that German might is such as to make the triumph of Germany inevitable, but, if not, we will all go down together. Whether that be for better or for worse." For Germany: one folk, one Reich, one Fuehrer. For the Allies: the cumbrous processes of democracy, the secure politeness of decision by committee.

Churchill cries in anguish, *I see such immense walls of prevention, all built and building, that I wonder whether any plan will have a chance of climbing over them.* His teeming imagination turns out plenty of plans. They die of strangulation by red tape.

For months the Germans have been shipping iron ore from northern Norway through the Leads—a sea lane between the coast of Norway and a string of offshore islands. Without the ore the munitions plants of the Ruhr will die. To Churchill the answer is simple: mine the Leads. But the Leads are Norwegian territorial waters, and Norway is neutral. The

Cabinet is shocked. Unabashed, Churchill seeks to do good by stealth. *Now that we are not allowed to interfere with the Norwegian Corridor,* he inquires privately of his right-hand man, the First Sea Lord, Admiral Sir Dudley Pound, *would it not be possible to have one or two merchant ships of sufficient speed specially strengthened in the bows and if possible equipped with a ram? These vessels would carry merchandise and travel up the Leads looking for German ore-ships or any other German merchant vessels, and then ram them by accident. . . .* But ingenuity and enthusiasm strike no spark in his colleagues.

Twelve times Churchill presents his original plan to the War Cabinet. Finally it is accepted, though reluctantly. On the night of 7 April 1940 the stubby mine layers, screened by a powerful task force, set off to close the Leads with a barrier of high explosives. They are detected by the wireless officer of the *Scharnhorst*. His captain staggers at the news. "What!" he cries. "Have they got the same idea as we?"

The *Scharnhorst* is escorting an invasion convoy destined for Narvik. All over Norway the vital ports are falling into German hands. Peaceable-looking merchant ships suddenly disgorge jack-booted infantry. Into Norwegian airfields drone long gaggles of troop carriers. *Operation Weser* is a walk-over. Boldly conceived, planned in exquisite detail, ruthlessly prosecuted, the operation owes at least part of its success to a unique piece of treachery. Each prong of the invasion is spearheaded by a party of "Wandervogels." These are Austrians who, as children, had been adopted by Norwegian families to rescue them from the famine and depression in their own country. Thus, generously fed, clothed and educated, they return an act of love with vile betrayal. More cankerous still are the actions of a man whose name will become synonymous with "traitor": Major Vidkun Quisling has prepared for this very moment a network of agents, saboteurs and turncoats who are delighted to sell their own country.

Once more the Allies have been outthought and outgen-eraled. Painstakingly they set about compensating for the inadequacy of their leadership and the ostrich policy of the thirties with slow and costly effort. Forlorn expeditions are dispatched to fight for Narvik and Trondheim.

Once more only the Navy is really effective. The tall cliffs of the fjords begin to echo to the thunder of its broadsides. By the end of June, so punishing is its offensive, all that is left of the German fleet is one eight-inch gun cruiser, two light cruisers and four destroyers.

On land there is failure. Units of the Chasseurs Alpins cannot maneuver in open country because they have no straps for their skis. Floundering about in snow far deeper than they have ever seen before, the British troops are green and unenthusiastic. An attack by a crack unit of the Guards is repulsed with relative ease by a body of tough young Nazi storm troopers. Cold, baffled and subdued, the Allies begin to withdraw. The retreat shadows a larger catastrophe.

Already undermined, Chamberlain's leadership is savagely attacked in full debate in the House of Commons. Churchill, as a member of the War Cabinet, feels bound to stand by his Prime Minister, but only blood will satisfy the angry members. Leopold Amery catches the Speaker's eye. As he rises the House is in babel, but his clear voice rings out in denunciation, echoing Cromwell's historic dismissal of an older government: "You have sat too long here for any good you have been doing. Depart, I say, and let us have done with you. In the name of God, go!" The Opposition press home their advantage and by the end of the second day of debate Chamberlain tells Churchill privately that he feels a National Government should be formed.

Chamberlain spends the next day trying to achieve this

aim. But the Labor Party will have none of him. In less than twenty-four hours, in any case, the whole question will be proved academic. For along the whole western frontier of Germany, waiting for the dawn, is poised the mightiest army seen thus far in the world's long history.

At eleven o'clock on the morning of 10 May Churchill is summoned to 10 Downing Street. Quietly Chamberlain admits at last that he must resign; the only question remaining is whom he shall advise the King to send for in his place. The choice falls between Halifax and Churchill. Facing the inevitable, Halifax defers in Churchill's favor. Quite against his custom Churchill remains unusually silent during most of the discussion.

At six o'clock Churchill is called to Buckingham Palace. George VI, by the Grace of God King, Emperor and Defender of the Faith, is in a joking vein. His eyes twinkling, he asks Churchill, "I suppose you don't know why I have sent for you?" Churchill catches his sovereign's mood and answers, "Sir, I simply couldn't imagine why!" His Majesty laughs. "I want to ask you to form a Government."

In the crowded moments of this great political crisis, Churchill has felt no unusual excitement, but that night, as he climbs into bed at 3 A.M., a profound sense of relief flows over him. His inheritance is chaos, but at last, at long last, he is master. *I felt as if I were walking with Destiny, and that all my past life had been but a preparation for this hour and for this trial. . . . I thought I knew a good deal about it all, and I was sure I should not fail. Therefore, although impatient for the morning, I slept soundly and had no need for cheering dreams. Facts are better than dreams.*

REAP THE WHIRLWIND

*. . . he that commands the sea is at great
liberty and may take as much or as little
of the war as he will, whereas those that
be strongest by land are many times
nevertheless in great straits.*

SIR FRANCIS BACON

HIGH ON Vimy Ridge the twin wings of the Canadian Memorial soar into a pink sunset, staring blindly across the flat plains of Flanders. From the Menin Gate rise the sad notes of the Last Post, floating through the still air as they have done every evening for twenty years in memory of the thousands upon thousands of dead who now lie neatly rank on rank in the cemeteries that checker the old, now gentle battlefields.

Wooden-wheeled carts trundle over the paving from their day's labor in the fields, down avenues of poplars as stiff as toy soldiers. Blue-smocked, hunched on their bumping carts, the farmers work under the threat of a war that never comes. This last winter has been the bitterest in living memory, but now spring is here and their pastures will be green again,

29

and in summer will come the blood-red poppies. But spring is also the start of the campaigning season.

France has two million men under arms. Many of them wait deep beneath tons of concrete in the mightiest defensive line ever conceived. The Maginot Line is impregnable, but it peters out two hundred miles from the sea, and these are the fatal miles, for they measure the ground over which France's enemies have marched in the past to invade her. Across them four French armies lie grouped, one to the left of the British Expeditionary Force, three to the right.

In front of these armies lies Belgium, in a state of armed neutrality so strict that she interns any roistering soldiers who wander across her border in search of an evening's sport. Beyond stretch the flat miles of Holland. The Dutch are stolidly prepared to flood their defense lines and render them impassable. The scene is set in the cockpit of Europe, but the combatants have not yet appeared. It is 9 May 1940, the ninth month of the Twilight War.

Through the gathering dusk of Germany a special train roars toward the hills south of Cologne. The antagonist is about to enter. As the train puffs into a little hamlet perched high on a hillside, Adolf Hitler laughs with his generals, steps out and enters his new *Fuehrerhauptquartier*, called, in the Wagnerian manner, *Felsennest*—the Eyrie. Set in a thin clump of scrubby trees, the headquarters is dug deep into the rock. Hitler calls his generals around the maps; there will be no sleep for Germans tonight.

Three hundred miles away, in the quiet of his Admiralty office, Churchill works steadily into the night at a mass of papers. His day has been spent at 10 Downing Street in fruitless negotiation. Neville Chamberlain, the reins of power slipping from his ineffective hands, has been trying desperately to form a coalition government. As he plows through the piles of dispatches, Churchill knows that for him the

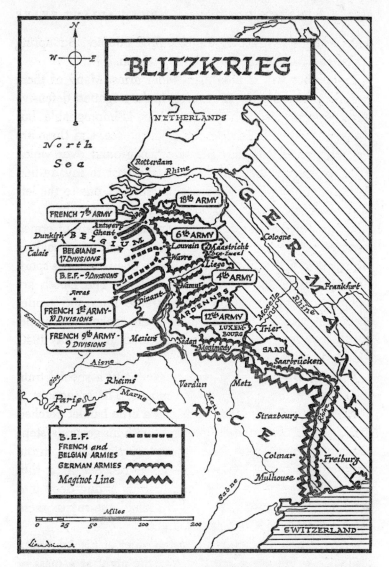

On May 10, 1940, the Germans invade Holland, Belgium and Luxembourg, by-pass the Maginot Line and strike toward France from the north. The blitzkrieg devours the Low Countries. As the Allies are forced to withdraw, the British Expeditionary Force is trapped on the Belgian coast. Under siege, the Allies evacuate over 300,000 troops in eight days at Dunkirk.

next day will be a day of decision. He has no time to reflect that it may also be a day of decision for millions in the Low Countries now innocently asleep. His thick shoulders hunch, the bright eyes scan line after line, the strong fingers make neat, incisive notes, the colossal will power surges on and on.

It is a hot, sticky night. Brigadier Sir John Smyth, commanding a brigade in the British Expeditionary Force, cannot sleep. "I lay awake and sweating in the enormous double bed in my huge bedroom and looked out across the beautiful grounds of the palatial and conspicuous château to the ridge where the concrete pillboxes of the defense line stood sharply etched against the night sky." It seems to the Brigadier, trained to fight and tuned to war, that the British are sitting on the edge of a volcano. It is just as well that he cannot see as far as the German frontier, for there the ground swarms with troops and the hot air is charged with menace.

All along the German border, for 180 miles, the last preparations are being made. Generals issue their final orders and fold their maps. Paratroops grouped on the dark perimeters of airfields file into their angular Junker transports. Tank commanders lagered in the sandy pinewoods opposite Eindhoven check the ammunition racks of their armored turrets. Infantry regiments shoulder their rifles and light machine guns and swing forward along quiet roads. Black-uniformed, dapper Gestapo officers pocket their lists of those about to be liquidated and load their automatics. In all ears ring the fanatic words of their Fuehrer: "The fighting beginning today decides the fate of the German nation for the next thousand years. . . ." Western Europe is about to pay in blood for its sins of omission.

At 2 A.M. Brigadier Smyth dozes off in his oppressive bed, "dreaming fitfully and uneasily of noise and confusion. About an hour later I was awakened by the sound of bombs and the hum of large numbers of aircraft. This was *it*."

A small party of German paratroops is at that moment floating down smack on top of the great brooding fortress of Eben Emael, cornerstone of the Belgian defense. Too late the Dutch flood their forward areas as an avalanche of fire and steel breaks across their frontier posts. *Fall Gelb*, Plan Yellow, has started. Its aim is the total destruction of the Allied armies in the West.

To the north, von Bock's Army Group B of twenty-eight divisions smashes toward Brussels, three armored divisions and one motorized division at its steel tip. But the main weight of the armor is concentrated in the south, where von Rundstedt's Army Group A of forty-four divisions, seven of them armored and three motorized, races toward the Ardennes, dismissed by the Allied staffs as impassable to tanks. Forming a column a hundred miles long, three thousand armored vehicles, a third of them heavy tanks, crash over the wooded ridges and pour toward the Meuse. The scream of Stukas and strafing fighters heralds their approach. In front of them the roads are clogged with hysterical refugees, swept from time to time by a mortal hail of machine-gun fire. Their advance is directed right at the hinge on which the Allied armies must turn when they move forward to support the Belgians. The hinge is composed of second-class troops.

Blooded in the savage annihilation of Poland, the Germans press home their attack with devastating fury. Holland and Belgium scream in the agony of complete surprise and the Anglo-French armies lumber forward to deploy in the open against a moving wall of steel.

To the south, Rundstedt's forward troops, among them Rommel's 7th Panzer Division, are slashing through the French cavalry in front of the Meuse. Next morning Rommel finds time to write to his wife, Lu, ". . . Everything wonderful so far. Am way ahead of my neighbors. I'm completely hoarse from orders and shouting." In two days his drive carries his division forward to the river.

As Rommel's engineers are hastily throwing across their bridges, virtually unopposed, wave after wave of German bombers are heading for Rotterdam. The later squadrons have no need for navigation, for in minutes the blue summer sky above the city is blotted out by dense climbing black columns of smoke. Between noon and two-thirty, twenty thousand people die in the ruins of twenty-six thousand buildings. They are mourned by Queen Wilhelmina, fled with her family to London. "There is now the desolation and stillness of death, broken only by the bitter weeping of those who have survived. . . . Yesterday's memory is today's oblivion. We pray that other nations will be spared."

But prayers are of no avail. Shortly after dawn on 15 May, the telephone by Churchill's bed rings. Paul Reynaud, French Premier, his voice tense with emotion, blurts out, "We have been defeated!" Churchill is mute. Reynaud says again, "We are beaten. We have lost the battle." Unable to believe him, Churchill asks, "Surely it can't have happened so soon?" But Reynaud, incredibly, is right. Rundstedt's ardent panzers have blasted a hole fifty miles wide through the French line at Sedan and are pouring through it in a cloud of dust, fanning out and clawing at the soft supply lines behind the Allied armies. By evening they are sixty miles behind the front.

The Dutch cease fire at eleven o'clock that morning. Crippled, the Belgians fight grimly on. Part of the BEF is heavily engaged, but so far has given no ground; others, in a parody of war, are lying peacefully on top of their earthworks, enjoying the baking hot weather and dreamily arguing about cricket.

Churchill decides that he must fly to France, boards one of the three government Flamingoes, and arrives in Paris in less than an hour. The officers who meet him say they expect the Germans there in a few days at most. At the Quai d'Orsay, Churchill and his staff meet the leaders of France— Reynaud, Daladier and Gamelin, the Commander-in-Chief. At one side of the room stands a pathetic little easel, bearing a map of the Allied front. Churchill notes "a small but sinister bulge at Sedan." Gamelin begins to explain the situation.

When he stopped, Churchill recalls, *there was a considerable silence. I then asked, "Where is the strategic reserve?" and, breaking into French, which I used indifferently (in every sense): "Où est la masse de manoeuvre?"* General Gamelin shakes his head, shrugs, and with a single word sounds the death knell of his country. *"Aucune."*

Silently Churchill walks to the great window. Below him in the formal garden there are clouds of smoke. Lines of old men are emptying wheelbarrow-loads of papers onto bonfires. The French are burning their archives. Summoning all his strength, Churchill turns back to seek a cure. But the only thing that can be done is the dispatch of ten British fighter squadrons to dominate the sky above the bulge at Sedan and give the French a last chance to rally their bravery and strength. After a sleep broken by minor air raids Churchill flies home.

But fighters are not enough. Next day, German tanks rumble into Cambrai, a bitter irony, for here the first tanks ever to throw a battle line into confusion were seen, and they were British. The list of fallen towns rings like the battle honors of an earlier war—Namur, Malines, Louvain, Antwerp, Brussels. That afternoon Churchill sets up a study of the problems that will arise if it becomes necessary to withdraw the BEF; with cold deliberation he requests Chamberlain to direct it.

Lord Gort, Commander-in-Chief of the BEF, is also considering the possibilities. His orders are to fight southward, but it is in the south that the German threat is strongest. It seems that nothing can stop the panzers. Brigadier Smyth contemplates his anti-tank guns, "excellent little weapons against anything not too heavily armored, and if they had only been given to us several months earlier, the men would have known how to shoot them." The Germans have taken thousands of French prisoners; they disarm them by piling their rifles in great heaps and driving tanks over them. Some of the prisoners are so dispirited that they still trudge along beside the panzers as they roll on to the coast.

Gort is a fighter. Five times decorated for bravery, once with the Victoria Cross, he is thickset, red-faced, belligerent and conspicuously fair. His nickname is "Fat Boy." His favorite sport is the fighting patrol and he is no man to shirk a battle. Neither is he a fool. He has in his care the cream of the regular army; if it is lost all hope of future armies dies with it. "He who fights and runs away lives to fight another day."

He is not the only one to think this. In Dover, Admiral Ramsay calls a conference to consider the emergency evacuation of very large forces across the Channel. By chance the Navy has begun, six days before, to carry out a census of small boats, intending them for coastal use to replace shipping losses caused by magnetic mines. As the conference disperses, the first German tanks reach the sea at Abbeville. If they turn north along the coast nothing can stop them rolling up the BEF like a carpet.

In the woods south of Cologne, Adolf Hitler too is in conference. Confident that the decadent French cannot withstand his dedicated legions for more than a few days, certain that the British will be swept like flotsam into the sea, the Fuehrer gathers his High Command to plan the best method of invading England. Though Admiral Raeder has conducted a staff study of this very problem six months before, the Fuehrer seizes on what to him is a new idea. He summons up all the fevered energy of his malevolent brain and Operation Sea Lion is conceived. It is to die stillborn.

In the early afternoon of Tuesday, 21 May, a valiant band of British attacks Rommel with such vigor that he is halted dead, south of Arras. Seventy-four dilapidated British tanks, their tracks threadbare, hurl themselves against the Germans. "Every gun, both anti-tank and anti-aircraft, was ordered to open rapid fire immediately," says Rommel, "and I personally gave each gun its target. . . . We ran from gun to gun." An SS division, elite of the new Germany, the silver death's head brave on its lapels, begins to panic in the face of the nerveless British infantry. The effect of the attack is far beyond its weight. It begins to seem to the cautious Rundstedt that his armor will be destroyed before his infantry can catch up. Slowly his confidence begins to ebb.

Allied hopes rise. Churchill again flies to France. Weygand, brisk, buoyant and incisive, has become Commander-in-Chief. Reynaud is now Minister of War as well as Premier. As he walks through the garden Churchill notices *a very tall cavalry officer . . . pacing moodily up and down.* It is his first glimpse of Colonel Charles de Gaulle, whose unpopular theories of mobile warfare are now so disastrously vindicated. Weygand proposes a vigorous new plan. But it is clear to Churchill, flying home, that its success depends wholly on the French armies' taking the initiative. Of this there is no sign. As a precautionary measure the BEF are put on half rations. They are the only formidable force left on the Continent, and they must carry the brunt of the battle.

Next morning naval officers in Admiral Ramsay's office in

the white chalk cliffs of Dover catch sight of tiny puffs of
black smoke above Boulogne. The Germans are pressing
home their attack. The evacuation of the port begins. The
destroyers carrying it out come under appalling fire from
field guns and mortars. *Venomous,* moored to a jetty, is almost surprised by a German motorcycle battalion, but blasts
it into oblivion with her pom-poms as it swarms across the
quay. Then, as dusk falls, a miracle. Rundstedt halts his
panzers.

Half his armored vehicles are out of action, some destroyed, some needing overhaul. Moreover, he must prepare
for *Fall Rot,* Plan Red, the *coup de grâce* across the Somme
and into the heart of France. Plan Yellow has succeeded
beyond all expectation; now, at the moment of exploitation,
the Teutonic military imagination gropes blindly for inspiration, finds none and falls dully back on a plan conceived
seven months before. The British are given a breathing space
and Gort decides that evacuation by sea is the only chance.

But first his flank must be guarded. In answer to the German thrust from the south Calais has been garrisoned. At
2 P.M. on 25 May a message is sent to its commander, Brigadier Nicholson. It ends: THE EYES OF THE EMPIRE ARE UPON
THE DEFENSE OF CALAIS, AND HIS MAJESTY'S GOVERNMENT ARE
CONFIDENT THAT YOU AND YOUR GALLANT REGIMENT WILL PER-
FORM AN EXPLOIT WORTHY OF THE BRITISH NAME. It is a message that carries the smell of doom for Nicholson and his men.
The next night he receives a second message:

EVERY HOUR YOU CONTINUE TO EXIST IS OF THE GREATEST
HELP TO THE BEF. GOVERNMENT HAS THEREFORE DECIDED
YOU MUST CONTINUE TO FIGHT. HAVE GREATEST POSSIBLE
ADMIRATION FOR YOUR SPLENDID STAND. EVACUATION WILL
NOT (REPEAT NOT) TAKE PLACE, AND CRAFT REQUIRED
FOR ABOVE PURPOSE ARE TO RETURN TO DOVER.

Sitting silently at the table, Churchill feels physically sick after the message has been sent.

Brigadier Nicholson has already refused a proposal to surrender " . . . as it is the British Army's duty to fight as well as it is the German's." The water mains are broken and his troops are critically short of water. Infantry can fight without water, without food or sleep, sometimes even without hope. But no infantry can fight without ammunition. When the German bombardment, reinforced with fresh guns, breaks out again at dawn, Nicholson knows his time is at hand. The Germans have to fight for every stone of Calais, but in the hour of twilight they break into the Citadel.

Now only Dunkirk is left. A short service of intercession and prayer is held in Westminster Abbey. In his stall in the choir Churchill can feel *the pent-up, passionate emotion, and also the fear of the congregation, not of death or wounds or material loss, but of defeat and the final ruin of Britain.*

The Belgians surrender, overwhelmed by von Bock's infantry, and Gort completes his plans for evacuation by sea from Dunkirk and the beaches nearby. Grimly the British hold their line, with one thought in their minds. They must fight their way to the sea, for at the sea's edge lies safety. The sea belongs to the Navy.

Already the small boats are setting out, the first of the Mosquito Armada. More are being called in. The smack *Seasalter* hauls into the estuary at Burnham-on-Crouch after a day of dredging oysters and is sent out to the beaches. "The soldiers were coming off the beach clinging to bits of wood and wreckage and anything that would float," recalls L. W. Salmons, her skipper. *Seasalter* plies to and fro taking the patient soldiers to the big ships standing by out in the deep channels.

More and more boats swarm across the Channel which,

many think by an act of God, is calm enough for a rowboat. The handiest of them are forty Dutch schuyts, bluff in the bows and round at the stern, built for working shallow waters. Master of one of them is Captain Pim, who has forsaken his duties in Churchill's own War Room and now ferries back eight hundred men. There are yachts and shiny little motor cruisers from the quiet backwaters up the Thames; bluff tugs from the Port of London; pleasure steamers with holiday names—*Royal Sovereign, Shamrock, Princess Maud* and *Royal Daffodil;* paddle minesweepers like *Brighton Belle* and *Medway Queen;* lifeboats from the sleepy ports of the south coast; graceful Thames barges with great red sails; Dover drifters strangely named *Yorkshire Lass* and *Ut Prosim;* the ferry boats *Southern Queen* and *Ferry Nymph* from Poole Harbor; six cutter-rigged cockle boats with heroic names—*Renown, Reliance, Resolute, Defender, Endeavour* and *Letitia*—from the Thames estuary; a Sea Scout training pinnace; fire-floats from the London Fire Brigade; and, strangest sight of all, four steel hopper barges from Ramsgate, with a single huge hold amidships to take the sludge from dredgers. Hour by hour the disreputable but gallant armada grows along the crowded beaches of Dunkirk.

Inland the roads are packed tight with transport. The matériel of an army crams into a perimeter twenty miles wide by five miles deep. Bulldozers clear the roads by pushing the empty trucks into the ditches. Red rivers of fire run through the fields as the army burns its supplies. The gunners fire off all stocks of ammunition, spike their guns or split the barrels, and march back to the dunes. The silver sand takes on a khaki hue. From the wet edge of the beach human piers stretch out into the shallow water, lines of silent men waiting without panic for rescue. Not all are lucky.

Allan Barrell, aboard the little *Shamrock*, picks up eighty men, then " . . . we were just making for our destroyer when I was brought to a standstill; my engine stopped, the propeller had fouled, I believe a human obstruction. There were many in the shallow water." Too weak to dive through the thick black oil covering the surface of the sea, Barrell and his charges are hauled aboard the destroyer. Barrell weeps as he leaves his boat; it represents his life savings.

By the end of the fourth day of the evacuation, 126,606 men are safe in England. On the last day of May Churchill flies once more to Paris for a meeting of the Supreme War Council. There he finds an ominous figure—for the first time Marshal Pétain is present. The hero of Verdun, France's most honored soldier, he is wearing civilian clothes. As the leaders sit discussing the prosecution of the war, another 132,000 men reach England.

For another four days the soldiers cluster calmly on the beaches, some even playing football. As dawn rises on Sunday, 2 June, a service of communion is held among the dunes and the cool and gentle breeze of early morning freshens the tired and dirty men. By tens and by hundreds they wade and swim to the bobbing boats. Their crews are haggard from days and nights of crippling toil and the constant harassment of shellfire and bombing.

Captain Read of Ramsgate, bringing his battered vessel home for the last time, finds one of his passengers has died. He feels something hard in a sandbag under the young soldier's head. It is a bottle of whisky. "Me and my mate drank this whisky, it seemed the best thing to do," says Captain Read. "And when we got home my wife says to me, 'Are you drunk or tired?' I says, 'Both!'" But his wife can see a deeper truth: "Some say it was one thing and some another, but I say it was the hand of God."

At the dead hour of 3:40 A.M. on 3 June the old destroyer *Shikari* pulls away from Dunkirk mole with the last men to be brought off. The total rescued stands at 338,226 Allied troops. At 2:23 p.m. on 4 June, a bright Tuesday afternoon, Operation Dynamo is declared completed.

Parliament assembles to hear the Prime Minister. He sums up in two pungent sentences: *We must be very careful not to assign to this deliverance the attributes of a victory. Wars are not won by evacuations.*

Hitler calls it "the greatest battle in the world's history" and orders an all-out attack on the pathetic remnants of the French Army. In twenty-five days he has conquered half a continent, humbled an empire, and almost changed the face of civilization itself. He has crossed every frontier in western Europe but the last. The old capitals have gone down into darkness. All save one.

In London the last champion speaks to his peers. Over the hushed, electric benches of the House of Commons roll the rich, pugnacious tones. The bright eyes peer above the precarious spectacles, the heavy jaw thrusts out, the sheaf of notes is shaken like a sword. Churchill is rallying his people: *Even though large tracts of Europe and many old and famous states have fallen or may fall into the grip of the Gestapo and all the odious apparatus of Nazi rule, we shall not flag or fail. We shall go on to the end, we shall fight in France, we shall fight in the seas and oceans, we shall fight with growing confidence and growing strength in the air, we shall defend our island, whatever the cost may be, we shall fight on the beaches, we shall fight on the landing grounds, we shall fight in the fields and in the streets, we shall fight in the hills; we shall never surrender, and even if, which I do not for a moment believe, this island or a large part of it were subjugated and starving, then our Empire beyond the seas, armed and guarded by the British Fleet, would carry on the struggle, until, in God's good time, the New World, with all its power and might, steps forth to the rescue and the liberation of the Old.*

EPISODE 3

THE FALL
OF FRANCE

Ye sons of France, awake to glory!
Hark! Hark! what myriads bid you rise!
Your children, wives, and grandsires hoary,
Behold their tears and hear their cries!
ROUGET DE LISLE: *La Marseillaise*

HALF HIDDEN in a tiny twisting street in Rouen, beside the broad and queenly Seine, there lies an ossuary. A narrow black-painted doorway opens into a silent courtyard, the cobbles unexpectedly smooth. Around three sides run galleries, carved in relief and daubed with the same somber black. This is the last resting place for the bleached and brittle bones of generations of Normans. From every pillar, and over the entrance porch, there stare the blank eyes of skulls. In June 1940, they are a hideous reminder that all flesh is dust. The citizens of Rouen, passing the ossuary's gate, regard the symbol with a new awareness, for over their city—as over all France—there broods the shade of death.

Hour by hour the cancer of defeat gnaws deeper into the hearts of the French. Hour by hour their troops fall back.

Behind the thin and desperate line, civilians scramble together a few belongings and flee in terror to the west, clogging the roads, flooding the towns. In less than a month the Germans have driven within striking distance of the Seine. The dim, perfumed calm of Rouen Cathedral rustles and murmurs with prayers. They are prayers of fear.

Confusion has become the norm. Among the population, in the army, even in the Government—misunderstanding, illusion, contradiction, error. Order, control, decision, action —these are mere words lost in the whirlwind of chaos. The walls of France are tumbling down. For twelve days one man struggles to buttress them, seeking in the midst of nightmare to light some spark of hope. And he is not even a Frenchman; he is Winston Spencer Churchill.

It is time for the jackal to sidle up to the kill. "I assure you," Mussolini confides to Ciano, his Foreign Minister, "the war will be over in September, and I need a few thousand dead so as to be able to attend the peace conference as a belligerent." At a little before five o'clock on the afternoon of 10 June declarations of war are handed to the British and French Ambassadors in Rome. From the Piazza Venezia echo the roars of the Roman mob, "Duce! Duce! Duce!" as their leader beams, gesticulates, juts out his ponderous jaw. It is a cheap and rather comic copy of the terrifying giant rallies of Nuremberg.

The news flashes around the world. President Roosevelt, about to address the graduating class of the University of Virginia, amends his speech to declare his condemnation of the treachery: "The Government of Italy has manifested disregard for the rights and security of other nations, disregard for the lives of the people of those nations which are directly threatened by the spread of this war." The noble head rises, the clear voice rings out in scorn: "On this tenth day of June 1940, the hand that held the dagger has struck it into the back of its neighbor."

When these words are brought to Churchill, working late at night in his War Room, he is greatly comforted. All day long secretaries have been hurrying in and out, and every message but this has carried bad news. Under the green shade across his forehead his eyes are tired. All day he has been waiting to fly to France, but the French Government has disappeared. Another message arrives. It has been re-established at Briare, near Orléans. Churchill orders his plane to stand by for an early flight. Silently in a corner of the room sits General Spears, Churchill's chief liaison officer with the French. More messages. Churchill thrusts them under the harsh light of his desk, scans them, looks up. There is no need for words.

The tiny remnant of the British Expeditionary Force left in France is still withdrawing. Its only effective unit is a proud one indeed—the 51st Highland Division, the cream of British infantry. Slowly it gives ground, but it fights with quiet fury, and unit after unit of the Wehrmacht hurls itself to destruction before it. But the sun is setting over the battle. The French High Command know that nothing can hold the Germans for long, except the slender chance of an all-out air assault. Again and again they appeal to the British for more squadrons. But they do not say where and how they are to be employed. Testily Churchill answers them: *We are giving you all the support we can, short of ruining the capacity of the country to continue the war.*

He has to summon up all his resolution as the little Fla-mingo carries him across the sunny Channel. The Anglo-French War Council meets in a hideous château of raw lobster-red brick. Reynaud the French Premier, Marshal

Pétain, General Weygand and de Gaulle, newly appointed to the government, are waiting for Churchill. Except for de Gaulle they are listless with the torpor of defeated men. Churchill bends all his energies toward awakening their courage. He has a single theme—fight on, whatever the cost.

In reply Reynaud nods to Weygand. The Commander-in-Chief begins a precise assessment of the battle state. His voice carries no emotion, his eyes are hard and cold. His very first sentence sounds the death knell of his country. He does not possess one single battalion in reserve; if the line breaks at any one point it cannot be patched. "The troops fight all day," he continues, "then fall back to new positions during the night. The men have neither food nor rest. They collapse into sleep when halted and have to be shaken in the morning to open fire." He ends, but with no apparent sense of drama, "I am helpless. I cannot intervene, for I have no reserves; there are no reserves. *C'est la dislocation*—the breakup." His slanted eyes flicker to Churchill.

There is a silence. Reynaud's face twitches nervously. Pétain has not yet uttered a word. De Gaulle smokes one cigarette after another, his eyes sardonic on Churchill. The onus is on the Prime Minister.

His head low, his mouth working, Churchill seeks the words of fire that will kindle these dying embers. Slowly the ponderous shoulders brace, the steady phrases begin to roll. With mounting passion he pleads with his allies to hold on. He promises fresh divisions. If only they will fight a little longer help will surely come. Can they not see that Paris could absorb an army if every street and every house were contested?

It is too much for the French. Imperceptibly they strain away from such a thought. Churchill suggests guerrilla warfare throughout France. Weygand snorts in disgust. Churchill is talking to the wind.

They will not turn Paris into a charnel house; they cannot imagine ill-organized partisans withstanding Prussian efficiency; they cannot envisage ultimate victory. The tracks of invincible panzers have broken more than their villages, more than their massed infantry. They have smashed the French will, hurled self-respect into the dust, humbled the glory of an empire.

That night Paris is declared an open city. Her streets are lifeless: the more timid citizens have fled, not a car moves through the silent boulevards. Those who stay behind wait dully in the ominous quiet for a future they cannot imagine.

Sadly, Churchill flies home to report to the War Cabinet. Below him, in a little town on the French coast close to Le Havre, the Highland Division draws in its battalions. Its rearguard, the Argyll and Sutherland Highlanders, wait in doorways and behind walls on the outskirts of St. Valéry for the panzers to make their last attack. They fix bayonets, having no ammunition to fire. In the distance rises a wall of dust from Rommel's tanks. By midday he has accepted the surrender of the division.

Still Churchill works for an understanding with the French. Next day he flies over again. The Government is now in Tours. The airport has been heavily bombed during the night and the Flamingo has to dodge between huge craters. No one is waiting to welcome the British party, so they borrow a car and drive to the prefecture. It contains only clerks. Churchill drives off again, this time to find lunch.

The meeting begins in the afternoon with a catastrophic report on the battle situation. The Germans have burst through the line in many places. Churchill reiterates his former arguments. Let the French carry on the fight from North Africa, let metropolitan France turn to guerrilla warfare, let a line

be held across Brittany to form a salient that can be supplied
and reinforced from the Atlantic. He pleads with all the passion at his command. Alive with authority and power,
charged with respect for a great ally, his voice surges confidently, but his heart is sick: *It must be borne in mind,* he
writes, *that I was haunted and undermined by the grief I felt
that Britain, with her forty-eight million population, had not
been able to make a greater contribution to the land war
against Germany, and that so far nine tenths of the slaughter
and ninety-nine hundredths of the suffering had fallen upon
France and upon France alone.*

Even as Churchill speaks so boldly, Ismay, his chief of staff,
recognizes the inner despair: "Churchill looked unutterably
sad. His love for France and her people was very real and
very long-standing and it was agony to him that we could
not do more to help her. Weygand said the end must be very
near. There was a long pause, then Churchill said, 'If you
think that it's best for France in her agony that her army
should capitulate, let there be no hesitation on our account,
because it makes no difference to us what you decide to do.
We are going to fight on for ever and ever and ever!' "

Leaving the conference room, Churchill walks down a
crowded passage into the courtyard. De Gaulle stands in the
doorway, expressionless as a stone statue. Peering up into his
eyes Churchill whispers, "*L'homme du destin*—Man of Destiny." The cold face shows no emotion, the hard eyes do not
flicker. The fire within de Gaulle is a remote and icy flame.

Churchill's escort of Hurricanes is already in the air.
Boarding his Flamingo, Churchill adjusts a black velvet
bandage over his eyes and falls asleep. He will not see
France again for four years. Piloting one of the Hurricanes
is Tony Bartley, who, on landing in London, discovers that
the Prime Minister's journey has not been entirely unfruitful.
"While he was saying goodbye to us," he recalls, "an ardent

mechanic opened the parachute container in the aircraft, not knowing we had concealed a very fine vintage champagne therein, and it fell to the tarmac and smashed to smithereens, which could have been an embarrassing situation. But Mr. Churchill straightaway put his hand to his own coat pocket and pulled out a bottle of the finest French brandy and said, 'I had the same idea.' " Next day, 14 June 1940, the Germans enter Paris.

Still Churchill does not give up hope. Within forty-eight hours he makes an offer to the French which has never been equaled in history. It is a Declaration of Union that will make of France and Britain one country with a single constitution, a single War Cabinet. It is too late. Reynaud resigns and is succeeded by the aged Pétain. Pétain dismisses the offer with a sneer: "It would be fusion with a corpse!" and Weygand adds his professional opinion: "In three weeks England will have her neck wrung like a chicken."

Churchill broadcasts a grim message over the BBC: *The news from France is very bad. We have become the sole champions now in arms to defend the world cause. We shall do our best to be worthy of this high honor. We shall defend our island home, and with the British Empire we shall fight on unconquerable until the curse of Hitler is lifted from the brows of mankind. We are sure that in the end all will come right.*

The few British troops left in France are hastily withdrawing from Brest, Cherbourg, St. Malo and St. Nazaire. Putting off from the quay at St. Nazaire, the liner *Lancastria*, crammed with five thousand men, is dive-bombed. More than three thousand are burned to death or are drowned in the oil-choked sea. General Alan Brooke, their Commander-in-Chief, boards an armed trawler which has rescued nine hundred men from the fuel oil. He finds the whole vessel "covered in that foul-smelling black treacly substance, heaps of clothes on the deck oozed out oil, whilst in the tiny cabin below the carpet was soaked with it, the walls covered with impressions of every part of the human anatomy printed in brown on the white walls; bandages, cotton-wool, iodoform, blood and the all-permeating smell of fuel oil." Churchill suppresses all news of the disaster.

Ending its melancholy pilgrimage in Bordeaux, the French Government at last reaches a decision. A motorcade of ten cars, each flying the white flag of surrender, heads north for Paris. They are to report to the Germans after five o'clock in what must now be called "German Summer Time." They have a shameful rendezvous. For twenty-two years there has stood in a remote clearing of the Forest of Compiègne a single *wagon-lit*. It still contains the long polished table at which in 1918 Marshal Foch received the surrender of the Kaiser's armies. Now it is the French who are suppliants, and the Germans see to it that they bend the knee in the full glare of Nazi publicity.

For Churchill the time for tears is over. Regrets vanish. What is done is done, what remains is to rally his nation. The British are alone, with their backs to the wall; they must fight to a finish. Sentiment, loyalty, friendship must be sacrificed to expediency, resolution, even ruthlessness. Churchill the leader never hesitates; Churchill the man suffers an agony of the soul.

Michel Saint-Denis, lunching with him, notices his anguish: "He got into a dreamy sort of mood and suddenly he said, 'What are they doing in France? What are they thinking?' I know them all. I know old Pétain—he's always been a defeatist. I know Darlan very well, he did a lot for the French Navy. I know Reynaud . . . what are they doing? What are they thinking?' And every time, tears were dropping from his cheeks. Every time he would say, 'I beg your pardon!' and wipe the tears with his napkin. You will know now how great was Mr. Churchill's concern for France. But his concern was of two kinds. There was the affection: he cried every time he spoke about France. There was admiration. And on the other hand there was his responsibility as a war leader and you can from that imagine in what torture he must have been when he had to take the cruel decision of attacking the French Fleet at Mers-el-Kebir."

It has been a cornerstone of the Allied grand plan that the main strength of the French Fleet shall operate in the Mediterranean and in the South Atlantic. Accordingly, its units are dispersed in Toulon, Alexandria and Algiers. Others are based on Oran, on British bases and in Martinique. Together they make up the fourth largest navy in the world; if they fall into German hands the island fortress of Britain will be isolated.

In operations rooms deep beneath London, plans are made and transmitted. At all costs, whatever the risks, the navy of France must not fall into enemy hands. Operation Catapult is born. Its aim is the simultaneous seizure, control, or effective disablement or destruction of all accessible units of the French Fleet. Principal of these is the French Atlantic Fleet lying at Oran.

At dead of night on 1 July forces of British marines and sailors mass stealthily alongside the piers where the French ships in Portsmouth and Plymouth lie moored. There is a brief and silent assault. On one of the warships, the giant submarine *Surcouf*, there is bloodshed, but the rest—two battleships, two cruisers, eight destroyers and two hundred smaller craft—surrender peacefully enough. They will soon join de Gaulle's Free French. Far off in Alexandria the story is the same.

While these secret struggles are going on, the Admiralty radio station sends a top-priority message to Gibraltar. It

reads: BE PREPARED FOR CATAPULT. Aboard his flagship Vice
Admiral Sir James Somerville is wakened. As he reads the
message, his face hardens. Only a month before, he has
sailed into the ravaged beaches of Dunkirk to rescue a hundred thousand French troops. Now he must destroy his
friends.

Churchill well knows the burden he has placed on Somerville. The next night he reinforces his orders. YOU ARE
CHARGED, the message says, WITH ONE OF THE MOST DISAGREE-
ABLE AND DIFFICULT TASKS THAT A BRITISH ADMIRAL HAS EVER
BEEN FACED WITH, BUT WE HAVE COMPLETE CONFIDENCE IN
YOU AND RELY ON YOU TO CARRY IT OUT RELENTLESSLY. Somerville is already at sea, hastening south at full speed. By nine-
thirty the next morning his great gray capital ships (a battle
cruiser, two battleships and an aircraft carrier) are riding
easily off Oran, their guns menacing the port, their gun crews
at action stations. In one thing at least the Italian Count
Ciano is right: "The fighting spirit of His British Majesty's
Fleet is alive and still has the aggressive ruthlessness of the
captains and pirates of the seventeenth century."

Somerville sends a captain to parley with the French Ad-
miral Gensoul. Gensoul will not meet him, but telegraphs the
British demands to Darlan in Vichy. All afternoon Churchill
paces the floor of his office. At 6:30 he sends a third order to
Somerville: FRENCH SHIPS MUST COMPLY WITH OUR TERMS OR
SINK THEMSELVES OR BE SUNK BY YOU BEFORE DUSK.

When it is received, Somerville is watching heavy black
pillars of smoke climbing lazily into the African sky. He has
unleashed the terrible power of his battle squadron on his
former comrades. In ten minutes he has sunk a battleship,
heavily damaged a battle cruiser and another battleship, sunk
two destroyers and a seaplane carrier. A second battle cruiser
has been torpedoed by aircraft from *Ark Royal*. More than a
thousand of their crews lie dead or dying on blackened

decks, behind twisted gunshields. *It was*, says Churchill, *Greek tragedy.*

As a result of the determined action, no French ship will ever be used against the British. And there is a more profound effect. *Here was this Britain,* Churchill writes, *which so many had counted out, which strangers had supposed to be quivering on the brink of surrender to the mighty power arrayed against her, striking ruthlessly at her dearest friends of yesterday and securing for a while to herself the undisputed command of the sea. It was made plain that the British War Cabinet feared nothing and would stop at nothing. This was true.*

Then, as after all great drama, comes a postscript so full of quiet and dignity that all are moved to tears. A few days after the massacre at Oran a humble funeral procession winds through the warm peaceful lanes of the countryside near Toulon. The mourners cannot afford the black plumes, the purple velvet and all the sable pomp of a haughty funeral. At the head of the column a few weather-beaten men carry two plain coffins. They bear the sons of two peasant families, caught by the British fire at Oran. Atop the coffins, at the wish of both families, the Tricolor and the Union Jack lie side by side. *In this we may see,* Churchill writes out of the depths of his sorrowing heart, *how the comprehending spirit of simple folk touches the sublime.*

BRITAIN MANS THE RAMPARTS

> *There is nothing more difficult to take in hand, more perilous to conduct, or more uncertain in its success, than to take the lead in the introduction of a new order of things.*
> NICCOLO MACHIAVELLI: *The Prince*

MURDER is seldom a professional matter. But few murders can have conformed less rigidly to whatever ethical and technical standards the profession boasts than the small and forever anonymous affair of 25 June 1940. This day marks the enforcement of the German-French armistice. It is also Amateur Night in the annals of legitimate assassination.

During the dead hours of darkness, a small party of quite unauthorized British soldiers approaches the French coast in motorboats manned by civilian crews. Spilling haphazardly onto the beach, they crunch over the gravel in most inexpert fashion and by a miracle encounter in the blackness

53

two German soldiers even more inept than themselves. The Germans allow themselves to be dispatched. Not thinking to search the bodies for papers, maps or other objects of intelligence value, but feeling they have struck a blow for freedom, the raiders melt away into the silence of the sea. Their completely amateur status is emphasized when, returning home with blackened faces in the blissful daylight, they are denied entrance to Folkestone Harbor because not one of them can establish his identity to the satisfaction of the stolid constabulary of Kent.

Yet this small odyssey reflects a new spirit—the giant aggressive force of Churchill's will, surging like new lifeblood through every artery and vein of British life. *Let us therefore brace ourselves to our duties, comes the challenge, and so bear ourselves that, if the British Empire and its Commonwealth last for a thousand years, men will say, "This was their finest hour!"*

No longer burdened by the necessity of flying to France to bolster his allies, Churchill bustles about his seagirt fortress encouraging, bullying, questioning, inspiring. One of his favorite projects is cross-Channel bombardment. He arranges for two fourteen-inch naval guns to be mounted on the cliffs above Dover. The first is christened "Winnie" and the second, inevitably, "Pooh." He orders that when their first shells are fired the results shall be reported to him direct. Soon, signals are exchanged.

Royal Marine Siege Battery to Prime Minister:
> WINNIE FIRED THREE ROUNDS TODAY. TWO DIRECT HITS OBTAINED.

Prime Minister to Royal Marine Siege Battery:
> DIRECT HITS ON WHAT?

Royal Marine Siege Battery to Prime Minister:
> DIRECT HITS ON FRANCE.

Elsewhere the Prime Minister is less prodigal of ammunition. In one sector of the south coast extending for four or five miles, a harassed brigadier tells Churchill he can only muster six rounds each for his three anti-tank guns. More in sorrow than in anger he asks whether he may order his men to fire off one round for practice, so that they may at least learn how the guns work. Sternly Churchill admonishes him. Practice rounds most certainly cannot be afforded. Fire must be held until the very last moment at the shortest possible range.

Among the divisions that Churchill visits is that commanded by a promising young general called Montgomery. It is disposed along the pebbly coast of Sussex, with Brighton as its hinge. Brighton is noted for its Pavilion (a fantasy of minarets and stucco built as a pleasance by the Prince Regent), the excellence of its fish restaurants and the profusion of its antique shops, and its pervasive air of a town still luxuriating in the gaiety of a wholly Edwardian attitude to the peccadilloes of the flesh. In the spring a young man's fancy lightly turns to thoughts of love—and Brighton.

Churchill enjoys schoolboy memories of the resort in a far-off, imperial age. But, he admits as he lunches with Montgomery in the Royal Albion Hotel overlooking the wedding-cake pier and the lazy sea, Brighton has not changed much. A platoon of the Grenadier Guards is busily making a sandbagged machine-gun post out of a kiosk where, as a ten-year-old, Churchill was once fascinated by the antics of some performing fleas.

Across the Channel the atmosphere is rather different. Thick-spectacled, pale-faced staff officers pore day and night over tables of logistics. Supercilious quartermasters requisition every shallow draft vessel on the waterways of northwest Europe, and order them all to concentrate at once on the Channel ports. Hard-eyed sergeants drill their eager troops endlessly in the techniques of sea-borne invasion. With all the ponderous thoroughness of the Teuton, the Germans prepare for Operation Sea Lion, in which they will administer to the decadent British the *coup de grâce*. *We expect*, Churchill writes to his friend the President, *to be attacked . . . both from the air and by parachute and airborne troops, in the near future, and we are getting ready for them.*

To help guard against such a descent the Home Guard is formed. All over England, men find a new comradeship and a new purpose in this people's militia. Churchill's superb oratory spurs them on.

By the middle of the year, the Home Guard numbers half a million men. Alongside the pitted dart boards in the tiny stone pubs in the Cotswolds hang duty rosters and parade states. Village halls deep in the wooded valley of the Avon blossom with maps and diagrams. The scrubbed wooden floors of workingmen's clubs in the dark north country quake under the hobnails of drilling boots. Over a pint of beer, men's blood runs hot again as they re-live the frightful battles in Flanders' mud, for these are veterans of a bloodier war. Social and sporting clubs pupate overnight into self-contained military units when their members join up as one man; employer and worker train shoulder to shoulder in the camaraderie of danger.

Not the least colorful of these volunteers is a sixty-three-year-old Zulu whose father led one of Cetewayo's impis against a troop of British at Isandhlwana, graduating later as a lion tamer. This black princeling is one of the first members of a unit in a coastal district of Glamorganshire, where it is hoped (as Peter Fleming records) "if the invaders landed, his appearance on the foreshore might suggest to them that a serious error of navigation had been made."

There is only one major problem. The Home Guard have no weapons to speak of. "I do not want you," their Commander-in-Chief, the gigantic General Ironside, sternly reminds them, "to misjudge the shotgun. I have now coming out over one million rounds of solid ammunition, which is something that will kill a leopard at two hundred yards!" The doughty general has overlooked the probability that his formidable solid shot, if fired through a choked barrel, will disintegrate the marksman before it ever dispatches the leopard.

Everywhere, zealous parties ransack the hiding places of anything that will shoot, cut or club. The dusty rooms where the stage properties are kept at Drury Lane yield four dozen rusty Lee-Enfields. Kukris, assagais, maces and battle-axes are torn down from manorial walls they have long decorated as reminders of a far-flung empire. The Zoological Gardens in Manchester donate several muskets last used in the Indian Mutiny. In Essex a whole cutlass platoon is armed out of who knows what hoard of piratical relics.

Churchill coins the slogan, "You can always take one with you!" and practices what he preaches. A target range is set up in the grounds of Chequers. Detective Inspector Walter Thompson, his bodyguard, remembers his attitude: "He himself intended that he would never be taken alive and he issued direct instructions to me. I was to have his .45 Colt fully loaded. He intended to use every bullet but one on the enemy, the last one he saved for himself. His favorite weapons were a Mannlicher rifle, a .38 Webley gun and the .45 Colt automatic. This was really his favorite weapon and with it he was a dead shot. Anyone who came within range of it would never survive."

Magazines and newspapers become engrossed in the arts of

guerrilla warfare. The *Picture Post*, staffed in part by veterans of the Spanish Civil War, leads the field with bloodthirsty expertise. It carries articles on fortifying houses, on turning villages into defense "hedgehogs," and on do-it-yourself tank destroying. The favorite anti-tank weapon is the Molotov Cocktail, a large beer bottle (*any* beer bottle will do) filled with petrol and plugged with a petrol-soaked rag. On the approach of the tank the rag is lit and the bottle thrown, with sufficient force to break it, at the unsuspecting steel side of the monster. The reward is a roar and a gout of angry flames.

Oliver Nickalls, a member of the Home Guard, is selected to demonstrate this simple weapon during a visit of inspection by the King. It works like a charm. "Elated by my success," he relates, "I said to the assembled staff and everyone present, 'Stand back! I'm going to throw another!' At that point the King looked up and said, 'No, no, for goodness' sake don't! We simply can't afford it!' "

No amount of ingenuity, however, can produce the weapons needed. Behind the soldiers, the war factories work all out. *Men and women toiled at the lathes and machines in the factories till they fell exhausted on the floor and had to be dragged away and ordered home, while their places were occupied by newcomers ahead of time,* Churchill writes. Still the output is not big enough or fast enough to fill the gap. Churchill turns to the United States.

The President orders the Army and Navy to give him lists of what they can spare for Britain. Within forty-eight hours he has his answer—half a million rifles with two hundred and fifty rounds apiece, nine hundred field guns, eighty thousand machine guns. Immediately the matériel is packed for shipment, and within a week six hundred freight cars are rolling heavily toward the Army docks at Raritan, New Jersey, where fast British merchant ships are waiting. Churchill is deeply grateful: *At that time it was a supreme act of faith and leadership for the United States to deprive themselves of a mass of arms for a country which many deemed already beaten.*

The rifles are a great prize. As the ships approach Liverpool, special trains steam into the marshaling yards to await their precious cargoes. In every town and village the Home Guard sit up all the night, waiting. They descend on the packing cases like Israelites upon the new day's manna. The rifles are still smothered in the thick black grease that has embalmed them since 1918. *Men and women worked night and day making them fit for use. By the end of July,* Churchill proudly reports, *we were an armed nation, so far as parachute and air-borne landings were concerned. We had become a hornets' nest.*

His thoughts turn to giving out a few stings. He has always inclined to the old belief that attack is the best means of defense. On 6 June he instructs Ismay, his chief of staff: *Enterprises must be prepared, with specially trained troops of the hunter class, who can develop a reign of terror down these [enemy-held] coasts, first of all in the "butcher and bolt" policy, but later on, perhaps as soon as we are organized, we could surprise Calais or Boulogne, kill and capture the Hun garrison, and hold the place until all the preparations to reduce it by siege or heavy storm have been made, and then away.*

These troops he christens "Leopards," later to become "commandos," and one of the first of them is Brigadier Young: "We were formed at the end of June 1940 after going around choosing our own men. We chose reservists—men who had been in action before Dunkirk, men who wanted to fight. We chose them from all units—including gunners, sappers and signalers—and we started training straight away. They were all volunteers and all picked men. Churchill said that every British soldier ought to take one Nazi with him. The commandos thought this was rather a bad business. They thought we might settle for ten. . . ."

One of the Leopards' duties will be to smash any German landings before they can take firm hold. Other novelties are also prepared. The beaches are sown with mines down to the tide line and covered by machine guns in blockhouses. Experiments are conducted to set the sea itself on fire by means of oil pumped by the ton from tankers drawn up on the cliffs. Every exit from the beaches is primed with fougasses—forty-gallon drums containing a mixture of tar, lime and gasoline which spews out in a flood of glutinous fire.

Secretly, in innocent-looking country houses, scientists and engineers devise new means of discomfiting the enemy. A Major Jefferis invents a sticky bomb for destroying tanks. Churchill becomes fascinated by the idea and urges it forward with all haste. It proves, however, not the most amenable of weapons. The attacker is supposed to advance smartly toward the tank and slap the bomb onto its armor with sufficient force to break a glass activator. Unfortunately, the force is occasionally enough to detonate the machine also; moreover, the clumsier soldier is apt to find the bomb sticking to his own uniform and has to undress with all speed before pressing home his attack.

Churchill's right-hand man in this "Wizard War" is Frederick Lindemann (later Lord Cherwell), formerly Professor of Experimental Philosophy at the University of Oxford. Always a controversial figure, a vegetarian, a bachelor, remote, sensitive, ingenious, at times vindictive, Lindemann makes few friends and many enemies. His association with Churchill forms the mainspring of his life. Certainly not the most gifted of scientists, nevertheless he offers two priceless assets to Churchill. First, his complete devotion, cemented during years of close association. Second, with associations everywhere, he hears of the latest developments in all fields of science, can assess their practical value very quickly, and has the knack of explaining them in simple terms to the layman.

Churchill himself has long before admitted his own deficiencies in this respect: *I had a feeling once about Mathematics—that I saw it all. Depth beyond Depth was revealed to me—the Byss and the Abyss. I saw—as one might see the transit of Venus or even the Lord Mayor's Show—a quantity passing through infinity and changing its sign from plus to minus. I saw exactly how it happened and why the tergiversation was inevitable—but it was after dinner and I let it go.* With Lindemann to explain things, Churchill puts his shoulder behind the devious, sinister war effort of the scientists. *I used their brains,* he explains, *and my power.*

Occasionally he uses Lindemann's orderly mind on less weighty issues. Returning one day to London in his special train he wonders what quantity of champagne he has drunk in his lifetime, at the not inconsiderable rate of a pint a day. Lindemann's notebook comes into play and his quick total delights Churchill, who then inquires how many coaches like the one they are traveling in would be needed to haul the crates. Lindemann calculates, with regret, that the load would occupy only a part of one coach. *I am very disappointed,* Churchill grumbles. *I had hoped it would have taken several coaches.*

By the middle of September, the island is fully prepared, and it seems to British Intelligence that this will be the likeliest time for the German attack. Virginio Gayda, Mussolini's mouthpiece, announces that it will take place on a Friday. *Friday,* Churchill replies cheerfully, *is as good as any day!*

But the Fridays pass and still nothing but rumors reach the English shore. The RAF smashes to driftwood the barges in the Channel ports, German bodies are reported floating in the North Sea. The British stand to for an attack that never comes. It is all rather disappointing, really.

Confident that all has been done to deny the enemy this last frontier, Churchill turns to an even deadlier threat. Money is running short, and especially dollars. Until November 1940 England can pay for everything she buys from the United States out of her dollar reserves. Now they have dwindled to two billion, mostly in investments that are not readily marketable. Without money there can be no munitions, without munitions there can be no war. What is to be done?

Already America has been generous almost to the point of losing her neutrality. Her weapons have armed the Home Guard. She has transferred fifty of her old destroyers to the Royal Navy in exchange for a series of bases in the West Indies. Clearly, her inclinations cannot be doubted. After long thought Churchill writes one of the most important letters of his life. Its effect on the President will decide England's fate.

Churchill points out that the cash is almost gone. Without appealing directly for aid, he lays out his country's case so plainly, expressing hopes but admitting to fears, that it becomes obvious that unless "ways and means" are found to help, the outcome will remain in doubt.

The letter reaches the President as he is cruising peacefully in the warmth of the Caribbean aboard the *Tuscaloosa*. In the shade of a gun turret he sits alone in his deck chair reading and rereading the letter. Silent, withdrawn, he spends two days in a dark labyrinth of thought. There is no one to consult, no one in whom to confide. For two whole days, in the dreadful isolation of his office, Franklin Delano Roosevelt wrestles with history.

Finally his face lightens. Once more he begins to joke with his staff. The decision has been reached. Now the problem is one in which he takes delight. Now he must persuade Congress. *Tuscaloosa* steams for home.

On 17 December the President holds a press conference. "Now, what I am trying to do," he begins, "is to eliminate the dollar sign." His audience gasps. Gratified, he provides an illustration. "Suppose my neighbor's home catches fire, and I have a length of garden hose four or five hundred feet away. If he can take my garden hose and connect it up with his hydrant, I may help him to put out his fire. Now, what do I do? I don't say to him before that operation, 'Neighbor, my garden hose cost me fifteen dollars; you have to pay me fifteen dollars for it.'—I want my garden hose back after the fire is over. All right. But suppose it gets smashed up. He says, 'All right, I will replace it.' Now, if I get a nice garden hose back, I am in pretty good shape." In the whole history of statesmanship it is the simplest explanation of a question that affects the future of civilization itself. It is also one of the noblest.

Twelve days later the President explains his policy to the whole nation, in a Fireside Chat. It ends, "We must be the great arsenal of democracy." On 10 January 1941 the Lend-Lease Bill is placed before Congress. Within 24 hours it becomes law. In the House of Commons Churchill calls it "the most unsordid act in the history of any nation."

Meanwhile, in the ominous twilight of Occupied Europe a megalomaniac mastermind begins to show the first tiny crack that spells ruin. Adolf Hitler's leaden legions sprawl from the edge of the Arctic to the lazy Mediterranean, from

the grim marshes of eastern Poland to the ancient cliffs of
Brittany. His New Year's message to them is a masterpiece
of political ingenuousness. It ends, "We are ready! . . . The
year 1941 will bring completion of the greatest victory in our
history."

EPISODE 5

DAYS
OF GLORY

*Methinks I see in my mind a noble and
puissant nation rousing herself like a
strong man after sleep, and shaking her
invincible locks: methinks I see her as
an eagle mewing her mighty youth, and
kindling her undazzled eyes at the full
midday beam.*

JOHN MILTON: *Areopagitica*

SUMMER in England is a gentle season. The hedgerows of
the country shires lie heavy and sweet with the bloom of
dogrose and blackberry. Even in the dark industrial towns
of Tyneside and the Black Country the sky between the
sooty smokestacks of the iron mills and the machine shops
stretches blue and clear. Across the Weald the rolling pastures stride like humped green carpets down to the glaring
cliffs, white as gulls' wings in the unaccustomed sun. An
English summer is a time of comfort, lighthearted, a time for
relaxation.

But in the summer of 1940 the English are only just
awakened from a nightmare. The brute fury of the blitzkrieg

is only just past; a tortured France lies quiescent under the Nazi jack boot. Behind her sea defenses England stirs, arms, waits. The dull unnumbered masses of the Wehrmacht cannot cross the Channel without command of the sea and air. It is obvious whence the assault will come.

His eyes turned to the sky, Churchill warns his people: *I expect the Battle of Britain is about to begin. Upon this battle depends the survival of Christian civilization.*

Stripped to the bone to meet the demands of the French, the RAF is outnumbered in fighter planes by eight to one. Churchill brings in the dynamic, ruthless publisher, Lord Beaverbrook, as Minister of Aircraft Production, and tells him, "Get the Spitfires off the blueprints and into the sky!" Beaverbrook answers, "If God will give me the time I'll produce the Spitfires for you."

Divine intervention aside, the question is, will there *be* any time? Already the German Air Force is regrouping on the airfields captured from the French and the Belgians. General Kesselring assumes command of *Luftflotte* 2 and beside him lies Sperrle's *Luftflotte* 3; together they can put more than nine hundred fighters and twelve hundred bombers into the sky.

In his new office Beaverbrook uses ferocious measures to gain the momentum of victory. Just after his arrival two of his senior civil servants feel the pressure of an iron will. "Surely," one of them is overheard saying, "surely he is producing the planes?" "Oh yes, my dear fellow," comes the uncomfortable reply, "but by *what methods!*" Soon the factories are turning out Spitfires so fast that the supplies of aluminum run out. Appeals are made to housewives. "Pots and pans make fighters!" scream the billboards, and before long there is not a house in England that cannot boast empty hooks in its kitchen.

The *Luftwaffe* completes its plans. First, the Channel will be swept clear of British shipping and the southern ports destroyed. Then the RAF's airfields, stores and installations will be wiped out, together with the factories that supply them. The final phase will be the annihilation of London by concentrated air bombardment, thus, in Goering's arrogant view, forcing the submission of the British Government and people.

But London is not so soft a target. Clear-cut against the blue summer sky the battlements of the Tower of London loom gray above the broad Thames. Beneath the heavy walls, their cotton dresses swirling as they skip, the children play their street games. Thin and sweet, their voices re-echo from the ancient stones an ancient song, "London Bridge Is Falling Down." These children are heirs to nine hundred years of freedom and these walls have guarded their ancestors for generations. There is a legend about the Tower. On a green lawn below the White Tower within the keep, there flutter some ravens, sagacious and long-lived. Only when the ravens leave the Tower will London fall. Calmly, in this ominous summer of 1940, the ravens stroll about their lawn with all the deliberation of a convocation of clergy.

Now comes the challenge. The dapper officers of Goering's elite drink to the imminent defeat of the British, smash the glasses, hurl down the gage. On 10 July 1940 their fighter squadrons rake the Channel, seeking to draw the RAF into battle over the sea. After a few days it becomes clear that the gambit has failed. They come in closer and sweep down onto the gracious old Channel ports. Gradually, but on its own terms, the RAF begins to accept the challenge.

The cream of England's and Germany's young manhood meet in a battle the like of which has never been seen before and will never be again. It is the last broad blaze of a glory that has vanished from war—the hand-to-hand encounter, incredibly swift, a deadly game played out five miles above the earth with no boundaries but the limitless blue horizons. Richard Hillary, a youngster straight out of school, sums it up: "The fighter pilot's emotions are those of the duelist— cool, precise, impersonal. He is privileged to kill well. For if one must either kill or be killed, as now one must, it should, I feel, be done with dignity."

Except for the disparity in numbers it is an even match. "The modern Vickers Supermarine Spitfire," German ace Adolf Galland reports, "is slower than our planes (Messerschmidt 109s) by about ten to fifteen miles an hour, but can perform steeper and tighter turns. . . . The British fighters usually try to shake off pursuit by a half roll or a half roll on top of a loop, while we simply go straight for them, with wide-open throttle and eyes bulging out of their sockets."

Sometimes the eyes bulge for a different reason, however; when the Spitfire's machine guns zero in, their effect is lethal. "The bullets from your eight guns go pumping into his belly," says Johnnie Johnson, the RAF's greatest ace. "He begins to smoke. But wicked tracers sparkle and flash over the top of your own cockpit and you break into a tight turn. . . . Over your shoulder you can still see the ugly, questing snout of the 109. You tighten the turn. The Spit protests and shudders, and when the blood drains from your eyes you 'gray-out.' But you keep turning, for life itself is at the stake. And now your blood feels like molten lead and runs from head to legs. You black out! And you ease the turn to recover in a gray, unreal world of spinning horizons. Cautiously you climb into the sun. You have lost too much height and your opponent has gone—disappeared."

It is an intensely personal fight. The pilots can even hear each other talk. Tuning to the German frequency one afternoon an English pilot baits the German with the choicest language he can find. His reward is a voice choking with rage, declaring: "You filthy Englishman, we will teach you how to speak to a German!" But the lesson must be postponed, for the English squadron flies high in the setting sun and the Germans are two thousand feet below. Like metal falcons the Spitfires swoop at their prey and scatter them into the golden evening.

In Hitler's mouth the fruits of victory begin to turn sour. He issues Directive No. 17: "The German Air Force will use all available means to destroy the British Air Force as soon as possible. Attacks will be directed primarily against the flying units, ground organization, and supply installations of the Royal Air Force, and, further, against the air armaments industry, including factories producing anti-aircraft equipment." It is a simple order, but between the wish and the deed there interposes still the tenacity of the RAF.

Goering hastens to send in his bombers. Eleven waves of them attack Dover. Then Portsmouth, razed by two savage raids. Number 11 (Fighter) Group, dispersed in a tight semicircle of airfields south of London, meets them head on. Every day the skies are crisscrossed with vapor trails, with now and then the sudden flicker of sunlight on an opening parachute. The apple orchards of Kent begin to shelter a strange fruit as the wreckage of aircraft screams and thuds between their ancient rows.

Then, on 15 August, the Germans try a new tactic. A hundred bombers, escorted by forty Messerschmitt 110s, sweep out over the gray North Sea to strike at the shipyards and heavy plant of Tyneside. They are forestalled, for Air Marshal Dowding has withdrawn seven fighter squadrons from the southern battle for the North, greatly to the disgust of their pilots. *They had suffered severely,* says Churchill, *but were nonetheless deeply grieved to leave the battle. The pilots respectfully represented that they were not at all tired.*

Now came an unexpected consolation. These squadrons were able to welcome the assailants as they crossed the coast. Thirty of the enemy are shot down into the sea and Churchill hails Dowding's generalship as "an example of genius in the art of war."

The same day sees a more threatening change in Goering's strategy. He carries the battle to the fighter stations themselves. Bombs rain down on Hawkinge, Deal, Lympne, Dover, Kenley, Middle Wallop and Biggin Hill. The next day seven more fields are raided by six hundred bombers. The Operations Room at Biggin Hill receives a direct hit and moves to the butcher's shop in the village.

The strain is almost unbearable, and a savage grimness begins to cloud the former gaiety of the English pilots. A doctor asks "Sailor" Malan as he sips his beer in the mess how he goes about shooting down a bomber. "I try not to . . . now," comes the startling reply. "You see, if you shoot them down they don't get back and no one in Germany is a whit the wiser. So I figure the right thing to do is to let them get back." He pauses. "With a dead rear gunner, a dead navigator, and the pilot coughing up his lungs as he lands. I think if you do that it has a better effect on their morale."

The day of crisis falls on a Sunday. Churchill is spending the weekend at Chequers. Enjoying the summer weather and remembering perhaps that the Battle of Waterloo was won on a Sunday, he calls for his car. He motors through the dreaming little villages of Sussex, the hedgerows swishing at the passing of the great black sedan. Just outside the quiet market town of Uxbridge lies the headquarters of Number 11 Group. It is a neat, mellow country house. In the great oak doorway, waiting to welcome the Prime Minister, stands

a tall sinewy New Zealander. Air Vice Marshal Park has commanded the Group throughout the battle.

Park ushers the Prime Minister and Mrs. Churchill down a
steep flight of stairs. "I don't know," he tells them, "whether
anything will happen today. At present everything is quiet."
He is anxious not to disappoint his visitor.

Fifty feet below ground they come to the Operations
Room. It is arranged in two stories, like a small theater. *We
took our seats,* Churchill remembers with relish, *in the dress
circle.* Below them spreads a huge table on which the symbols of battle are grouped and shifted, spelling out the
tactics of victory and defeat, of survival and extinction.
Opposite is a wide board showing the condition of Park's
squadrons. Lamps of different colors light to indicate which
squadrons are refueling, which are air-borne, which are engaged. To Churchill's right, a battery of telephones receives
constant reports as enemy planes are sighted.

Park strolls about the room working out his dispositions.
Churchill watches him through a thin haze of cigar smoke
and glances about from time to time at the ordered and
pleasing bustle. Soon, to Churchill's delight, the action begins. Concentrations of German bombers are reported over
the coast. Gradually the stream becomes a torrent.

One by one Park commits his precious squadrons. Still the
bombers come. Churchill utters no word, but his expression
grows serious. Park calls to the North for reserve squadrons.
They fly in and at once are thrown into the battle. Uneasily
Churchill glances at the board. All along the top line, against
every squadron, there glow the red bulbs that spell IN AC-
TION.

If the fight continues for even ten minutes more, the
squadrons will have to land to refuel and rearm, and a new
German attack will catch them helpless on the ground. The

battle assumes a shape familiar to Churchill. It is the black shape of disaster.

Keeping his voice low, he turns to Park. *What other reserves have we?* Park, the lines on his face as deep as swordcuts, stares him in the eye. "Sir," he says, "there are none." Churchill's eyes cloud with tears.

But in that moment of agony a strange thing is happening. Climbing, forever climbing, the Spitfires quarter the sky like hawks riding the wind. They spiral up and up into the sun, but the white pastures of the clouds are empty. There is nothing left to fight. In that crucial moment the Germans have turned for home. One by one the tired English squadrons slide down to their fields.

On the great table in the Operations Room the ugly black symbols of the enemy coagulate into a stream, flowing south and away. The headquarters is in holiday mood. In the sudden freedom Park tells Churchill how frightened he has been. Churchill grins at him like a schoolboy, gathers his entourage and heads for the open air. For a moment his face is thoughtful, then, as he climbs into his car, Park hears him murmur, *Never in the field of human conflict was so much owed by so many to so few.* The thick shoulders sink back into the leather seat, the bright eyes twinkle, the stubby thumb points upward in the Cockney's sign of cheer. For Winston Churchill it has been a profitable day.

If proof is needed that the German air offensive will eventually fail, this glorious Sunday will provide it. But already Goering has begun the third and final phase of his grand strategy.

The jeweled baton of his rank clutched in one fat hand, his garish uniform creased across his obscene belly, Reichs-

marschall Goering stands late one September afternoon on
the cropped sea-grass of a French cliff. Beside him is Kesselring, the thickset commander of *Luftflotte* 2, whose smile is
as wide and as deadly as a shark's. Silently they gaze upward
as there rolls thunderously over them the distinctive, irregu-
lar throbbing of their Heinkels and Dorniers. It is a sound
that Londoners will learn to dread. Flight after flight claws
toward the north, heavy with high explosive and fire bombs,
flashing now and then with the blood-red reflection of the
setting sun. The two Nazis turn to each other and smile. It
is a historic occasion for the Third Reich. Tonight the execution of London will begin. It will be Warsaw and Rotterdam
all over again.

Right in the path of the bombers, plumb center of their
target, Churchill is wallowing like a sportive leviathan in his
bath. Number 10 Downing Street has been declared quite
unsafe, and a bombproof annex is being built to protect the
Prime Minister and his staff. So far there have been no inci-
dents. Tonight he is looking forward to dinner with a small
circle of friends.

As they sit at table in Stornoway House overlooking the
Green Park, the great French windows are lit by the glare
of exploding bombs. Finishing their brandy, they decide to
adjourn to the huge Imperial Chemical Industries building
on the Embankment. They enjoy a commanding view of the
action. Churchill observes: *At least a dozen fires were burning on the south side, and while we were there, several
heavy bombs fell, one near enough for my friends to pull me
back behind a substantial stone pillar. This certainly confirmed my opinion that we should have to accept many re-
strictions upon the ordinary amenities of life.*

Churchill broods on the vulnerability of the city. For the
ruthless Germans it presents a vast target, sprawling out on
both sides of the river (a perfect aiming point) through

ninety-five boroughs and districts. He has been warning everybody about the necessity for adequate air defenses since 1935. And now the blitz has come and, save for the courage and endurance of its citizens, London seems unprepared.

For the first three nights neither night-fighters nor flak meet the intruders. The people of London begin to look fearfully at the sky; are they powerless after all? Then . . . *Suddenly, on September 10,* says Churchill, *our whole barrage opened, accompanied by a blaze of searchlights. This roaring cannonade did not do much harm to the enemy, but gave enormous satisfaction to the population.* The darkness is ripped open by the gun flashes of massed batteries. Windows shatter, roof tiles clatter down, the earth shakes at the recoil. The hissing shards of shrapnel raining down suddenly seem more dangerous than the screaming bombs. For General Sir Frederick Pile, commanding the defenses, it is a triumph.

"The next day at eleven o'clock," he recalls, "when I attended my usual daily meeting with the Prime Minister at the War Council, he noticed me for the first time.

" 'Pile,' he said, 'you fired a lot of rounds last night. I hope you were successful?'

" 'Not very, sir,' I replied.

"He looked at me. 'Did you fire a lot of rounds?'

"I said, 'About sixty thousand.'

" 'Oh dear,' he said, 'that's a lot! Have you got a big reserve still?'

" 'Well,' I told him, 'we've got enough to go on a little longer.'

"He smiled. 'You've heartened the people, and their morale has been greatly improved by this night's work.'

"But it wasn't such fun for me, really, because that night

I thought to myself that perhaps we *had* fired too many rounds, so I told the batteries to be a bit more canny about what they fired at. Sure enough, at half past seven, when the raid had just started, my telephone rang. A voice said:

" 'This is the Prime Minister speaking. Is that Pile?'

" 'Yes, sir,' I said.

" 'Have you taken the guns away?'

" 'No, sir.'

" *'Then why aren't you firing?'*

"That went on every night for about a week. First I'd fired too many, the next night I hadn't fired enough."

During that week General Pile's men serve their guns virtually without sleep. Pile cannot slacken his fire, because the Londoners are comforted by the umbrella of steel they imagine he has placed between themselves and the enemy. Yet he knows that if his present rate continues he will have none of his heavy guns left in action by December, and no 3.7s either by February. Every single barrel will have been worn smooth. However, the first part of the blitz lasts for fifty-seven nights, and then there is a lull.

Thus embattled, Churchill is in great spirits. *Life at Downing Street was exciting,* he writes. *One might as well have been at a battalion headquarters in the line.* Detective Inspector Walter Thompson, his bodyguard, spends all his time pestering his charge to take cover, or at least to wear a steel helmet. But do what he will, Churchill cannot be prevented from clambering onto the roof of the annex as soon as the fun begins, remarking pleasantly to the worried Inspector, *I am sorry to take you into danger, Thompson. I would not do it, only I know how much you like it.* He adopts a habit, on colder evenings, of sitting on a little chimney that pokes through the annex roof. Until one night a very senior civil servant puffs up to report, with respect, that unless the Prime

Minister shifts position his staff below will be suffocated by smoke.

It is soon clear to everyone that, as they suspected, Churchill scorns the bombs. He declares, *The people should be accustomed to treat air raids as a matter of ordinary routine. . . . Everybody should learn to take air raids and air-raid alarms as if they were no more than thunderstorms.* In a speech to the House he growls, *On that particular Thursday night 180 persons were killed in London as a result of 251 tons of bombs. That is to say, it took one ton of bombs to kill three-quarters of a person.* As if in days of peace, he even announces the time and place of his public speeches. Goering screams, "We will stop this man speaking!" But neither friend nor foe has been able to do that in sixty-six years.

Darkness comes early during an English winter, and the cold months of the winter of 1940–41 seem long indeed. There are some nights so cold that the roaring jets of water freeze as they leave the fire-hoses, others so hot from the blinding furnace heat of blazing warehouses that it seems that old Thames itself could not cool them. The royal standard still flies over Buckingham Palace, a sign that the King and Queen are still in residence, but it waves over bomb craters and shattered glass.

Number 10 Downing Street is hit. Mrs. Landemare, the cook, is busy in her kitchen "preparing the sweet, Mr. Churchill's favorite sweet." In rushes the Prime Minister to ask why she is not down in the shelter. Mrs. Landemare is not easily perturbed. "Well, sir," she replies firmly, "if you'd been on time I *would* have been there!" Abashed, Churchill ushers her below ground. Two minutes later the kitchen is a mass of rubble.

London becomes a city of cave dwellers. Every night at

dusk long lines of quiet people file down into the shelters and the Underground. The Tube stations become dormitories packed with rows of steel bunks where whole families stake out their claims for weeks on end. As they lie asleep, rolled in their harsh gray blankets, they seem already wrapped in shrouds. In the dim light their close-packed ranks people the platforms like catacombs lined with dead.

The devastation mounts. The Germans begin to drop heavier bombs, fitted with time fuses. These have to be dug out deep in the clay, and emptied of explosive by means of steam hoses. It is a deadly game. The men of the Bomb Disposal Units, whose task this is, develop their own grim humor. Asked what qualifications are needed, one of them suggests, "A member of the squad should not be indispensable to the factory. He should be of excellent character and prepared for the after-life."

Then comes a new weapon, a mine weighing a ton and a half that floats down on the end of a parachute. One of them explodes a few yards away from a BBC engineer: "I had a momentary glimpse of a large ball of blinding, wild white light and two concentric rings of color, the inner one lavender and the outer one violet, as I ducked my head. The ball seemed to be ten to twenty feet high. . . . The explosion made an indescribable noise—something like a colossal growl—and was accompanied by a veritable tornado of air blast."

These mines lay waste vast areas of the poorer parts of London. Churchill constantly visits those hardest hit, scrambling over the rubble, noting the pathetic little Union Jacks sticking out among the broken beams and crumbled brick. More often than not, he weeps at what he sees. Lord Ismay, his chief of staff, hears an old woman call out, "You see, he *really* cares. He's crying!"

To the boys of Harrow, his old school, he says, *Never, never, never, never give in.* In an aside to one of his secretaries, he mutters, *We must go on and on like the gun-horses, till we drop*. He watches the blitz spread to the provincial cities—Bristol, Liverpool, Coventry, Manchester, Birmingham. Like London, they are indomitable. The pride swelling in his heart, Churchill cries, *It did not matter where the blow was struck, the nation was as sound as the sea is salt*. He is on record as having seen the outcome of an air offensive as long ago as 1917, writing then: *Familiarity with bombardment, a good system of dugouts or shelters, a strong control by police and military authorities, would be sufficient to preserve the national fighting power unimpaired. In our own case we have seen the combative spirit of the people roused, and not quelled, by the German raids.*

The slogan is GRIN AND BEAR IT! For one famous theater in London it is particularly apt. Boasting the funniest comics and the least-dressed chorus line in the country, the Windmill puts on its nonstop revue come what may. To this day its proscenium arch carries the legend WE NEVER CLOSED. One night, however, they almost capitulate. The bombing is very fierce. As it draws closer to the center of the city the audience begins to thin. At last only one small elderly man remains, square in the middle of the front row. Unable to close while they still have an audience, the girls force smiles and dance on. At the end of the evening they discover that their solitary audience is as deaf as a post.

The House of Commons maintains its decorum. When the bombers come too close the Speaker interrupts the debate, though in seemly fashion. "I am informed," his deep voice rolls over the oaken benches, "that an air raid is now considered imminent and I will accordingly suspend the sitting."

Churchill's impish wit delights his colleagues. *Statisticians*, he tells them, the *s* impediment in his speech making the word both a trap and a triumph, *statisticians may amuse themselves by calculating that after making allowance for*

the law of diminishing returns, through the same house be-
ing struck twice or three times over, it would take ten years
at the present rate for half the houses in London to be de-
molished. After that, of course, the progress would be much
slower. Churchill's mood is infectious. One day the BBC reports that Monkey Hill at the Zoo has received a direct hit.
Gravely the announcer adds, "The morale of the monkeys
remains high."

The night of 29 December 1940 sees the worst fire raid of
all. Six of the elegant old churches built by Sir Christopher
Wren, each a national treasure, are set ablaze. The water
mains burst. London is a holocaust, but still she will not die.
Churchill broadcasts to his tired people: *This monstrous*
product of former wrongs and shame has resolved to try to
break our famous island by a process of indiscriminate
slaughter and destruction. What he has done is to kindle a fire
in British hearts which will glow long after all the traces of
the conflagration he has caused in London have been re-
moved.

But the end is in sight. The black smoke of desolation begins to disperse. Once more the people can see the spring
arrive. As the delicate blossoms break in a white mist in the
orchards of the south and the daffodils wave in seas of yellow
the skies grow strangely quiet. What has happened to the
Luftwaffe?

The answer is not long in coming. As spring touches the
flat marshes of eastern Poland the fields bloom with German
troops. The *Luftwaffe* has been withdrawn to prepare the
road to Moscow. London's ordeal is over.

Churchill congratulates the nation: *A million Britons died*
in the First World War. But nothing surpasses 1940. . . . We
had not flinched or wavered. We had not failed. . . . Alone,
but upborne by every generous heartbeat of mankind, we
had defied the tyrant in the height of his power.

SINK HER
BY GUNFIRE

The sea is Death's garden, and he
sows dead men in the loam . . .
FRANCIS MARION CRAWFORD: *The Song of the Sirens*

SLICING the gray waves with their proud, beaked longships, the Normans came to England in an age when Germany was a land of petty tribes, and founded a seafaring nation. They spoke lovingly of the sea, calling it "the whale-road" and "the gannets' bath" and their keels furrowed it as plows lay open the land. Alfred, the English king who mastered them, built the first navy since the Roman galleys harried the coasts of Carthage, Tyre and Egypt. Norseman and Anglo-Saxon fought upon the sea, traded across it, felt its sudden anger, learned its inscrutable ways. The sea had moods and mysteries and deep down, down in the green depths, there lived the Kraken. From time to time he would surface in a cold froth of spray, engulf a ship, and sink back slowly to the dim bed of the sea.

•   •   •

In 1940 there lurk in every sea lane leading to England the steel hulls of modern Krakens. U-boat warfare is the noose that will strangle Britain, and the slim shapes of the *Unterseebooten* wait like shadows for the fat convoys that carry Britain's future. The island cannot survive in isolation: since the time of the Phoenicians maps of the world's trade routes have carried lines from all points of the compass, all converging on Britain. Through the centuries the lines have thickened, conjoining into pulsing arteries as they approach her coast. It is to protect these arteries that for centuries the Royal Navy has been manned and armed.

In 1940 the Royal Navy bears the longest tradition of any force in the world. Her captains are the heirs of heroes who burned the hulking galleys of Spain, sundered the French battle line at Trafalgar, humbled the German Grand Fleet in the thunderous dawn of Jutland. Her squadrons have sailed invincible from the muddy waters of the China Sea to the sullen wastes beyond Cape Horn, maneuvered through the mountainous icebergs off Ultima Thule, lain threatening in the sweating heat of the Guinea Gulf.

From fat-bellied bomb boats to sleek destroyers, from lumbering eighty-gun men-of-war to steel dreadnoughts, the names of glory have passed from generation to generation of the trim ships that fly the white ensign: *Royal Sovereign* and *Repulse, Iron Duke* and *Arethusa, Illustrious, Havock* and *Revenge.* The drum beats of history echo through the muster roll.

When war breaks out, the Navy is at its battle stations, as it was twenty-five years before. But now the scene is different: the emphasis has shifted away from the squadrons of great capital ships. There is no German Grand Fleet. The war at sea will be fought along the supply lines; the menace will come from U-boats and surface raiders, and Churchill, remembering the desperate winter of 1917, when the British looked famine in the face, knows how real this menace is. *The only thing that really frightened me during the war,* he admits, *was the U-boat peril. . . . Here was no field for gestures or sensations; only the slow, cold drawing of lines on charts, which showed potential strangulation.*

One of the deadliest effects of the fall of France is that the Atlantic ports of Brest and Lorient pass into German hands. No longer need the U-boats undertake the long and perilous haul from the Baltic through the North Sea, or run the gauntlet of destroyers from the Dover patrol hunting in the Channel. The moment France is overrun, the Germans mass their battalions of forced labor to build submarine pens and storehouses on the edge of the Atlantic itself.

Fall of 1940 is dubbed "the happy time" by Admiral Doenitz's Submarine Command. For the beginning of a campaign the figures are terrifying: one hundred and forty-four unescorted merchant ships sunk, and seventy-three more sailing in convoy. The cost to the Germans is six submarines. The British crowd all their ships into convoys, for no lone ship, however fast, can sail unchallenged through the wide screen of U-boats.

To counter this, Doenitz introduces a new tactic, the wolf pack. One submarine sights a convoy and immediately calls in others; there is no attack until seven or eight of them have grouped. Then the sea boils with waterspouts as torpedoes crisscross the tight-knit convoys, slamming into freighters and tankers. Week after week, month after month, the convoys beat their way eastward, losing ships, sometimes accounting for a submarine, but always struggling somehow into the Clyde or the Mersey to discharge the cargoes on which Britain lives and fights. Some ships are so old their

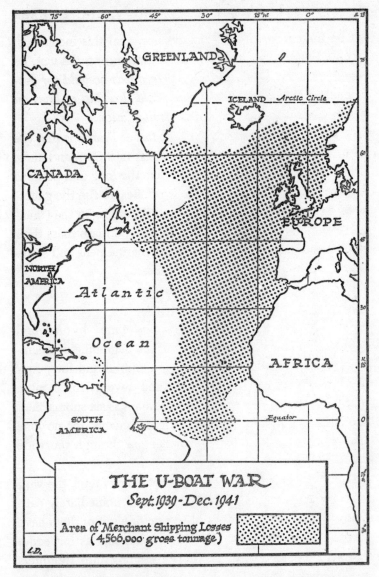

With the outbreak of war, German U-boats, first hunting separately
and then in "wolf-packs," ravage Allied shipping in the Battle of the
Atlantic. In March 1941, the Allies suffer losses of 243,000 tons by
U-boats alone. By December 1941, on orders of Adolf Hitler, the
U-boats extend their attacks into American coastal waters with imme-
diate success.

strakes twist and groan at every surge of the sea; at the torpedo strike they burst like rotten plums.

It is a lonely battle, fought far out of sight of land, upon the cruel winter waters of an ocean dangerous enough in times of peace. In the war rooms of headquarters in London and Berlin it is fought on maps and charts, with symbols and graphs and little colored pins. But, like every battle, in the last analysis it is won or lost by the men whom it engulfs. To the men of the merchant navy it is as personal a war as any fought by infantry.

Admiral Sir Kenelm Creighton, Commodore of Ocean Convoys, is climbing up to the bridge when "she staggered like a stumbling horse and shuddered to a lurching stop. . . . My ears were buzzing from the crash of the exploding torpedo. . . . My left arm was numb from being flung against the side of the bridge ladder. The vicious scream of escaping steam smothered some of the unearthly gargling sounds coming from the drowning and the tearing squeals of those trapped in the scalding agony of the engine room."

Nor are the escort ships immune. "The sky suddenly turned to flame and the ship gave a violent shudder . . ." reports Commander D. A. Rayner. "Looking ahead, I could see something floating and turning over in the water like a giant metallic whale. As I looked it rolled over farther still and I could make out our own pennant numbers painted on it. I was dumfounded. It seemed beyond reason. I ran to the after side of the bridge and looked over. The ship ended just aft of the engine room—everything abaft had gone. What I had seen ahead of us *had really been the ship's own stern.*"

From time to time there are further hazards. These are the "ghost ships," fast raiders that slip past the British cordons to range the Atlantic, sink as much tonnage as possible and sneak back to port. *Atlantis,* the first of them, steams north along the Norwegian coast disguised with the colors of neutral Russia, cuts through the Denmark Strait and heads for the South Atlantic, where she becomes a Japanese merchant-man. Changing again, she repaints en route for the Indian Ocean and appears there as a Dutch cargo steamer. Her bag numbers thirteen ships, totaling 94,000 tons. Another raider, *Orion*, cruises 112,000 miles in 510 days. Tankers and supply ships rendezvous with the raiders in mid-ocean, or establish bases on tiny remote islands. The raiders themselves carry telescopic smokestacks and topmasts, dummy derricks, false bulwarks, deckhouses and deck cargoes, and an unlimited supply of flags and paint.

The problem they pose is not so much that they exact crip-pling losses (in 1940 they account for 366,000 tons), though every cargo sunk means another notch to be taken in Brit-ain's belt. They hinder shipping movements, since no mer-chantman is safe outside a convoy when they are abroad. More seriously, they disrupt the concentration of escort and patrol vessels that the U-boat war demands.

In the fall of 1940, as nights begin to lengthen in the northern hemisphere, the threat suddenly intensifies. Two pocket-battleships, *Admiral Scheer* and *Admiral Hipper*, ap-pear in the North Atlantic. On 5 November *Admiral Scheer* encounters the homebound convoy H.X.84, numbering thirty-seven ships. Dusk is falling as the convoy hurriedly makes smoke and scatters like a flock of fat hens. Their escort, the merchant cruiser *Jervis Bay*, closes desperately but is sunk with all hands. One of the surviving ships, the tanker *San Demetrio*, yaws in the waves like a floating bon-fire. Her crew have abandoned her, but the second officer and a handful of brave men reboard her, douse the flames and bring her limping home.

Admiral Hipper is less successful. Sighting a troop convoy, she pounces avidly. However, the convoy's escort includes three cruisers. *Admiral Hipper* receives their eager and unexpected attentions and has to return at once to Brest for repairs.

At the end of the year Churchill glumly sums up: *We could not regard the state of the outer oceans without uneasiness. We knew that disguised merchant ships in unknown numbers were preying in all the southern waters. The pocket battleship* Scheer *was loose and hidden. The* Hipper *might break out at any moment from Brest, and the two German battle cruisers* Scharnhorst *and* Gneisenau *must also be expected soon to play their part.*

This last is no idle prophecy. In February 1941 the two great ships are unleashed into the Atlantic. Admiral Lutjens has orders to avoid action with any equal opponent. Lurking near the busy convoy routes he picks off five ships and moves south. There he summons a wolf pack of U-boats and they take five more. A few days later Lutjens sinks sixteen ships, all from the same convoy. Thus gorged, he runs for Brest: his raid has been a fantastic success. Twenty-six ships lie on the bottom of the sea, and not an inch of paint on his two battle cruisers has been scratched.

Churchill sees the German threat at sea as a mortal danger, and it gnaws at his bowels. Early in March he declares to Admiral Pound, his First Sea Lord: *We have got to lift this business to the highest plane, over everything else. I am going to proclaim "The Battle of the Atlantic."*

Its effect is not felt immediately. In March, April and May of 1941 the losses amount to 1,700,000 tons. Gradually, however, the balance begins to swing. The United States Navy starts to convoy American ships carrying supplies to outpost bases. American planes alert convoys to the presence of enemy ships. Aircraft are launched from makeshift carriers to fight off Focke-Wulf Condors and to spot submarines. The first radar sets are installed. More air cover is provided from bases in Iceland and Newfoundland.

The Navy is confident that in the long run it will win the Battle of the Atlantic. It will be a long haul, but in the end the Navy will win. What it longs for is something to sink its teeth into. The frustrations of chasing ghost ships, invisible submarines, and pocket battleships that will not stay to fight drive the British captains into a cold and sullen anger. Huddled on their spray-soaked bridges, drinking their endless cups of thick cocoa, they scan the gray wastelands for a sight of an enemy they can *attack*.

On 18 May 1941 such a target puts forth her armored snout. *Bismarck*, pride of the Third Reich, takes aboard the last ton of supplies from the quaint quays of Gdynia and sets sail. She is the heaviest warship afloat, and most of her weight is in guns and armor. Ten thousand tons heavier than the latest British battleship, she mounts eight fifteen-inch guns. The Germans claim she is unsinkable.

All through the spring she has been cruising the Baltic, exercising her crew and perfecting her gunnery. North she steals now through the Kattegat, westward through the Skagerrak. Beside her steams her consort, the new eight-inch gun cruiser *Prinz Eugen*. Three days later they are refueling within the towering rock walls of a fjord close to Bergen. These clearly are the final preparations for a deadly odyssey.

Inside the Home Fleet's base at Scapa, the winches roar and the heavy ships make ready for sea. The cruisers *Norfolk* and *Suffolk* are patroling the icebound Denmark Strait, and out from the Orkneys the battle cruiser *Hood* and the battleship *Prince of Wales*, so new that she carries civilian fitters aboard her still, sail to join them. Every capital ship that can steam is alerted. *Bismarck* must not escape, or the Navy's honor is lost.

Across the North Sea an icy rain whips the racing waves,

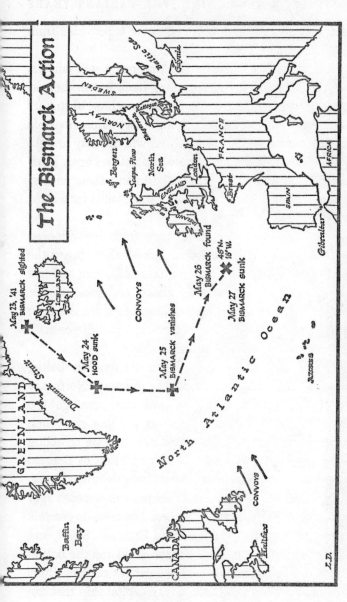

The Bismarck Action

Greenland · *Baffin Bay* · *Denmark Strait* · May 23, '41 BISMARCK sighted · ICELAND · May 24 HOOD sunk · May 25 BISMARCK vanishes · May 26 BISMARCK found · May 27 BISMARCK sunk 48° N.-15° W. · CONVOYS · North Atlantic Ocean · AZORES · CANADA · Halifax · CONVOYS · SWEDEN · NORWAY · Bergen · Scapa Flow · North Sea · Skagerrak · Kattegat · Baltic Sea · Gdynia · ENGLAND · London · IRELAND · Brest · FRANCE · SPAIN · Gibraltar · AFRICA · L.D.

On May 22, 1941, the German battleship *Bismarck* dashes through the Denmark Strait toward the open sea and Allied shipping. Intercepted by the battle-cruiser *Hood* on May 24, she opens fire, sinks the *Hood* and disappears into the trackless wastes of the North Atlantic. On May 26, Allied aircraft sight her. Brought under attack by British planes and warships, the *Bismarck* bursts into flame and founders.

the clouds pressing down black and impenetrable. By the time a reconnaissance plane can reach Bergen the fjord is empty. Somewhere in that gray wilderness *Bismarck* and *Prinz Eugen* have broken loose. At once Admiral Tovey, Commander-in-Chief of the Home Fleet, puts to sea in the battleship *King George V*, with the great carrier *Victorious*, four cruisers and a screen of seven destroyers. Next morning the battleship *Repulse* joins him. If *Bismarck* runs into them it will be a hard meeting.

But *Bismarck* is far to the north, heading for the Denmark Strait. There the pack ice is thick and the seaway only eight miles wide. Great bands of fog shift and eddy unpredictably. Uneasily the cruiser *Suffolk*, aware in this nightmare seascape only of the reality of *Bismarck's* guns, tacks in and out of the swirling mist. A single salvo from *Bismarck* can lift her out of the water, but it is *Suffolk's* duty to watch—and wait.

On her bridge Captain R. N. Ellis suddenly hears a shout. "When the lookout hailed that he had sighted an enemy battleship, I went to the edge of the bridge because it was important to be sure it was a battleship. There is a tendency in the fog for a ship to seem much larger than it really is. But it was the *Bismarck* all right!" Remembering dryly, "it is the business of the cruiser not to fight battleships but to follow them until you can bring them into contact with your own heavy forces," Captain Ellis hurriedly alters course, increases speed and heads for the fog. *Bismarck* is only seven miles off, almost point-blank range for her enormous guns. Within half an hour *Suffolk* is astern of the quarry and settles down to dog her.

During these maneuvers Churchill had been harassing the Admiralty War Room by telephone from Chequers. His weekend guests, among them the President's envoy Averell Harriman, sweat out the tension until three in the morning.

*   *   *

As the Arctic twilight brightens slowly into the dawn of Saturday, *Norfolk* and *Suffolk* are plunging doggedly through driving rain and snow. In a few hours *Bismarck* and *Prinz Eugen* will be in the open, and perhaps clear away. Then, on the southeastern horizon, the smoke of heavy ships. *Hood* and *Prince of Wales* are turning to engage; they open fire at twenty-five thousand yards. At once *Bismarck's* batteries open, bracketing *Hood*.

One of *Hood's* seamen, Robert Tillbourn, sees the great spouts of *Bismarck's* salvo lurch skyward in *Hood's* wake. He does not know that his ship is most vulnerable at this extreme range; her deck armor is insufficient defense against the plunging fire of a longer—and therefore higher—trajectory. *Bismarck's* next salvo strikes aft and starts a fire. As the blaze spreads, another salvo hurtles through the deck below the bridge, ripping into the main magazine deep inside the ship.

Tillbourn, crouching behind his gunshield, feels the blast slam around beside him, killing his two mates. "Feeling sick," he says, "I crawled to the side, but the angle of the deck was so steep I slid into the water. The ship began to roll over on top of me and some of the wireless aerials, which were loose, began to wrap around my feet. They started to pull me down with the ship. I kicked my boots off and surfaced and realized I was only fifteen feet away from the ship. She was sinking fast and had her bow in the air. I struck out for some wreckage. The sea was colder than anything I'd ever imagined. I remembered somebody saying it was easy to die in such cold just by going to sleep. So I found a float or something and lay on it, trying to go to sleep." Rescued eventually, Tillbourn is one of three survivors out of *Hood's* complement of 1,419 officers and men.

On *Bismarck's* bridge Admiral Lutjens, the veteran raider, loses his Prussian reserve. His binoculars reflect the angry red and yellow glare as an immense explosion splits *Hood* in two. With five salvoes, after only eight minutes of action, he has sunk a battle cruiser. *Bismarck*'s guns train around on *Prince of Wales* and again Lutjens feels her heel beneath him with the recoil. Within minutes she scores four hits.

The bridge of *Prince of Wales* is a slaughterhouse. Her forward turret and rangefinders are out of action. She is holed underwater aft. Captain Leach, stunned by the blast that has annihilated his officers, drags himself to the speaking tube. Making smoke, *Prince of Wales* turns slowly away. The action is broken off.

But those few minutes have sealed *Bismarck*'s fate. Two shells from *Prince of Wales*'s main armament have pierced her underwater. Though *Bismarck* loses little speed, one of them has ripped open an oil tank, and the oil seeps out of her like a scent for hounds to follow. As Lutjens jubilantly speeds on his course the hounds are still with him.

At seven o'clock that Saturday morning Averell Harriman wakes in his bed at Chequers with a hand shaking his shoulder. Faintly he discerns a stocky figure. "*Hood*'s blown up," it says, then adds grimly, "but we've got *Bismarck* for certain." But Churchill is in for a shock: an hour later comes the appalling news that *Prince of Wales* has broken off the action. At once he wonders desperately whether Lutjens has turned back for Germany with victory glistening in his pocket.

Saturday is a day of horror at Chequers. Dully Churchill plods through the stream of papers that follows him everywhere. But his mind is far away. *Bismarck* is rushing south, toward the convoys that now lie defenseless. Can Admiral Tovey's force cut her off? Admiral Somerville has left Gibraltar with *Renown* and the carrier *Ark Royal*, but suppose *Bismarck* alters course? To be sure, the net is forming, but there are still huge gaps in it. The cruisers *Norfolk* and *Suf-*

folk and the chastened *Prince of Wales* are still in prudent contact, but the weather is worsening. What, moreover, might not happen during the night?

In the early evening *Bismarck* suddenly turns and shows fight. In the melee *Prinz Eugen* slips away to the south. *Bismarck* resumes her ominous course as twilight begins to fall. Far to the northwest, *Victorious* flies off nine Swordfish torpedo aircraft, at extreme range, against a strong head wind, and in rain and low cloud. It is an impossible gamble, but in the last gleam of light one of their torpedoes runs in and strikes under *Bismarck*'s bridge. *Bismarck* does not falter. Is she really unsinkable? It is now pitch dark. What *will* happen during the night?

What does happen that night is like an evil dream. *Suffolk* is patiently tracking *Bismarck* by radar and zigzagging as ordered on an anti-submarine course. As she tacks on an outward leg, *Bismarck* vanishes. The British begin a frantic quartering and find—nothing. The first glimmer of dawn illuminates an empty sea.

Lutjens is the only one unaware of the situation. His more powerful radar still shows ships within range, and he cannot therefore know that he has been lost. Admiral Tovey has turned east, on a guess, believing *Bismarck* is making for the North Sea. Innocently Lutjens breaks radio silence to make a signal to Berlin. Jubilantly the Admiralty pick up the signal and relay it to Admiral Tovey. Then another mistake. Aboard *King George* V there is an error in the decoding. Though puzzled by the bearing given, Admiral Tovey steams for nine hours in hot pursuit, but in the wrong direction. By six in the evening, however, the Admiralty has guessed again, and this time correctly. *Bismarck* is headed for Brest. Now Admiral Somerville from Gibraltar is coming within range.

Coastal Command is ordered to make ready every aircraft that can fly. Flying Officer Denis Briggs takes off in his Catalina in the early morning of 26 May. "We were in the clouds," he remembers, "but we suddenly hit a break and for a while we were buffeted about the sky by a certain amount of shrapnel. A large number of holes began to appear in our aircraft. I looked down and there we were in a clear sky over a battleship. The fact that she was firing on us was no proof she was an enemy ship, though. The Royal Navy had instructions to fire on all aircraft approaching too close. In my experience we were fired on more often by the Royal Navy than by the Germans, especially if the captain had had a good lunch . . ." However, recollecting that it is too early for lunch, and taking a steady look, Flying Officer Briggs concludes that it really is *Bismarck*.

Once more the Navy has a chance, but now there are more problems. *Bismarck* is almost within reach of air-cover from France, is apparently almost unmarked, and rapidly gathering a thick screen of submarines. *Prince of Wales* and *Repulse* have turned away to refuel. *King George V* and *Rodney*, still far behind, are both dangerously low in fuel. Admiral Somerville's force is only seventy miles to the east, but he has nothing heavy enough for a killing blow. The only hope of success is for Somerville to slow *Bismarck* down until *King George V* and *Rodney* can come up.

Ark Royal flies off her Swordfish with torpedoes and there ensues a moment of high comedy. The cruiser *Sheffield*, part of the same force, has been sent on ahead at high speed, and the Swordfish pilots have not been warned. Ardently seeking their target, they catch sight of a dangerous gray shape below and attack at once. *Sheffield* fortunately realizes the mistake and dodges, elegantly but with all speed. So too, at last, do the pilots. One of them signals *Sheffield*, with a flippancy that is not immediately appreciated, "Sorry for the kipper!"

At 7:10 P.M. a second strike is flown off and in the fading light they make their steady runs. One torpedo hits *Bismarck's* thick armor and does negligible damage. But a second carries *Bismarck's* death. It catches her low in the stern, blows off her propellers and jams her rudder into a vicious tangle of steel. In a flurry of spray *Bismarck* turns two complete circles, like a wounded dog.

Also heading for the fight is a force of five destroyers, led by the resolute and daring Captain Vian. He conceives his duty to lie in "the delivery of the enemy to the Commander-in-Chief." White water creaming over their sharp bows, the destroyers circle *Bismarck* all night, attacking with torpedoes. They score two hits, but still *Bismarck* is afloat.

Churchill spends four hours that evening in a favorite haunt, the Admiralty War Room. Spotting the Controller of the Navy, Admiral Fraser, who is not normally so closely involved in such belligerent matters, Churchill asks rather unkindly, "What are *you* doing here?" "I am waiting," the Admiral thoughtfully responds, "to see what I have got to repair."

Admiral Tovey signals that his fuel is now so low that unless *Bismarck* is slowed he will have to abandon the chase at midnight. Churchill tells the First Sea Lord to order him to go on even if he has to be towed home. Eventually Churchill leaves, convinced that the end is now certain; it is an enormous relief, for in the morning he must report to the House of Commons.

At midnight Admiral Lutjens faces his fate. "Ship unmaneuverable," he signals Berlin. "We shall fight to the last shell. Long live the Fuehrer!"

Bismarck's main armament is still intact, though she cannot maneuver. But there is a tiny flaw. Her guns are laid by stereoscopic rangefinders, and the system depends on the gunlayers being at the peak of physical condition. After four days' constant action they are haggard. When *Rodney* and *King George V* unleash their broadsides at 8:47 in the morning, *Bismarck* is slow to reply. The British ships hit at once. *Bismarck*'s third salvo straddles *Rodney*, but the British are closing, closing. Fire breaks out amidships, and one by one *Bismarck*'s four turrets fall silent. *Rodney* turns across her bows in the classic maneuver, closes to four thousand yards, and rakes her with a tornado of shell. By 10:15 *Bismarck*, her guns silent and her mast shot away, is wallowing in an inferno of flame and smoke. And still she will not sink.

King George V and *Rodney* turn away, anxious about their fuel. The cruiser *Dorsetshire* is ordered to administer the *coup de grâce* with torpedoes. *Bismarck*'s flags are still flying as she goes down. A hundred and ten of her crew survive.

At that moment Churchill is telling an expectant House the details of this quietus. A slip of paper is passed to him and thankfully he announces, *I have just received news that the* Bismarck *is sunk.* Looking round, he notes, *They seemed content.*

Next day Churchill telegraphs *Bismarck*'s epitaph to President Roosevelt, and points a moral as well. *She was a terrific ship, and a masterpiece of naval construction. . . . The effect upon the Japanese will be highly beneficial. I expect they are doing all their sums again.*

THE
INLAND
SEA

The meteor flag of England
 Shall yet terrific burn
Till danger's troubled night depart
 And the star of peace return.
 THOMAS CAMPBELL: *Ye Mariners of England*

IN THE torrid noonday even the pariah dog lying in the shade is asleep. The heat shimmers off the tawny earth, at the horizon merging sand and sky in the metallic illusion of the mirage. Under the straggling palms a few camels lie tethered, a green foam caking on their lips, flies clustered thick on their saddle sores. The sky is a light hard blue and in it the sun blazes white and savage. The air stands absolutely still.

Outside the oasis, to the east, the low white fort seems inhabited only by the dead. Its flag, limp as a rag on the staff, throws a rumpled black shadow aslant the wall. From the shadow the wary jade eyes of a lizard regard a hostile world. Suddenly the lizard scurries across the wall and into a dusty crevice. Nothing else moves. The fortress is asleep and the desert dreams at midday.

This is the frontier of an empire, the new Italian empire of Benito Mussolini, Father of Fascism, a new Caesar leading his Romans to the domination of the lands of the sun. This is the frontier post of Capuzzo, the end of the line. It lies in the center of the Western Desert, soon to be the arena for a kind of battle never seen before and unlikely ever to be seen again, the swift fluid battle of devastating machines maneuvering like fleets at sea.

This is the wasteland. Waterless, rock-strewn, baked iron-hard by the sun, the Western Desert is a tableland stretching four hundred miles along the Mediterranean shore from the powdery dunes of El Alamein in the east to the harsh cliffs of Derna in the west. The frontier between Libya and Egypt runs roughly down its center. Its eastern end is blocked by the Qattara Depression, a deep escarpment tumbling down to a flat immensity of salt marshes that glisten like quartz in the sun. To the west it merges with the gentler cultivated settlements of northern Libya. A hundred and fifty miles southward from the coast lie the great oases of Jarabub and Siwa, twin centers of a spider's web of camel tracks, the last vestiges of civilization on the edge of the Sand Sea. Beyond the Sand Sea yawns the limitless desolation of the Sahara, a land forgotten by God.

Along the edge of the Mediterranean, a tiny thread in this vastness, runs the coast road, a strip of macadam the width of two trucks. Seaward, a line of telegraph poles march alongside it, landward, only the drab dun miles of rock and sand and camel thorn. From Tripoli to Bardia the road is Italian, and dignified at discreet intervals with concrete monuments to the glory that is Rome.

On this day of 10 June 1940, in the blank hours of afternoon, the road is deserted, though it is the main supply artery of the Italian garrison of Libya. France is in her death agony, and Mussolini has seen fit this day to enter the war. The legions of Italy, however, see no cause to alter their habit of siesta. After all, they are two hundred thousand strong, heavily supplied with artillery and tanks, supported by crowded magazines at Benghazi, Derna, Tobruk and Bardia. Their positions are solidly fortified, their generals energetic, their troops spirited and well fed.

On the other side of Egypt are three hundred thousand more men, under the command of no less than the Duke of Aosta, Viceroy of Ethiopia. He has only to come down from the hills, subdue the Sudan, and Egypt will be caught in the jaws of a vise. In the whole of the Middle East there are only fifty thousand British. They are outnumbered ten to one. What need of military activity on this first glorious day of a victorious war? Sleeping off their farinaceous lunches, the Italians are unconscious of their fate.

For across the border, not far from their railhead at Mersa Matrûh, the British are assembling one of the most formidable divisions ever to command a battlefield, the 7th Armored, later known as the Desert Rats after their divisional crest, a red jerboa, the little jumping rat of the desert. Moreover, two of the British commanders will make names for themselves that will echo down the history of war.

Sir Archibald Wavell, the Commander-in-Chief, is a stocky, hard-muscled man, with a face ravaged by deep lines of experience and thought. Silent, unpredictable, he is blessed with the most penetrating military intuition since the great Duke of Marlborough himself. His subordinate, Major General Richard O'Connor, a diffident, shy spirit, in command of the Western Desert Force, is soon to prove himself a past master at the punitive battle: the guileful approach, the murderous sudden assault, the ruthless pursuit. O'Con-

In December 1940, the British open their first offensive in the Western Desert of North Africa, held by Mussolini. Mersa Matruh is captured on December 10; Tobruk falls on January 21, 1941. By the spring of 1941, the Italians are routed. In March 1941, Britain comes to the aid of Greek patriots fighting the Italians and then the Germans in the mountains of Greece. The German armies overrun the country, forcing the British to retreat to Crete.

nor's tactics in the next few months will provide the Italians
with a textbook on the battle of annihilation. On this day of
10 June Major General O'Connor still wears the Silver Medal
for Valor he won fighting beside the Italian Army in 1918.

During the first few hours of the war against Italy the
Duce's forces remain an unknown quantity. In the Spanish
Civil War they fought with courage. Now it is time to test
their mettle. The armored cars of the 11th Hussars, with a
few tanks, are ordered out to the southwest and disappear
in a plume of dust.

In the cooler hours of the late afternoon the frontier post
at Capuzzo begins to stir. Men yawn and stretch, and from
the kitchens comes the clatter of buckets and canteens as
the evening meal is prepared. A line of camels plods slowly
north on its lethargic business. A few soldiers gather around
a radio set to hear the news on their first day of war. It is
also, unfortunately for them, to be their last.

Tucked comfortably out of sight in a trough of ground
little more than a mile away, the Hussars await the darkness.
They have cut the frontier wire and their commander has
been gazing at the fort from behind a convenient thorn bush
for the past hour. He considers there is time for a light meal
before the attack. They are, after all, on the imperial soil of
Italy and it would be a pity to rush things.

In the soft darkness of the desert night the garrison is
suddenly and unkindly awakened by the crack of tank guns.
A few delayed-action shells soon persuade them to capitulate. The British move on to a second fort at Maddalena.
Their total bag for the night is seventy prisoners and one
frontier. Encouraged, they push on to the west.

There, barreling down the fine road, they are pleased to
encounter a long and succulent Italian column. Cruising

parallel with the crowded road, the tanks destroy the soft-skinned vehicles and forty inadequately armored tanks as well. They capture another eighty-eight prisoners, the most distinguished of them General Lastucci, chief engineer of the Italian 10th Army. It is a propitious beginning and the Hussars return to the frontier with their guests.

By such skirmishes and sudden raids the British quickly dominate this barren no man's land. But it is clear that soon the Italians must launch upon them an offensive to gain the glittering prize of Alexandria and the fertile delta of the Nile. Strategically, all hangs in the balance. England is alone, her army stripped of its weapons by the somber disasters of May and June in northern France: she must rearm to face the threat of invasion of her soil, inviolate for almost nine hundred years.

Yet the Middle East must be held, not so much because of the Suez Canal, or because the fall of Egypt opens the road to India. The Middle East must be held because beneath its arid soil spreads the black gold of the Gulf, the coin of life itself—oil.

Above all these considerations—the defense of the British Isles, the import of arms and raw materials, the curbing of Italian power in North Africa, the buildup of force in Egypt —one factor, as always in British strategy, is of prime importance. The Navy must dominate the sea. As early as May Churchill has seen this need, writing (not without irony) to General Ismay: *It is important that at the outset collision should take place both with the Italian Navy and Air Force, in order that we can see what their quality really is, and whether it has changed at all since the last war.* Thus encouraged, Admiral Andrew Cunningham, commanding the Eastern Mediterranean, puts to sea and stays there. *Mare dolce*, as the Italians call it, "the gentle sea," becomes for them a bitter pasture.

Pleased with Cunningham's successes in the first weeks, Churchill sends him reinforcements of heavy ships, and on 11 November the Admiral is ready to call on the Italian Fleet at home. In a night attack torpedo bombers from the carrier *Illustrious* slice into the heavily defended harbor of Taranto. Within minutes three battleships and a cruiser have been hit. In a single stroke the balance of naval power in the Mediterranean has been altered.

By coincidence, this same day the Italian Air Force has made its debut against the RAF. A force of bombers flies insolently if imprudently up the Medway River, toward London, by personal command of the Duce, and there meets a cruelly efficient reception. *This was*, Churchill records, *their first and last intervention in our domestic affairs.*

One of Churchill's greatest concerns in this theater is the defense of Malta. Historically a staging post for fleets passing to the Crusades, the home of an Order of Chivalry, in Nelson's day the base commanding the Central Mediterranean, Malta in 1940 boasts a naval dockyard, a few light anti-aircraft guns and three senile Gloster Gladiators for air defense. Her people, it will be seen, are made of iron.

Seventeen miles long and nine miles wide, a flattened hummock of rock, treeless and waterless, Malta is no magic island in the sun. Her harbor at Valletta has a certain rickety charm, but no style whatever. A system of tunnels, caves and galleries runs through the rock, and it is within their protection that her citizens will be spending a great deal of their time. The three Gladiators, their fabric so riddled that it looks like lace, fly off on endless sorties against the Italian bombers. They are aptly christened *Faith, Hope* and *Charity.*

In time they are joined by Hurricanes, and eventually by Spitfires, but nothing can end the ordeal of the ordinary, humble people of Malta. Their casualties from bombing are in proportion twice as heavy as those of the British. Father

Hugh Attard remembers one hideous incident: "One day a tragedy occurred. The cinema in the town was packed to capacity when it was hit. We soon realized that hundreds of people were lying under the debris. We ran to the spot, digging out the victims and anointing them, at the same time comforting and consoling their relatives. I shall never forget the dilemma in which I found myself. Who, amid the carnage, was I to help first?" Month after month the siege and the bombardment of little Malta continue, but she will not break.

Meanwhile, the British suffer their only defeat at the hands of the Italians. In a campaign lasting only five days they are swept ignominiously out of Somaliland by a larger, but not necessarily more powerful, force. Churchill considers it a "vexatious" episode. Compared with what is impending in the north, however, it is hardly a major setback.

Through the months of summer, British strength in the Delta is reinforced. The armored division is brought up to strength. An Indian division arrives, and brigades of Australians and New Zealanders; another armored division is promised. As the likelihood of a German invasion of Britain recedes, the flow of arms to Wavell increases. There is a sudden change in the Italian command. Marshal Rodolfo Graziani succeeds Marshal Balbo when the latter flies over one of his own anti-aircraft batteries and, in a sudden access of zeal and accuracy, is shot down.

Graziani, in spite of his superiority of force, is not anxious to attack. By the beginning of September, however, Mussolini, avid for victory, has grown tired of procrastination and orders him forward. Against his will, Graziani attacks on 13 September with his main body of six divisions of infantry and eight battalions of tanks. The British number three battalions of infantry and a battalion of tanks.

O'Connor's men, staring out across the desert at this impressive array, are somewhat amused. The Italian battle line is drawn up in review order, as if about to march in triumph up the Appian Way and onto the Field of Mars. In the van a screen of motor cyclists keeps immaculate formation, followed by orderly phalanxes of light tanks and mechanized infantry. Not without admiration for this showmanship, but made thoughtful by this evidence of power, the British withdraw. Their barrage tears holes in the dense Italian columns and after four days, having reached Sidi Barrâni, Graziani is glad to call a halt and lick his wounds. The British have lost forty men.

Graziani now threatens Mersa Matrûh. He has also extended his lines of communication by sixty miles; there are gaps in his defenses and he is uneasy. Wavell and O'Connor determine not to wait for him, but to start an offensive of their own. They report accordingly to Churchill, whose reaction is instantaneous: *I purred like six cats. Here was something worth doing.*

On 6 December 1940 O'Connor begins his first devastating battle, the opening of a breathless onslaught. That night twenty-five thousand men, desert-hardened and eager, sweep forward unopposed (and indeed undetected) for forty miles, lie up under camouflage during the day, advance again the next night. A red dawn sun climbs over an armada of steel on the morning of 9 December. Squadron after menacing squadron of tanks blankets the desert, behind them the compact batteries of field artillery and among them the thin files of infantry on whose bayonets the dawn light winks red and angry. Guns, tanks and men are blanketed with the dust of the desert wind, but through their tawny masks of sand the troops gaze relentlessly upon their prey.

The hard land thunders with a sound the world never thought to hear again, the opening barrage of a British attack. It shreds the Italian camps and the heavy tanks churn through them with murderous ease. By ten o'clock the next morning, a battalion of the Coldstream Guards, asked to report the number of prisoners, replies, "About five acres of officers and two hundred acres of other ranks."

Churchill is in Downing Street, greatly excited, reading signals hot from the battlefield. Though unable to gain a clear picture of events, he is much struck by the general air of success. One message, transmitted by a tank officer, reads: "Have arrived at the second B in Buq Buq."

O'Connor has already begun his deadly pursuit, loosing the 7th Armored and a division of Australians in a hook along the coast road. In this moment of victory, however, he loses one of his divisions, transferred to fight in Ethiopia. Undaunted, he cuts his way to the west in a relentless pattern of classic actions. By 15 December he has cleared Egypt of the enemy, taken thirty-eight thousand prisoners and isolated the first of their fortified towns, Bardia.

Three days later, speaking with the voice of the New Testament, an elated Prime Minister dispatches a cable to his Commander-in-Chief and receives an answer in kind:

Prime Minister to General Wavell: ST. MATTHEW, CHAPTER VII, VERSE 7.*

General Wavell to Prime Minister: ST. JAMES, CHAPTER I, VERSE 17.†

Bardia falls on 5 January 1941, yielding 45,000 prisoners and 462 guns. Next day Tobruk is isolated. But now far away a fanatic mind begins to take heed, apprehending

---

* "Ask, and it shall be given you; seek, and ye shall find; knock, and it shall be opened to you."

† "Every good gift and every perfect gift is from above, and cometh down from the Father of lights, with whom there is no variableness, neither shadow of turning."

danger. On 11 January Hitler decides to intervene in North
Africa and sends a warning order to his 50th Light Division
that they must make ready at once for desert war. O'Connor
has a month in which to gain complete control of Libya; if
he fails he may forfeit all his brilliant gains.

Tobruk falls on 22 January, and with it 30,000 prisoners
and 236 guns. In five weeks O'Connor has advanced two
hundred miles. Westward he presses into Cyrenaica, the
northern province of Libya, leaving the harsh desert for the
gentler grain fields and olive orchards the Italian settlers
have planted and tended. On 7 February he invests Beda
Fomm and opens his last great battle.

The fury of his assault crushes the Italians in hours and,
fleeing along the coast road, they are once more caught in
the terrible trap of an armored hook. The plain is crowded
like a fairground with abandoned trucks, tanks, tents and
piles of supplies and ammunition. Through the confusion
O'Connor rides to meet his beaten adversary and finds him
poorly accommodated.

"I'm sorry you are so uncomfortable," he says shyly, "We
haven't had time to make proper arrangements."

Touched by this considerate approach, General Bergonzoli
is very understanding.

"Thank you very much," he replies. "We do realize you
came here in a very great hurry."

There is good reason for hurry. O'Connor's time is almost
spent. His advance has now covered five hundred miles. In
ten weeks he has wiped out an Italian army five times his
own strength. He has captured 130,000 prisoners, 400 tanks,
1,290 guns and a sea of trucks. His own losses in men total
1,744. He shows a profit of eighty to one. He has shattered
Italian morale. He has executed an armored offensive faster
and more effective than the German's own blitzkrieg. What
is left of Italian power in North Africa cowers like sheep

in the fold waiting for the wolf. O'Connor prepares for the final lunge to Tripoli, the last bastion. With Tripoli secured, there will be no place for the Germans to land in Northeast Africa.

But he is too late. The draining of units from his desert army to serve elsewhere as strategy demands and the exhaustion of those left rob him of the fruit of his brilliant fighting tactics. And in the meantime there comes upon the scene another master of the pursuit battle, an adversary more worthy of his steel. On 12 February 1941 Hitler's favorite, a veteran of the annihilation of France, the panzer general Erwin Rommel, arrives in Africa.

The emphasis has now shifted ominously away from O'Connor and the dusty heroes of his Western Desert Force. Their victories have brightened the British winter, but strategic thought now concentrates on Greece and the Balkans. Moreover, there is the campaign against the Italians in Ethiopia. Already Indians and British are fighting in the sickening heat of the foothills on the eastern edge of Sudan. Coming out of the desert they have to maneuver through miles of elephant grass dried into tinder by the sun so that it catches fire at the first blast from the guns. Above them, tier after tier, threaten the bare mountains of Ethiopia. In a series of savage engagements, often fought hand to hand and at night along the rocky escarpments, they drive back the Italians and at last reach the plateau. On 6 April they take Addis Ababa. Haile Selassie, Lion of Judah, King of Kings, Emperor of Ethiopia, is restored to his throne. Mussolini's African Empire has vanished.

Though heartened by this victory, British eyes, and especially Churchill's, are fixed on events in Greece. Mussolini, with lunatic logic, has decided to attack this ancient country "to put her out of action and to assure that in all circumstances she will remain in our politico-economic sphere." His troops attack on 28 October and greatly to their surprise are immediately thrown back by the evzones, whom previously they had regarded as fancy-dress soldiers in little skirts and white stockings. Hitler, more realistic, is not amused. Churchill, fearful of German intervention, decides to send forces to Greece and orders Wavell to strip the Middle East. Harassed and apprehensive, Wavell complies.

Churchill's concern is not unfounded. Already the Germans are established in Rumania. On 14 February an arrogant summons reaches the Yugoslavian Minister for Foreign Affairs: he must come at once to Berchtesgaden. There he is told that unless his country signs a pact with the Third Reich it will be destroyed. He retires to consult his government. On 1 March the Wehrmacht moves ponderously into Bulgaria. Two weeks later the worried Yugoslavs sign the pact. But when the news reaches Belgrade the people rise in patriotic anger. At this Hitler is convulsed with insane fury. Choking, he orders "Operation Punishment" and on the morning of 6 April 1941 waves of low-flying bombers swoop down on defenseless Belgrade. For three days, sickeningly methodical, they pulverize the city, piling its streets with seventeen thousand dead.

This same day the worst happens in Greece. At the end of March British and New Zealand troops have reached their Greek allies in the line and the Italians, already half beaten, begin to crumble. But now the gray uniforms of the Wehrmacht appear in the mountains, and in the rumble of their panzers sounds the old familiar threnody of defeat for the Allies. Within eleven days it becomes clear that evacuation is inevitable. The Allies begin their withdrawal past Mount Olympus, from whose snowy peak the gods are no longer smiling. Once more the Navy's flotillas assemble to carry off

a defeated army. Greece surrenders on 24 April and smiling
Germans strut along the sunny quays of Piraeus.

Now the tide of war has turned with a vengeance. Boiling
with energy, Rommel has already begun his first campaign
by driving back the frustrated British on the first few re-
luctant miles of their withdrawal to Egypt. Directing his
scattered units, O'Connor drives straight into a German
patrol in the desert darkness and is captured. Tobruk is
hastily fortified and garrisoned by angry Australians. By-
passing it, Rommel attacks Bardia.

Tobruk has held, and continues to. Fortified by a repertory
of their native songs—the only printable ones being "Waltz-
ing Matilda" and, unaccountably, "The Wizard of Oz," the
slouch-hatted Australians, most of them fighting stripped to
the waist, discuss the ancestry of the enemy in their flat
Cockney accents and nonchalantly halt every assault dead
in its tracks. They are well supplied with food and ammunition by sea, but water is as precious as gold. It is not comfortable for the infantry, for the rocky ground makes digging
difficult, so that defenses must be built from the boulders
that strew the desert as if scattered from some indiscriminate
giant hand. Every shell that lands erupts in a vicious cloud
of stone splinters. Grimly, the Australians accept their casualties and hold. As long as Tobruk remains a stronghold Rommel dare not advance too far.

But Rommel is receiving reinforcements, and soon he will
have an Afrika Korps. More immediately, there are insistent
signs that the Germans are about to descend on Crete. Their
8th Air Corps moves onto Greek airfields, strong in Stuka
dive bombers, the harbingers of the sudden assault, and—
even more significant—mustering more than five hundred
large transport aircraft and a hundred gliders. With them,

swinging confidently down through the mountain passes, come three fresh divisions, one of paratroops, the other two of mountain troops.

The paratroops are the very cream of Germany. Young, physically superb, nurtured and disciplined by Nazi youth organizations, they are more formidable even than the SS. Issuing them their gilt bronze badges—depicting a plunging eagle in a garland of oak and laurel leaves—Baron von der Heydte, commander of the 1st Battalion of the 3rd Parachute Regiment, tells his men: "Our formation is young. We have not yet any traditions. We must create tradition by our actions in the future. It depends upon us whether or not the sign of the plunging eagle . . . will go down in history as a symbol of military honor and valor." They fight, not for any perverted racist idealism, nor out of commitment to a black circle of Nazi elite, but impelled by utter devotion to the Fatherland. They gaze now at the sapphire sea as their black Junkers trundle toward Crete and they laugh with joy.

Waiting for them is a man born for war. General Bernard Freyberg wears the crimson ribbon of the Victoria Cross—the mark of unusual courage displayed in four years of front-line fighting in Flanders. His body also carries the marks of battle. Once, in the twenties, Churchill asks to be shown his wounds and counts twenty-seven separate scars. Freyberg explains in a matter-of-fact voice, "You nearly always get two wounds for every bullet or splinter, because mostly they have to go out as well as go in." In the present war he suffers three more wounds. Still as resolute as a fighting bull, Freyberg prepares to withstand the shock of an all-out airborne attack.

His fortress is the cradle of Western civilization. In a distant dreaming age its brooding palace at Knossos housed the Minotaur, the bull-god for whom the Cretan kings exacted tributes of living sacrifices. Youths and maidens perished in that maze in whose deadly center lived the monstrous bull, until the golden hero Theseus came from Greece to slay him. The power of its great piratical kings passing into dust, the island has slept for centuries in the warm Mediterranean sun, beautiful, serene, and full of memories.

The sky above Crete on this morning of 20 May 1941 is a clear, unbroken blue. The first fighters howling down from it bring Brigadier Howard Kippenberger from his breakfast at the run. He is still grumbling about the quality of his porridge when one of his men looks up and shouts in astonishment.

"Almost over our head were four gliders, the first we had ever seen, in their silence inexpressibly menacing and frightening. Northwards was a growing thunder. I shouted, 'Stand to your arms!' and ran upstairs for my rifle and binoculars. . . . As I ran down the prison road to my battle headquarters, the parachutists were dropping out over the valley, hundreds of them, and floating quietly down." One of the parachutists is the chivalrous Baron von der Heydte. Another is boxer Max Schmeling.

Speedily the little groups of Germans coalesce into companies, then into battalions and brigades. Their attacks grow in intensity and strength. They fight by the book. Colonel Robert Laycock is leading a unit of commandos against them: "I was sitting at my headquarters on a small hill watching the Stuka dive bombers in formation knocking the blazes out of the next position. I turned around to my liaison officer, Captain Evelyn Waugh, the author, and I said, 'You know, I can't help admiring the precision with which the Germans do things.' They were peeling off, diving, releasing their bombs, and flying back to Scarpanto for more ammunition. He turned round and remarked rather aptly, 'Yes, but like everything Teutonic, it goes on far too long.'"

Twenty troop carriers and transports an hour drop more and more troops and keep them supplied, and the RAF are powerless to stop them. Skirmishes become raids, raids develop into battles. At the end of the sixth day General Freyberg begins a report to General Wavell: "I regret to have to report that in my opinion the limit of endurance has been reached by the troops under my command. . . ." The long evacuation to Egypt across three hundred and fifty miles of sea begins.

The outcome of this unique battle is neither a victory nor a defeat for either side. The British have lost thirteen thousand men and considerable naval force, including three cruisers, but for them Crete is a tactical and not a strategic reverse. Crete costs the Germans fifteen thousand men, but in the intensity of the struggle they have lost their only operational air-borne division (the most mobile of all striking forces); for those who remain on the mountainous island are no longer front-line units and their former strength lies in the freshly turned earth of new cemeteries.

The Mediterranean is still a battleground with no man its master. Though Rommel has made the Western Desert his domain, Tobruk threatens his side like a poised spear. Malta, seared by the iron shards of innumerable bombs, remains indomitable. The Navy still dares all and the Army, driven from pillar to post, is still resilient and aggressive. As the great sun sets on the Gentle Sea it still stains its shores with a lurid and foreboding red.

TAKE UP
THE SWORD

It was mirk, mirk night, there was nae starlight.
They waded thro' red blude to the knee;
For all the blude that's shed on the earth
Runs through the springs o' that country.

THOMAS RHYMER

FOR THREE HOURS the roosters have been bragging to one another across the silent morning miles as the slow dawn spreads over a June countryside in the year 1941. Now and then a random dog barks at some fancied intruder. The dew shines clear on opening flowers, bright with the summer in their veins. Inside the great house, isolated in its broad and ordered parkland, there are as yet few signs of life. The Prime Minister of England is still asleep.

On duty at Chequers this promising morning is Jock Colville, Mr. Churchill's private secretary. And already Mr. Colville has been posed a difficult problem. On the one hand he has the Prime Minister's personal order that he is never to be awakened prematurely, save in one exceptional circumstance. On the other, there has just come to Mr. Col-

110

ville's hand a most secret, and certainly most urgent, message. Rapidly the precise mind of Mr. Colville reaches its conclusion. Quietly, but with some alacrity, he heads for the staircase.

"The Prime Minister had told me," he explains, "that he was never to be wakened except in the event of invasion. It seemed to me, however, that the message fell within this category, and so I went up to Mr. Churchill's bedroom. I woke him and told him that the Germans had invaded Russia. His immediate reaction was to disappear completely beneath the bedclothes." Knowing where his duty lies, Mr. Colville waits beside the bed. "After about half a minute he emerged and said, 'Tell the BBC I shall broadcast tonight.'" Mr. Colville then retires to make arrangements.

The news is really no surprise to Churchill. Deep in his heart he has always known that the two tyrannies must eventually fly at each other's throats, and during the weeks of early summer his agents have been reporting massive troop movements eastward through Germany and Poland. Not only has he warned Stalin—without acknowledgment— but he has cabled the President his prediction and notice of the action he expects to take: *From every source at my disposal, including some most trustworthy, it looks as if a vast German onslaught on Russia was imminent. . . . Should this new war break out, we shall, of course, give all encouragement and any help we can spare to the Russians, following the principle that Hitler is the foe we have to beat. . . .*

The previous evening, strolling after dinner across the close-cropped croquet lawn, Jock Colville has mentioned a curious paradox. Mr. Churchill is, after all, the arch anti-Communist. If he allies Britain with the USSR will he not be "bowing down in the House of Rimmon"? Mr. Churchill does not agree: *Not at all,* he tells Colville. *I have only one purpose, the destruction of Hitler, and my life is much simplified thereby. If Hitler invaded Hell I would make at least a favorable reference to the Devil in the House of Commons.*

This Sunday night, 22 June 1941, with the entire population of the country waiting by their radios, Churchill's speech leaves no doubt about the direction he proposes to follow. It has taken him all day to write it and, greatly to the alarm of his secretaries, it is ready only twenty minutes before the broadcast is due, but it is worth the labor. *No one,* Churchill tells the people, *has been a more consistent opponent of Communism than I have for the last twenty-five years. I will unsay no word that I have spoken about it. But all this fades away before the spectacle which is now unfolding. . . . I see the Russian soldiers standing on the threshold of their native land, guarding the fields which their fathers have tilled from time immemorial. I see them guarding their homes where mothers and wives pray. . . . I see the ten thousand villages of Russia where the means of existence is wrung so hardly from the soil, but where there are still primordial human joys, where maidens laugh and children play. I see advancing on all this in hideous onslaught the Nazi war machine, with its clanking, heel-clicking, dandified Prussian officers, its crafty expert agents fresh from the cowing and tying down of a dozen countries. I see also the dull, drilled, docile, brutish masses of the Hun soldiery plodding on like a swarm of crawling locusts.* He ends with a clear call, *The Russian danger is, therefore, our danger, and the danger of the United States, just as the cause of any Russian fighting for his hearth and home is the cause of free men and free peoples in every quarter of the globe.*

*　　　*　　　*

June 22, 1941: The German-Soviet Non-Aggression Pact of 1939 is abruptly severed with a three-pronged invasion of Russian soil by the German war machine. Striking hard and swift, the German Army Groups A, B and C cut deep into Soviet territory. By November, their targets—Rostov, Moscow and Leningrad—are besieged. By this action, Germany creates a deadly foe and Great Britain gains an ally.

The Russians have been taken by surprise. From the Germans has come neither an ultimatum nor a formal declaration of war. Hitler's legions have massed for this ultimate blow from the Baltic to the Black Sea along the whole length of the artificial frontier that splits Poland at the point where, in 1939, the troops of two conflicting ideologies met. Though alert to Hitler's political designs, Stalin has not heeded the signs of military danger.

Hitler has been preparing for months, for some cogent reasons as well as through his driving megalomania. Almost overnight Russia annexes the Baltic States and thus extends her northwestern frontier. Threateningly, she then occupies the Rumanian province of Bessarabia, which can mean only one thing—she has designs on the Rumanian oil fields on which Germany's existence depends. Hitler resolves on the only solution he knows. On 18 December 1940 he issues Directive No. 21, which begins: "The German armed forces must be prepared to crush Soviet Russia in a quick campaign before the end of the war against England."

Already the first German troops have arrived in Poland. Army Group B, particularly strong in infantry, is ordered to the east from France, where it has helped shatter the Allies in the brutally swift summer campaign. Its commander, the Prussian Field Marshal von Bock, a lean, tall man with a sour wit and an ailing stomach, shifts his headquarters to Posen. Through the fall and winter of 1940 unit after unit, some battle hardened, some newly trained, all superbly equipped, climb aboard the troop trains and ride secretly eastward. They are to be in position on the battle line, says Hitler's directive, by 15 May.

Two factors, unfortunately for Nazi hopes, upset the schedule. The Duce, eager as a puppy to join in the general melee, had invaded Greece and now finds himself in such straits fighting its sinewy mountaineers that a jaundiced

Hitler must intervene. Some German divisions have to be drained off for this Balkan adventure. Second, the thaw comes later than expected in 1941. The invasion of Russia must be put off for a few weeks.

Hitler's generals, never enthusiastic about the idea, grow even more uneasy. They remember 1914–18, when Germany's losses on the Eastern Front were heavier than those in the west. Now, under the Bolsheviks, the Russians are likely to prove even more formidable: for one thing, they have been rearming longer even than the Germans. Their reserves of manpower make the imagination boggle. And their country is a sickening place to fight in.

To begin with, there is the weather. June to September, certainly, are ideal for mobile campaigning. But early in October heavy rains bring in the season of *Rasputitza*, the autumn mud, when the hard clay of the steppes is turned into a quagmire. A month later, in November, come the first frosts, and for a while movement is again possible. But then the terrible Russian winter sets in. In spring the thaw again softens the ground—and the clay turns to mud. The *timing* of such a gigantic attack as Hitler plans, therefore, is vital. The generals reflect, debate, and shake their heads.

But they cannot persuade Hitler to change his mind. He declares expansively to his staff after an explanation of the problems one February evening: "When Barbarossa commences, the world will hold its breath and make no comment." Operation Barbarossa is named after a legendary German emperor who sits enthroned forever in a cave in the Harz Mountains, with his Teuton knights at either side of a mighty stone table. When Barbarossa's red beard has grown three times around the table he will come forth and start the crusade that will liberate Germany from her oppressors until the end of time. The name of the operation says much for Hitler's hopes.

Its chief end is to secure the rich wheat fields and industrial areas of the Ukraine, open a road to the Caucasus
and then to the oil fields of Baku, and incidentally to destroy
the holy cities of Leningrad and Moscow. To accomplish this
Hitler has amassed a host the like of which has not been seen
in Europe since the savage Golden Horde of Genghis Khan
It consists of three main forces.

In the north, under Field Marshal Wilhelm von Leeb, two
armies and a panzer group are to take Leningrad and then
swing south. They face Marshal Voroshilov. In the center
Field Marshal von Bock, facing Marshal Timoshenko, musters thirty infantry, fifteen panzer or motorized, and one
cavalry division; they will drive straight for Moscow. In the
south, below the Pripet Marshes, the wizened Field Marshal
von Rundstedt, with four armies and a panzer group, has
orders to defeat Marshal Budenny (a veteran Cossack general), capture Kiev and master the Ukraine. Supporting each
of these massive groups is an Air Fleet, including Air Fleet 2
(Field Marshal Kesselring), recently withdrawn from the
Battle of Britain. German intelligence has collected few details of what lies in front of them, but Hitler is so utterly
confident of immediate victory that he is about to order a
cut in the production of munitions.

About midnight of 21 June 1941 the international train
from Berlin to Moscow suddenly blazes with lights as it
passes through the waiting lines on its peaceful way to Brest
Litovsk. The German gunners stare at it in surprise: their
guns are already zeroed in, the shells piled ready beside
them. As the sky begins to lighten to a bilious yellow a
thousand commanders glance at their watches. At 3:30 A.M.
the frontier erupts with the red glare of massed artillery.

There is no retaliation whatever from the Russians! One
Russian message picked up asks querulously, "We are being
fired on. What shall we do?" Tartly the answer comes from

headquarters: "You must be insane. Why is your signal not in code?" Grinning through the clouds of ocher dust kicked up by their surging transport columns, the troops of the leading panzers roll through village after village. Nothing can stop them. Plodding behind them with their horse-drawn supply trains, the infantry divisions mop up what little resistance remains. By 2 July they have taken 150,000 prisoners, 1,200 tanks and 600 guns.

In the somber wars of modern democracy, writes Churchill, *chivalry finds no place. Dull butcheries on a giant scale and mass effects overwhelm all detached sentiment.* Hitler allocates "special tasks" in the territories newly occupied in the east, and appoints Himmler to carry them out. Elegant and perverted groups of the SS prowl in the wake of the fighting troops, shooting, burning, hanging, torturing. Their duties are conceived on an unbelievable scale: the transfer of Ukrainian wheat to Germany will mean that "many tens of thousands of people in the industrial areas will become redundant and will either die or have to emigrate to Siberia." The SS try their evil best to settle the question, but it is only when their *einsatzgruppen*—their highly trained specialists in mass extermination—arrive that the job is done with any real efficiency and speed.

Across the endless steppes, sweating in the heat of high summer, the ponderous armies roll farther and farther into Russia. All through July, mile after mile, covering the flat plains with their squat black tanks, they press toward Moscow. But they have not yet succeeded in bringing any major Russian force to bay. And at the end of the month the going gets harder, the spearheads slow down. The generals begin to worry.

Adolf Hitler sees no problem, will not alter his objectives.

A high-level argument develops and continues through August. It is an argument that will cost Germany a million dead. For in that short time four things happen: General Zhukov assumes command in front of Moscow, a fresh new army corps arrives from Siberia, the first heavy rains begin to fall, and for the first time the Russian T-34 tank enters the battlefield. The infantry are powerless to stop it and the German tanks and heavy guns that can are beginning to slide off the unsurfaced roads into oceans of mud. They have to be abandoned.

In mid-November the first frosts solidify the mud, and for two weeks the Germans can move again. Tugging free their equipment, they grind forward once more toward Moscow. Smolensk has fallen to them, and Kiev, and graceful Leningrad is besieged. Early in the morning of 3 December the Reconnaissance Battalion of the 258th Infantry Division finds a gap in the Russian defenses and dashes through it, reaching the southwestern outskirts of Moscow. There they are fallen upon by tanks and the furious workers of the city, and forced back. They are the only Germans to catch sight of the glittering domes of the Kremlin.

Hitler's armies are halted. Their breath hangs in clouds on the dead air, ice freezes in their eyebrows and on the stubble of their haggard chins. Weapons stick to bare flesh, and to touch the armor of a tank is like grasping a searing iron. For now the weather has broken and the thermometer shows thirty degrees of frost. Silently the first heavy flakes of snow come drifting in from the north, and beating through their flurries the Germans hear the icy wings of Death. Within three days 100,000 of them are suffering from frostbite, and still the temperature falls.

It is a nightmare of darkness and snow. Through the night and early morning a thick fog blanks out the endless featureless landscape, through which the rising sun stares like a great crimson globe. By four o'clock in the afternoon it is as dark as the grave again. And as cold. The Germans have to keep fires burning under their tanks or they will not start. A consignment of wine arrives from France with every bottle burst and the wine compressed into uniform blocks of red ice. There is no winter clothing.

Then, upon this horror, Zhukov launches a counteroffensive, slashing out of the white darkness with seven armies. The blitzkrieg has failed. Caught deep inside Russia, with the worst winter in forty years about to settle on them, matched at last with foes as ruthless as themselves, the Germans are now in the same plight as Napoleon's Grand Army which in 1812 struggled back from Russia a shattered collection of ghosts. Hoping for time to maneuver, the German generals begin to withdraw. But at once a direct order from *Wolfschanze* (the Wolf's Lair), the Fuehrer's headquarters in eastern Poland, cancels all their plans. The Wehrmacht will stand and fight. The Battle of Moscow begins; in less than six months the turning point of the war in the east has been reached.

No one can prophesy what the outcome will be, least of all Winston Churchill. He has never boasted a complete understanding of the Soviets. *I cannot forecast to you,* he has written, *the action of Russia. It is a riddle wrapped in a mystery inside an enigma.* But he is well able to assess the malignant doom that has fallen upon his new allies: *Since the Mongol invasions of Europe . . . there has never been . . . butchery on such a scale. . . . And this is just the beginning. Famine and pestilence have yet to follow in the bloody ruts of Hitler's tanks. We are in the presence of a crime without a name.*

He arranges for supplies to be sent to Murmansk—weapons, food, raw materials, aircraft. Many of them are American in origin, and if Britain is to continue passing them on it is clear that the situation must be discussed with the President. Churchill is relieved, therefore, when Harry Hopkins, the Lease-Lend Administrator President Roosevelt has sent to London, broaches the possibility of a meeting. That sunny afternoon in the garden of 10 Downing Street, Churchill tells Hopkins he will be delighted to make the journey. Aides are immediately summoned to arrange it; to Churchill there is nothing to touch a little trip in a battleship.

On 4 August 1941 a special train bears the Prime Ministerial party, with champagne supplies, to Scapa Flow. There they embark joyfully on *Prince of Wales*. The seas are high for the time of year and soon the battleship's destroyer escort falls back; the destroyers cannot maintain her speed with safety. So the great ship shoulders ahead alone, maintaining absolute wireless silence. *Thus*, says Churchill, *there was a lull in my daily routine and a strange sense of leisure which I had not known since the war began.*

This sense of leisure is not, however, communicated to his staff. The harassed General Hollis, his military aide, is constantly being called from his office to Churchill's quarters behind the bridge. It is no mean journey along the lurching decks, as the General recalls: "Being at war, we were all battened down, with many watertight doors. He would ring me up and say, 'I want to speak to you in my bridge cabin at once!' Well, it meant opening and shutting no fewer than seventeen watertight doors and securing them behind you. And when I arrived at last in his cabin he would say, 'Why have you been so long?' I would say, 'Well, sir, after all there are *seventeen* watertight doors between where I live and where you live.' But all I got was 'Well, you could have been much quicker.'"

On the morning of 9 August *Prince of Wales* smoothly rounds the cape that shelters Placentia Bay from the ocean's wild surge and there sees before her, bright and surprising in peacetime dress, the United States cruiser *Augusta*. As *Prince of Wales*'s cables roar out of their lockers, there rise clear from her foredeck the noble cadences of "The Star-Spangled Banner." Then, echoing from the hills guarding the bay, *Augusta*'s band answers with "God Save the King." Anxiously Churchill stares from the bridge for his first glimpse of the man to whom he owes so much . . , and there, wearing a light suit and leaning on the arm of his son, his hat doffed in salute, a figure of quiet power and authority.

At once a barge lowers away from *Prince of Wales* and heads for *Augusta*. Not one to scoff at ceremony, Churchill climbs aboard with a letter in his hand. Solemnly he greets Mr. Roosevelt: "I have the honor, Mr. President, to hand you a letter from His Majesty the King." But then the high spirits cannot be held back, and a grin of sheer pleasure bursts across the chubby face. It is good to be here.

That afternoon gifts arrive aboard *Prince of Wales*, a box of fruit, cigarettes and cheese for every member of her crew, each containing a message from the President. The news-paperman in Churchill cannot resist the challenge. He bustles about posing with groups of sailors, positioning camera-men, crying now and then to the uncomfortable, "More tooth, more tooth!"

Next morning, a Sunday, the ship is made ready for divine service. Two lecterns bear the flags of the two great nations and the moving phrases of the service roll over the mingled crews of the two fighting ships: "I will not fail thee nor for-sake thee. Be not afraid, neither be thou dismayed, for the Lord thy God is with thee wherever thou goest . . ." Two thousand voices thunder out the old and mighty hymns.

This historic meeting is a short one, but still long enough

to cement a close and warm friendship, and to prepare the draft of a document that descends directly in spirit from the Magna Charta and the American Constitution. Like them, it is a reaffirmation of human rights—the Atlantic Charter. It looks forward to a future of peace: "After the final destruction of the Nazi tyranny, America and Great Britain hope to see established a peace which will afford to all nations the means of dwelling in safety within their own boundaries, and which will afford assurance that all men in all lands may live out their lives in freedom from fear and want."

One of the parties to the declaration is at war, the other in a state of armed neutrality. Her brass dulled, her paint dark, her magazines crammed and her crew at action stations, *Prince of Wales* slips out of the bay and into the embattled Atlantic. Looking back for a last glimpse of the President, Churchill again wonders at the contrast with these trim vessels that have not yet felt the harsh necessity of war. Though neither he nor they can know it, in a few weeks they will have lost the innocence of peace and their guns will be roaring at a new enemy.

On the way home *Prince of Wales*, crashing through the waves at twenty-two knots, overtakes a convoy of seventy or eighty ships. Immediately "Good luck, Churchill!" breaks out on every halyard. As the battleship steams through the lines, causing no little confusion, the ships' sirens blast out the V-sign and cheering seamen line their rails. Churchill is so diverted by this novel experience that he orders *Prince of Wales* about. Once more her thousands of tons hurtle through the convoy, completely disrupting its careful order.

Back in England, Churchill watches the slaughter in Russia with grave concern. Then, on 6 December, comes the shock of Zhukov's massive offensive. The incredible has hap-

pened. *The Russian Army, far from being beaten, was fight-*
ing better than ever . . . For the first time Nazi blood flowed
in a fearful torrent . . . All the anti-Nazi nations, great and
small, rejoiced to see the first failure of a German blitzkrieg.

Much comforted, Churchill settles back to enjoy the rest
of his weekend in the country at Chequers. It is something
of an American occasion, for his two guests are Ambassador
Winant and Mr. Averell Harriman. On this evening of Sunday, 7 December 1941, they have dined together, pleasantly
warm and quite drowsy after an evening of conversation. It
is Churchill's habit, in spite of his many official channels of
information, to listen every evening at nine o'clock to the
BBC's broadcast of the news. To this end, shortly before
nine, his butler carefully places before him a little black box.
It is a neat portable radio, a gift from Harry Hopkins and a
toy of which Churchill is extremely fond.

The lid of the box is lifted and the rounded tones of the
BBC announcer, syllable by impeccable syllable, proceed im-
passively through the day's news. No one speaks. Churchill
sits hunched, his elbows propped on the table, his hands
covering his eyes. Toward the end the well-educated voice
mentions quite casually that some American ships have been
attacked at a place called Pearl Harbor.

Harriman cries out, "What was that?" as Churchill suddenly slams down the lid.

"Something about Pearl River . . ." murmurs one of the
secretaries. "Isn't that in China?"

"No, no," Winant insists, "it was Pearl *Harbor!*" At that
moment another secretary rushes in to confirm it.

Churchill gets up and strides toward his office, picks up the
transatlantic telephone and asks for the President. A pause,
then tensely—"Mr. President, what's this about Japan?"

Back comes the tired, but still resonant, voice: "It's quite true. They have attacked us at Pearl Harbor. We're all in the same boat now."

Not unmindful of the suffering this will mean, Churchill is nevertheless profoundly relieved. No longer is there the slightest doubt about the outcome. *The United States was now in the war, up to the neck and in to the death. England would live. . . . Once again in our long history we should emerge, however mauled or mutilated—we would not be wiped out. We were no longer alone. The British Empire, the Soviet Union, and now the United States were bound together with every scrap of their life and strength.*

DEADLY SUNRISE

Across the sea,
Corpses in the water;
Across the mountain,
Corpses heaped upon the field;
I shall die only for the Emperor,
I shall never look back.
    JAPANESE POPULAR SONG: *Umi Yukaba*

FIFTEEN shopping days to Christmas," the sergeant reflects, and pictures idly the laden shoppers crowding Fifth Avenue, tramping through the gray snow and puddles of a New York winter and gazing with a faint sense of impending doom into the twinkling windows of massive treasure-house stores. The sergeant is relieved that this year at least he will not have to endure the wintry ordeal; his packages have long since been shipped and this year he will be enjoying the festive season far from the possibility of wet feet and head colds. A warm breeze wafts against his tanned cheek, bearing with it faintly the heavy scent of pineapples. The sergeant glances through the porthole beside him, watching the sunlight dance on the little chopping waves of Pearl Harbor.

124

All around him are the familiar sounds of the unhurried routine of Sunday morning aboard a battleship of the United States Pacific Fleet in time of peace. One detachment of 1st Sergeant Emmons' U.S. Marines is carrying through the ceremony of Colors on the fantail. Other men flick a last shine on their already immaculate shoes before going ashore. Some are enjoying a slow after-breakfast smoke in the freshness of early morning. The sky promises another beautiful day: a few clouds sail high in its clear, deep blue. In his office on the second deck of USS *Tennessee*, Sergeant Emmons, satisfied that all is for the best in this best of all possible worlds, turns to see how soon his clerk will have finished the Morning Report.

It is a report that will never be completed, for "suddenly we felt a violent bump which gave us the feeling that the ship had been pushed bodily sideways, and as I did not hear any explosion I remarked that some ship had run into us." As the Sergeant is considering this possibility an even more astonishing event interrupts his thoughts. All over the ship brazen alarm gongs clang out the call to General Quarters.

Rushing up to his battle station Sergeant Emmons sees that the sky is full of black puffs. The scream of diving aircraft assaults his ears, the rising shriek of falling bombs, then the awful thunder of their detonation. All over the harbor there grows a staccato cracking as the anti-aircraft gun teams wake to this incredible challenge. It is 7:55 A.M. on the morning of 7 December 1941.

In a simple bedroom in Honolulu, furnished austerely but with exquisite taste in the Japanese fashion, a young vice-consul opens his eyes as the first explosions echo over Oahu. His hand reaches out to the radio, already tuned to Tokyo's short-wave station. A hiss, a crackle, and a guttural voice begins the eight o'clock news. There is nothing in it to destroy the delicate calm of a Japanese morning, but it is followed by the weather forecast, and that spells storm. Twice the announcer reads, without special inflection, "East wind, rain." This is the code signal telling all Japanese agents that the attack on the United States has begun.

Of all these agents the young vice-consul should be the least surprised. For it is he who has sent the decisive signal less than nine hours before. He is in fact Takeo Yoshikawa, no consular official but an ensign in the Imperial Navy, and his training for this mission has taken four long years. Throwing aside his quilt Yoshikawa peers out of his window, notes with satisfaction a couple of columns of heavy black smoke like exclamation marks on the horizon and walks calmly down to his office to destroy his code books and intelligence reports. On top of the pile lies his last message:

VESSELS MOORED IN HARBOR: NINE BATTLESHIPS; THREE CLASS-B CRUISERS; THREE SEAPLANE TENDERS; SEVENTEEN DESTROYERS. ENTERING HARBOR ARE FOUR CLASS-B CRUISERS; THREE DESTROYERS. ALL AIRCRAFT CARRIERS AND HEAVY CRUISERS HAVE DEPARTED HARBOR. NO INDICATION OF ANY CHANGES IN U.S. FLEET. ENTERPRISE AND LEXINGTON HAVE SAILED FROM PEARL HARBOR.

As it begins to burn Ensign Yoshikawa composes himself for the meeting with the FBI that he knows will soon come.

On the bridge of the great aircraft carrier *Akagi*, 230 miles to the north and slightly east, Admiral Chiuchi Nagumo glances once more at a copy of the signal relayed from Tokyo. Whipped by the rising wind there flutters above him the very flag flown by the Japanese flagship thirty-six years before when a Russian fleet was sent to the bottom of the Pacific off Tsushima. Ever since he left the fog-shrouded Kurils the Admiral's nerves have been on edge. He wonders

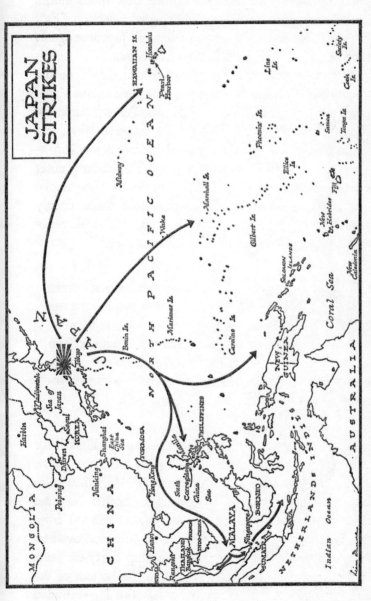

December 7, 1941: By land, sea and air, the military forces of the Japanese Empire brutally attack Pearl Harbor, the Philippines, Malaya and Thailand. On December 8, the United States and Great Britain declare war on Japan as Japanese forces attack Hong Kong, Guam, Midway and Wake Islands.

anxiously now how the planes of his First Air Fleet are faring over Oahu.

They are succeeding beyond all possible expectation. As Sergeant Emmons dashes over the steel decks of the *Tennessee* he sees waves of mustard-yellow aircraft gliding in from Merry's Point, low on the water, their bellies heavy with torpedoes. From high above, dive bombers rip down through the thin curtain of flak, the red Rising Sun glaring from their fuselages as they skid triumphantly past the superstructures of the helpless lines of ships.

Within five minutes the battleship *Arizona* blows apart: a heavy bomb has dropped down her funnel and penetrated her magazine. Flaming from end to end, her back broken, she settles in the shallow water and spreads the surface with a huge lake of burning fuel oil. More than a thousand men lie dead within her riven decks.

Oklahoma, torpedoed on her port side, capsizes. *Nevada* gets under way to gain fighting room but is torpedoed almost at once and runs aground. *West Virginia*, listing to port and afire, is settling by the bow; her captain, mortally wounded, still struggles feebly on a bridge ringed by searing flame. *Maryland* is holed in the port bow, *Pennsylvania* is badly hit in one of her casements, *California* shows a heavy list and thick smoke billows out of her. The pride of the Pacific Fleet is being blasted into utter impotence and men weep with futile rage.

Inland, supply depots, air fields and barracks are under heavy attack from high-level bombers. As their sticks of bombs crump down across runways and into hangars and ammunition dumps the Zeros streak in machine-gunning anything that moves on the roads, slicing along lines of parked aircraft with incendiary shells that leave behind them leaping flames and twisted fuselages. Now and then the ground quakes as a dump flares and blows up. The Zeros twist back

and forth through the climbing smoke like evil birds threading the black pillars of some monstrous ruin.

In the harbor the water is choked with oil and debris. Two
of the eight battleships are sunk, the remaining six damaged.
As their gun crews search the deadly sky for targets, shooting
at shadows, the stricken ships wallow at their moorings like
iron mammoths dealt a mortal blow by the hunters. In all,
18 ships are sunk or seriously damaged, 188 planes have been
destroyed and 159 more damaged. The dead number 2,403.
It has cost the Japanese 29 planes, one submarine and five
midget submarines, and 80 or 90 men. Scarcely scratched,
the attacking force is already heading jubilantly back to its
carriers. The time is 10 A.M. on a beautiful morning.

In Japan it is the eighth day of the twelfth month of the
sixteenth year of Showa, the Propitious Year of the Serpent.
From the holy inner cloisters of the little god-king has issued
an Imperial Rescript. "We, by the grace of heaven, Emperor
of Japan, seated on the Throne of a line unbroken for ages
eternal, enjoin upon ye, Our loyal and brave subjects: We
hereby declare war on the United States of America and the
British Empire. The men and officers of Our Army and Navy
shall do their utmost in prosecuting the war, Our public servants of various departments shall perform faithfully and
diligently their appointed tasks, and all other subjects of
Ours shall pursue their respective duties; the entire nation
with a united will shall mobilize their total strength so that
nothing will miscarry in the attainment of our war aims."
To observers the ordinary folk of Tokyo seem awed by this
daring. But the samurai are in control; their long swords are
drawn and before they are sheathed again they will have
blood.

Shortly after noon next day in Washington ten glossy black

limousines halt at the south entrance to the Capitol, the
first one guarded by three enormous open tourers, affection-
ately nicknamed Queen Mary, Normandie and Leviathan by
their Secret Service occupants. From this leading car, supported by his son, steps the President, come to seek the support of Congress for a declaration of war. The chamber is
charged with high emotion as he stands alone at the rostrum. Quietly he opens a common black loose-leaf notebook.
The powerful hands come forward, grip the dark wood in
a familiar gesture, the head sweeps up. The clear, vibrant,
unforgettable voice begins: "Yesterday, December 7, 1941—
a date which will live in infamy—the United States of America was suddenly and deliberately attacked by naval and air
forces of the Empire of Japan . . ." Suddenly the race of
funny little yellow men has become a swarm of deadly
fanatics.

In London Mr. Winston Churchill cannot hide his delight.
He knows, as he has always known, that the entry of the
United States into the war can mean only one thing. In these
hours of what seems hideous and shameful defeat he sees
only victory. *Silly people,* he announces with emphasis, *silly
people—and there were many, not only in enemy countries—
might discount the force of the United States. Some said they
were soft, others that they would never be united. They
would fool around at a distance. They would never come to
grips. They would never stand blood-letting. Their democracy and system of recurrent elections would paralyze their
war effort. They would be just a vague blur on the horizon
to friend or foe. Now we should see the weakness of this
numerous but remote, wealthy and talkative people. But I
had studied the American Civil War, fought out to the last
desperate inch. American blood flowed in my veins.*

On this wintry morning Mr. Churchill's blood is quite
definitely up. He finds he has a pleasant duty to perform. By

great good chance his Foreign Secretary is en route for Moscow and the duties of that office therefore fall upon the Prime Minister. Mr. Churchill is deliciously aware that one of these duties this morning will be the composition of a letter to the Japanese Ambassador at the Court of St. James. Its subject will be a declaration of war. The letter is not without some distinction.

FOREIGN OFFICE, December 8

SIR,

On the evening of December 7th His Majesty's Government in the United Kingdom learned that Japanese forces without previous warning either in the form of a declaration of war or of an ultimatum with a conditional declaration of war had attempted a landing on the coast of Malaya and bombed Singapore and Hong Kong.

In view of these wanton acts of unprovoked aggression committed in flagrant violation of International Law and particularly of Article I of the Third Hague Convention relative to the opening of hostilities, to which both Japan and the United Kingdom are parties, His Majesty's Ambassador at Tokyo has been instructed to inform the Imperial Japanese Government in the name of His Majesty's Government in the United Kingdom that a state of war exists between our two countries.

I have the honor to be, with high consideration, Sir,

Your obedient servant,

WINSTON S. CHURCHILL

Sitting back, the Prime Minister regards his handiwork with satisfaction. *Some people did not like this ceremonial style,* he notes, *but when you have to kill a man it costs nothing to be polite.*

What is happening on the forlorn battlegrounds of the East, however, is far from polite. In Pearl Harbor the battleship *Arizona* is still burning after two days. Thailand has ceased all resistance within twenty-four hours of the first whine of bullets at her borders. Six battalions in Hong Kong, two of them Canadian, are besieged by three divisions from the mainland of China. Japanese columns are threading through the jungles of Malaya toward Singapore, and more troop convoys and supply ships are streaming toward the peninsula.

Two of Britain's finest battleships, *Prince of Wales,* veteran of the *Bismarck* action, and *Repulse,* have sailed hurriedly from Singapore to annihilate the Japanese invasion fleets. It is not expected that they will meet any serious resistance from the Imperial Navy in the area. With a screen of four destroyers they dash northward with all speed. But unseen submarines are shadowing them, and soon they are also sighted by reconnaissance aircraft.

Through the pea-green sea, cleft with broad whiteness where their sharp bows plunge, the two battleships hasten toward an easy prey. All gun crews are at action stations, uncomfortably muffled in the heat with anti-flash gear. At 11:07 the Tannoy clicks, announces metallically: "Enemy aircraft approaching!" Out of the yellow sun, in line astern at twelve thousand feet, lumber nine serene bombers, leisurely passing from bow to stern over *Repulse.* Lazily their bombs tumble down, growing . . . growing. Suddenly huge gray geysers spout towering from the sea and *Repulse* shudders through all her length. She is hit on the catapult deck.

Now they are surrounded by torpedo bombers curling in from all angles. Little splashes mark the release of torpedoes as the pilots coolly run the gauntlet of flak, machine-gunning as they press in. On *Repulse*'s deck, littered with empty shell cases, an officer turns to War Correspondent Cecil Brown and remarks quietly, "Plucky blokes, those Japs. That was as beautiful an attack as ever I expect to see." He has only minutes to live.

The captain of *Repulse* signals to *Prince of Wales* during a brief lull: "Have you sustained any damage?" The reply chills him: "We are out of control. Steering gear is gone."

Commander Harland, an engineer officer, is on the bridge when the first torpedo strikes *Prince of Wales* on the port side aft. He makes his way down to view the damage: "There was a terrific explosion. Then I heard a lot of what I might call expensive noises going on aft, which made me realize we were in a bad way." The battleship is stopped almost dead, begins to circle like a buck wounded in the quarters. The hounds concentrate, circling and grouping around her. She is hit three times and the powerful new Jap torpedoes rip her open. Sinking by the stern, she heels over to port.

As the horrified crew of *Repulse* watches, their deck lurches under them. A torpedo has burst open *Repulse's* port side. It is a fatal hurt. Screws still turning, her stern sinks into the oil-blackened sea. The bow swings up high as a steeple, showing her underplates blood-red against the sky. Within minutes *Prince of Wales* follows her. "I remember my last feeling before leaving the ship," says Commander Harland, "was the hush after the throb of the engines. Everything was absolutely silent."

At a single stroke the Japanese have destroyed all naval opposition in the South China Sea and the Indian Ocean. It is a second triumphant vindication of the tactical principle of using aircraft carriers as assault units. In a matter of days their naval air power has cleared the road to those treasure houses of the East, to gain which they embarked on a war. *In all the war*, Churchill records, *I never received a more direct shock. . . . As I turned over and twisted in bed the full horror of the news sank in upon me. There were no British or American capital ships in the Indian Ocean or the Pacific except the American survivors of Pearl Harbor, who were hastening back to California. Over all this vast expanse of waters Japan was supreme, and we everywhere weak and naked.*

In spite of this disaster, however, the arrangements of war

must be carried forward, and it is imperative that the new
allies meet at once. Churchill has already suggested it, and
on 12 December he embarks on the recently completed *Duke
of York*, sister ship to *Prince of Wales*. One of his party is a
newcomer who more than once is to save his life—his medical
adviser, Sir Charles Wilson. Churchill is not the best of
patients, but *Although I could not persuade him* [Wilson] *to
take my advice when he was ill, nor could he always count
on my implicit obedience to all his instructions, we became
devoted friends. Moreover, we both survived.* Ten days later
Churchill arrives in Washington.

During the voyage he has transacted a great deal of business. The situation in Hong Kong is dire, and the slender
garrison is now fighting on the island itself. Churchill signals
the gallant Governor: *The enemy should be compelled to
expend the utmost life and equipment. There must be vigorous fighting in the inner defenses, and, if the need be, from
house to house. Every day that you are able to maintain your
resistance you help the Allied cause all over the world, and
by a prolonged resistance you and your men can win the
lasting honor which we are sure will be your due.* Even as
the messages are passing, the Canadian Brigadier in Hong
Kong is dying heroically with all his headquarters staff,
fighting hand-to-hand against impossible odds.

President Roosevelt meets the Prime Minister at Washington Airport as he flies in from Hampton Roads, greets him
warmly with a firm and infinitely comforting handclasp. Dinner at the White House proves quite a social occasion, and
Churchill accepts the somewhat strange Presidential cocktail
that precedes it with good grace. As a mark of respect
Churchill makes a point of wheeling the President in his
chair to the elevator, mindful of Sir Walter Raleigh's prece-

dent. *I formed a very strong affection, which grew with our years of comradeship, for this formidable politician who had imposed his will for nearly ten years upon the American scene, and whose heart seemed to respond to many of the impulses that stirred my own.*

With the traditional White House tree sparkling through the darkness of Christmas Eve, Churchill, oddly at home on the balcony of the President's residence, makes a seasonal speech to a friendly crowd: *I spend this anniversary and festival far from my country, far from my family, yet I cannot truthfully say that I feel far from home. . . . Let the children have their night of fun and laughter. Let the gifts of Father Christmas delight their play. Let us grownups share to the full in their unstinted pleasures before we turn again to the stern task and the formidable years that lie before us, resolved that, by our sacrifice and daring, these same children shall not be robbed of their inheritance or denied the right to live in a free and decent world.*

Christmas Day 1941 is overcast by black news from Hong Kong. Overwhelmed at last, its defenders exhausted and almost without ammunition, the island surrenders. Fighting men and civilians throw themselves on the doubtful mercy of the Japanese and are led away on this holy morning of Christ's birth into a bestial captivity.

Next day Churchill addresses Congress. Despite the ruin in the Pacific he faces the august assembly buoyantly. *I cannot help reflecting,* he remarks from the dais, *that if my father had been American and my mother British, instead of the other way round, I might have got here on my own.* His message is one of *hope and faith, sure and inviolate, that in the days to come the British and American peoples will, for their own safety and for the good of all, walk togther side by side in majesty, in justice and in peace.* Referring to the Japanese he thrusts out his jaw and growls, with an air of puzzlement, *What sort of people do they think we are?* It brings down the house.

Sir Charles, the Prime Minister's physician, is delighted to see his charge in such great shape. But next morning, returning to his hotel after an early stroll, he is surprised by an emergency call to the White House. He finds the Prime Minister sitting on his bed, his confidence evaporated. The doctor inquires what has happened.

Churchill tells him that during the night, finding the room oppressively hot, he got up and tried to open the window. It was hard to move, so he exerted greater effort and suddenly felt harsh pains score through his chest. Breathing hard, he managed to stagger back to his bed and lay there until the pains passed.

Sir Charles looks keenly at his patient. "Well," he begins slowly, "we'd better just give you a check. Shouldn't think it was anything serious." He takes out his stethoscope. His brain is racing, for he is now faced with a very intricate problem indeed. The symptoms Mr. Churchill has been describing with such clarity are those of coronary thrombosis.

To gain time the doctor carries out a very thorough and lengthy examination. Shall he tell the Prime Minister the truth and hospitalize him to make *sure* he rests? What comfort would this afford the enemy? On the other hand, if he conceals what he knows and does not advise immediate treatment, might not his patient succumb to another attack? The one just passed was not severe. Will there be more? Will they be more serious? A hundred factors bear on the problem. Sir Charles's incisive mind examines them all, reaches its decision. He draws in his breath. Churchill is looking gloomily at him, growing impatient. Sir Charles hopes he has come to the right conclusion.

"I threw down my stethoscope on the bed," Sir Charles recollects, "and when I raised my eyes he was looking at me.

" 'Is my health all right?' he asked.

" 'Well,' I said, 'you've just been overdoing things a bit . . .'

"He broke in. 'Now, Charles, you're not going to tell me to rest, are you? I won't. Nobody else can do my job. I must.'

"Of course, he was right. No one else *could* do his job. He had to. That meant I had been right."

But there will be many occasions in the future when Sir Charles will wonder. And grow tense.

Churchill breaks his stay in Washington for a short visit to Canada, where he addresses the House of Commons. Looking back on the disastrous summer of 1940 he recalls his offer to the French. *But their generals misled them. When I warned them that Britain would fight on alone whatever they did, their generals told their Prime Minister and his divided Cabinet: "In three weeks England will have her neck wrung like a chicken!" Some chicken! Some neck!*

Returning to the White House on New Year's Day, his first duty is to sign the United Nations Pact. Another signatory, M. Litvinov, the Soviet Ambassador in Washington, has been experiencing a hard time at the hands of the President over the inclusion of the words "religious freedom." He retires gracefully and exhausted after the President takes him aside for "a long talk with him alone about his soul and the dangers of hell-fire." The pact, embracing the principles of the Atlantic Charter, draws together twenty-six nations with the single purpose of defeating the Axis Powers.

When Churchill prepares for home he has accomplished the main object of his journey. From the first moment of the news of Pearl Harbor he had feared that the whole fury of America would at once be unleashed upon Japan. The question was: *Should we be able to persuade the President and the American Service chiefs that the defeat of Japan would not spell the defeat of Hitler, but that the defeat of Hitler made the finishing off of Japan merely a matter of time and trouble?* Now his apprehension has been proved groundless. The Americans are resolved. Hitler first (and incidentally his junior partner in Italy) and then His Imperial Majesty.

Churchill holidays briefly but happily in Palm Beach before facing once more the rigors of an English January. It becomes his habit, wrapped about with a sturdy towel, to take frequent bathes from his private beach. Until one day a large shark is reported cruising the area. Churchill is not to be fooled. *They said it was only a "ground shark" but I was not wholly reassured. It is as bad to be eaten by a ground shark as by any other. So I stayed in the shallows from then on.* Much rested, he arrives in Bermuda, where *Duke of York* lies at anchor, ready to carry him home.

On the way there, however, he has discovered a new love. It is a Boeing flying boat. He has an idea. Would it not be advantageous to *fly* home? Kelly Rogers, her captain, blenches. But the question comes from such eminence, is put with such directness, that he must at least work it out. Pressed, he admits the flight is possible. An unenthusiastic entourage accompanies Mr. Churchill aboard. Not many planes have attempted such a crossing of the Atlantic. The Prime Minister settles comfortably into the bridal suite in the stern and surveys the luxury surrounding him with satisfaction.

They pass within inches of utter disaster. The flying boat is in the air for more than twenty hours. During the night she suddenly alters course: another five minutes and she would have emerged from the darkness of the sea smack above the searchlights and massed anti-aircraft batteries of German-held Brest. Thus, approaching the English coast from an unexpected direction, the flying boat is now declared a hostile bomber and two flights of Hurricanes are dispatched to destroy her. *However,* Churchill records with calm, *they failed in their mission.*

The great conference just finished—known as "Arcadia"—has set the cornerstone for Allied victory. But the rising yellow tide of Nippon still batters at the ill-prepared foundations. Passing from the triumphant Year of the Serpent to the equally auspicious Year of the Horse, the Japanese swarm victoriously over all the Pacific. They have bottled up General MacArthur's Philippine Army in the devastated peninsula of Bataan. They have invaded Burma and the Celebes. They are clawing nearer and nearer, island by island, to the vast and defenseless continent of Australia. Malaya is overrun and the Japanese have almost reached the all too narrow strait that protects the hinge of Britain's Far East defenses—the luxuriant island of Singapore.

On 30 January 1942 two hundred infantrymen, all that are left of the Argyll and Sutherland Highlanders, march wearily across the causeway behind their pipers. As the last man steps onto the island the strand that connects Singapore to the mainland is blown. There are no British left on the farther shore. Civilian life in the city is carried on much as usual, though of course there are irritating shortages. At the fashionable Raffles Hotel the planters and businessmen gather in their daily routine to sip their customary *stengahs* as the sun drops red on the horizon. A small orchestra still plays daily for tea dances. Singapore wears unconsciously the doomed air of those Cities of the Plain in the Bible, but without the sins, except possibly for some of omission.

Doomed Singapore most certainly is, in spite of Churchill's exhortations. The news of Japanese assault landings on the island on 8 February provokes a blunt message to General Wavell, over-all commander in Southeast Asia: *There must at this stage be no thought of saving the troops or sparing the population. The battle must be fought to the bitter end at all costs. . . . Commanders and senior officers should die with their troops. The honor of the British Empire and the British Army is at stake.* At 8:30 P.M. on Sunday, 15 February 1942, in the velvet, tropic darkness, the Singapore garrison surrenders unconditionally to its exultant Japanese conquerors.

Bitter in itself, the ghastly shame of this defeat is intensified for Churchill because the Americans on Corregidor, no less severely invested, are still desperately holding on. He feels they have been let down.

Tense in their foxholes in the gritty soil of that humped rock, the Americans grimly await the final assault they know must come. Deep underneath them run the arteries of the Malinta Tunnel, the nerve center of the defense. It reeks of blood and creosote and sweating bodies. By 5 May the bombardment has stripped every scrap of vivid green from the island and it looms gaunt and blackened, a modern Golgotha. On that day the Japanese transports mass gunwale to gunwale and at last scrape ashore. The last radio message is tapped out from the Tunnel.

It ends: "They are piling dead and wounded in our tunnel . . . Tell my mother how you heard from me . . . God bless you and keep you . . ." Corporal Irving Strobing, the Brooklyn boy who has sent it, hears the firing begin to die away. Knowing the battle is almost done, he smashes his equipment and goes to look for the Japanese. "After the fighting had ceased on Corregidor," he recalls, "we were all assembled on a steep hillside below the Malinta Tunnel when General Wainwright and his staff came out on their way to Manila to sign the formal surrender terms. The men were utterly exhausted, but as the General walked slowly down the road every man who could rose and stood at attention. Some of us saluted, and some didn't. But I think most of us cried at that moment, not for ourselves—we cried for General Wainwright. On that day he was the most forlorn man I have ever seen."

Now the Japanese stand at the very zenith of their success. They have the Philippines and all the Dutch East Indies. With Malaya and the great naval base at Singapore beneath their heel, they menace India and Ceylon, and even the sea routes up the coast of Africa upon which the survival of the Middle East depends. They prowl toward Australia flushed with victory. But they have left two factors out of their calculations.

The Japanese have never been able to envisage the enormous latent power of the United States, and they have underestimated the hard aggressive qualities of her fighting men. Only weeks after Pearl Harbor a renascence of U.S. strength becomes apparent. Then at the end of April and early in May two actions make it clear that the nation that can boast a long roster of formidable seafarers is still well supplied with tough and ruthless captains eager to carry the battle to the enemy. Learning quickly, the Americans take a leaf from the Japanese book and begin to deploy their carriers offensively in fast task forces.

On 18 April 1942 General Doolittle (piloting the *Ruptured Duck*) appears above a startled Tokyo with a group of sixteen B-25 bombers, slashes in and disappears. The aircraft have been flown off carriers at tremendous risk. It is America's first offensive punch and it lands right on the heart.

The Japanese press on through the Solomons with an invasion fleet intended for New Guinea, and thence for Australia. Rapidly Admiral Nimitz concentrates his forces to cut them off. On 8 May he brings them to bay in the Coral Sea. The action is the first ever to be waged exclusively between carriers. Though inconclusive, it results at least in averting the threat to New Guinea. More important, the damage inflicted on two of the Japanese heavy carriers will have a possibly decisive effect on the outcome of one of the great fatal battles of history that is about to be fought.

Still puzzled by General Doolittle's unexpected visit to their capital, the Japanese look about for his base. A few days after the attack some senior officers bend over a map table in the naval headquarters in Tokyo. Their faces are blank as they gaze at the islands speckling their chart. Suddenly a hand plunges down, a hand from which two fingers are missing. They look up into a harsh black-browed face, then down again at the chart. Admiral Isoroku Yamamoto has decided. He is indicating a remote atoll 2,250 miles to the east, here indicated as a point about the size of a random pencil mark. Their slant eyes peer at the name. "Ah, so!" they exclaim. "Midway!"

The capture of this humble stretch of coral and sand that nowhere rises more than thirty-five feet above the broad waters of the ocean will give them two advantages. The first is that its use as an offensive base by the Americans will be terminated. Second, it will serve as a jumping-off point for the assault on Hawaii that will precede the invincible advance against the west coast of the United States itself.

Yamamoto's design is to sail north for the Aleutians, so drawing after him such naval forces as America can muster. Then he will unleash his main power against Midway. He assembles a mighty armada, arranged in three principal divisions. The assault force carries the troops for Midway in sixteen transports escorted by two battleships and thirty-eight smaller warships, under command of Vice-Admiral Nobutake Kondo aboard the battleship *Kongo*. The striking force, commanded by the victor of Pearl Harbor, Admiral Chiuci Nagumo, musters two battleships, four carriers, two heavy cruisers and a light cruiser and sixteen destroyers. Admiral Yamamoto himself sails in the new battleship, the *Yamoto*, with the main body, comprising seven battleships (two of them, at 63,700 tons, the most powerful afloat) and seventeen lighter vessels.

To oppose this awesome array the Americans dispatch two battle squadrons. The first, Rear Admiral Raymond A. Spruance's Task Force 16, numbers two carriers (*Enterprise* and *Hornet*), six cruisers and nine destroyers. The carrier *Yorktown*, two cruisers and five destroyers make up the second, Rear Admiral Frank J. Fletcher's Task Force 17. Midway itself is hurriedly reinforced: additional aircraft are flown in, light patrol vessels are detailed to the lagoon and its vital supplies are replenished. But in this vital moment the most important weapon of all is something not a single Japanese is aware of. Navy Intelligence has broken their secret codes.

Nobody on the American side is taken in by Yamamoto's elaborate game. The Task Forces rendezvous by a happy irony at Point Luck, northeast of Midway. The battle opens early on 4 June when planes from Midway spot Nagumo's ill-fated striking force.

Aboard *Hornet* Ensign George H. Gay, a husky Texan and one of the fifteen pilots of Torpedo Squadron 8, lounges in the briefing room wondering whether his ancient Devastator will get him close enough to the Japs to do a little damage. He hears the din of *Hornet*'s bombers roaring away. Shortly afterward his own group is flown off. Formating at low level, mainly because they carry torpedoes, but partly because they cannot climb very high anyway, they head for the rising sun. After about an hour they sight smoke on the horizon. Believing the Japanese have been set afire by *Hornet*'s bombers, the men of Torpedo 8 conclude they have failed to rendezvous as ordered, and squeeze the last ounce of speed out of their laboring engines.

In fact the damage has been done by Marine flyers from Midway. *Hornet*'s bombers, which should now be attracting the Japanese air cover circling high above the target as the fearfully vulnerable Devastators plow in, have temporarily gone astray. Quivering with strain the Torpedo 8 planes rattle toward Nagumo's carriers. Approaching the point where they must begin their dangerously straight runs they are suddenly flailed by more than seventy Zeros. They have drawn upon themselves the whole savage weight of the air cover.

One by one the Devastators begin to plummet helplessly into the sea. Ensign Gay hears his gunner scream, "They got me!" A bullet slams into his left hand, another into his arm. The latter he squeezes out and pops into his mouth.

In front of him is the long shape of the carrier *Kaga*. Gay flies on straight and true. Glancing right and left he observes calmly that he appears to be alone. His torpedo is of ancient design. If it is to be at all effective Ensign Gay must drop it within a thousand yards of his target, from not more than thirty feet above the water, at a speed not exceeding eighty knots.

"I got in to about a thousand yards," he says, "and tried to drop my torpedo. It missed fire. So I pulled the cable loose with my good hand and away it went, straight for the carrier. As I started in there was a fellow on a pom-pom gun trying to get my range. So I flew right down his throat and ran him off his gun. I banked under the carrier's bridge, flew down her deck and out over her stern, where I figured there'd be less guns. As I was weaving my way out of the Jap fleet on the other side, the Zeros jumped on me again and I ditched. Out of the fifteen airplanes and thirty men in Torpedo Squadron 8, I was all that was left."

Facing such gallantry the Japanese are overwhelmed. Floating in the warm sea that day Ensign Gay watches one of their carriers flame like a blowtorch. The mortal blow is dealt by a group of dive bombers from *Enterprise*. They come upon the enemy fleet at the very moment when Nagumo is about to launch an air strike. The decks of the carriers *Kaga* and *Soryu* are crammed with planes. As the first bombs plummet among them they spew blazing gasoline everywhere. A pillar of solid fire howls sixteen hundred feet into the air from *Kaga*. *Soryu's* magazine explodes and her captain orders his men to abandon ship, screaming, "Banzai, banzai!" as the flames sear the flesh from his bones.

Still far from the engagement, the irresolute Yamamoto, hearing of the slaughter of Nagumo's force, orders immediate withdrawal. In so doing, it is historically interesting to note, he acknowledges Japan's first naval defeat since that of 1592 at the hands of the Korean Yi Sunsin. Even more important historically, this majestic American battle of Midway, which may be reckoned one of the three decisive battles of the war, has turned the Pacific tide. *At one stroke*, as Churchill thankfully sums it up, *the dominant position of Japan in the Pacific was reversed. . . . The glaring ascendancy of the enemy . . . was gone forever. . . . In the East I expected terrible forfeits, many disasters, immeasurable cost and tribulations . . . but there was no doubt about the end.*

A TIME
OF HOPE

And not by eastern windows only,
 When daylight comes, comes in the light;
In front, the sun climbs slow, how slowly,
But westward, look, the land is bright.
ARTHUR HUGH CLOUGH: *Say Not, the Struggle*
 Naught Availeth

THROUGH the thin traffic of early morning a small but elegant carriage clip-clops down the Mall from a side gate of Buckingham Palace. As beetle-black taxicabs, bearing prim civil servants to their dark and peaceful offices fragrant with tea and ancient documents, swing around it, the carriage proceeds sedately but handily to the imposing purlieus of Whitehall. Holding the reins lightly in his white-gloved hand, its coachman swings it into Storey's Gate and draws up precisely opposite a small green door. The carriage bounces as the footman behind jumps down, bright in his royal livery, and raps peremptorily upon the door. It opens and he steps inside, doffing his cockaded hat. The horse snorts briefly in the manner of all horses, royal or otherwise.

In a few moments the footman emerges with a dispatch box of scarlet leather. It bears the royal crest.

A quiet click from the coachman's tongue and a flick of the reins and the spruce little equipage is wheeling away back to the Palace with a day's work for His Britannic Majesty. It is a small, unnoticed ceremony enacted every morning at 8:30 exactly, through all hazards of weather or enemy action, outside this unassuming door that leads down to the underground War Room whence issue the orders for the conduct of a global war.

Inside the box are piled the memoranda, the files, the letters, reports, dispatches and enactments that crave the Royal assent or bring to King George VI the latest intelligence of his armed forces. Among them is a sheet of fine paper bearing a short letter from the King's First Minister. It reads:

> SIR,   16 June 1942
>   In case of my death on this journey I am about to undertake, I avail myself of Your Majesty's gracious permission to advise you that you should entrust the formation of a new government to Mr. Anthony Eden . . . who I am sure will be found capable of conducting Your Majesty's affairs with the resolution, experience and capacity which these grievous times require.
>   I have the honor to remain
>   Your Majesty's faithful and devoted servant and subject,
>   WINSTON S. CHURCHILL

Its author is bustling about in the last stages of preparation for what is by now quite his favorite method of travel. At midnight the long inlet at Stranraer is bisected by the white wake of a Boeing flying boat taking off for the west.

Round and brilliant in a dark heaven shines the full moon, spreading the sea with silver. Fascinated, Churchill sits silently in the co-pilot's seat gazing at the metallic gulfs glistening below him and turning over in his mind the problems of state, seeking the best means of gaining the ends for which his journey is made. The pale radiance of that ghostly seascape calms and comforts him.

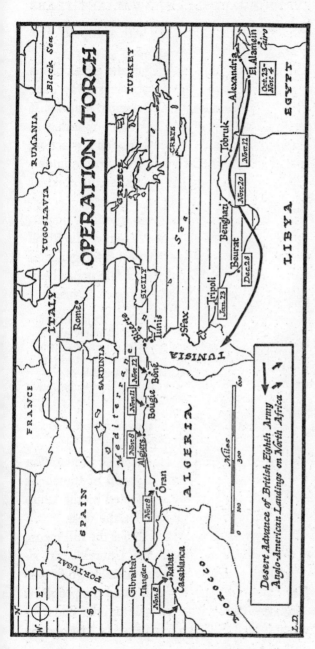

With "Operation Torch," the Anglo-American invasion of French North Africa scheduled for November 8, 1942, the "desert rats" of General Montgomery's British Eighth Army open the Battle of Alamein on October 23, firing a thousand guns on the batteries of General Rommel's Afrika Korps. On November 4, the Eighth Army cracks the German lines opening the way for British armor to pursue Rommel across the open desert to Tunisia. In the west, at Casablanca, Oran and Algiers, the "torch is lit" as the Allies land their forces in the invasion of North Africa.

Three meals later, 18 June 1942, the great aircraft is approaching Washington. *As we gradually descended toward the Potomac River I noticed that the top of the Washington Monument, which is over five hundred and fifty feet high, was about our level, and I impressed upon Captain Kelly Rogers that it would be peculiarly unfortunate if we brought our story to an end by hitting this of all other objects in the world. He assured me that he would take special care to miss it.*

The President has quit the summer heat of Washington and, surrounded by his family, awaits the Prime Minister at his Hyde Park estate. Delightedly he drives Churchill out to one of its boundaries, where sheer bluffs command superb views of the Hudson River. Churchill is surprised to see his old friend actually in the driver's seat. *I had some thoughtful moments. Mr. Roosevelt's infirmity prevented him from using his feet on the brake, clutch or accelerator. An ingenious arrangement enabled him to do everything with his arms, which were amazingly strong and muscular. He invited me to feel his biceps, saying that a famous prize fighter had envied them. This was reassuring; but I confess that when on several occasions the car poised and backed on the grass verges of the precipices over the Hudson I hoped the mechanical devices and brakes would show no defects. All the time we talked business, and though I was careful not to take his attention off the driving, we made more progress than we might have done in formal conference.* In these preliminary discussions the two great men are able to cover the two principal topics Mr. Churchill wishes to broach.

The first of these is the decision on what operations to undertake in the current year. With their native simplicity of approach, the Americans are eager to get at German throats by the most direct means possible. That is, by headlong assault across the English Channel into northern

France. There is some need for haste, and the reason lies along the thawing steppes of Russia.

The brute hordes of Hitler's eastern armies have lived through the long darkness of an inhuman winter. At the end of March, as the breeze betrayed a faint warmth, they scented the coming of spring and the new campaign season. A directive from Hitler on 5 April 1942 outlined the strategy: "It is intended to hold the central part of the front, in the north to bring about the fall of Leningrad . . . and on the southern wing of the army front to force a breakthrough into the Caucasus . . . To begin with all available forces are to be combined for the main operations in the southern sector, the objective being to destroy the enemy before the Don in order to gain the oil region of the Caucasian area and to cross the Caucasus mountains. . . . We must try to reach Stalingrad, or at least to subject this city to bombardment of our heavy weapons to such an extent that it is eliminated as an armament and traffic center in the future." The occupied wastes of Russia begin to bustle with the heavy gray trucks of a colossal field army. Soon Field Marshal von Bock, commanding in the crucial south, controls a hundred divisions. Behind them group fifteen hundred first-line aircraft.

Aware of this mighty preparation, the Russians are understandably alarmed. Josef Stalin sends the impassive Vyacheslav Molotov, he of the grizzled beard and the schoolmaster's rimless spectacles, on a mission. Late in May the People's Commissar of Foreign Affairs arrives in London. Coldly he outlines Russia's fears, then asks for the establishment of a second front menacing enough to draw off at least forty of the German divisions. Explaining the difficulties to him, Churchill nevertheless tells him there are hopes of preparing a landing on the Continent in the fall of 1942.

During these talks the Russian party is housed at Chequers, the Prime Minister's weekend retreat among the quiet orchards of Kent. Their habits arouse mild surprise among Churchill's staff. When the beds are made pistols are found under every pillow. Mr. Molotov's room is searched by his secret police; instead of being tucked in, his sheets and blankets are so arranged that an opening is left in the center of the bed that allows instant egress in case of sudden malicious attack by night. His pistol is laid out beside his brief case every night on a bedside table.

Even as the conversations are concluded, the Eastern front flares into activity and a brutal slogging match, surpassing even the slaughter of Barbarossa, begins. To mitigate this, it becomes clear that Anglo-American forces must be committed. The question *now* was—where?

There is a choice between the Cherbourg Peninsula (Operation Sledgehammer) and North Africa (Operation Gymnast, later Operation Torch). Neither Churchill nor his Chiefs of Staff are anxious to assault the Continent until the Allies have built up sufficient forces in England and the Germans have been bled in Russia. They realize it will be no help to the Soviets to land forces unless there is a reasonable certainty of their staying put. Remembering perhaps the bloody beaches of Gallipoli that tumbled him from office in another war, Churchill is not eager to attempt the hazard before all conditions indicating a favorable outcome are met. Though the issue is not decided until late in July in London, one thing even now, in this session at Hyde Park, is abundantly clear. The President later expresses it in a single sentence, part of a massive directive: "It is of the highest importance that United States ground troops be brought into action against the enemy in 1942." America is spoiling for a fight.

Having searched the President's mind on this main object of his visit, Churchill broaches a second, mysteriously referred to as the "Directorate of Tube Alloys." Within the slim folder that contains his brief lies the seed of an unimaginable power, a force that will soon change the lives of all mankind, irrevocably, forever. Long before this, Churchill has experienced an odd prescience. In 1925 he wrote: *May there not be methods of using explosive energy incomparably more intense than anything heretofore discovered? Might not a bomb no bigger than an orange be found to possess a secret power to destroy a whole block of buildings —nay, to concentrate the force of a thousand tons of cordite and blast a township at a stroke? Could not explosives even of the existing type be guided automatically in flying machines by wireless or other rays, without a human pilot, in ceaseless procession upon a hostile city, arsenal, camp, or dockyard?*

When war breaks out in 1939 scientists are already working out practical means of producing energy by atomic fission. By the summer of 1941 they report their belief that an atomic bomb can be produced. Not without a sense of foreboding Churchill writes to his Chiefs of Staff: *Although personally I am quite content with the existing explosives, I feel we must not stand in the path of improvement* . . . and sets up the secret directorate known as "Tube Alloys." On 11 October 1941 he receives a suggestion from President Roosevelt that American and British research be joined. Churchill agrees. Now, in the summer of 1942, the research has advanced so far that the two men must decide whether or not to establish the huge production plants that will be needed. The fruit of their decision will later appear over two Japanese cities as a mortal light brighter than a thousand suns. The monstrous birth of this new weapon on the desert proving grounds of Nevada will provide all men with a vile inheritance—a unique and pervasive fear they have never known before.

But in this hot summer of 1942 these things lie beyond knowledge. President and Prime Minister leave Hyde Park for Washington for more detailed discussions with their advisers. One of the latter's entourage is not sorry. Detective Inspector Walter Thompson, that long-suffering bodyguard, has found the numerous and boisterous Roosevelt clan an exacting challenge. "Of all the places that I visited during the war, with Winston Churchill, in my opinion Hyde Park was the worst," he says with feeling. "The place was very vulnerable, which meant it had to be covered by security officers for the whole twenty-four hours, and everybody that moved about, either entering or leaving the premises, had to be checked by these men. I hated the place. There was no peace there for anyone. The Roosevelts were always on the move. If they wanted something they meant to have it. Day and night I had to be on the alert, walking about the grounds all over the damn place with a creel on my hip, a hot dog in my hand and often a parcel of sandwiches on my head and my trousers covered with mustard. And to add to all this, very often half a dozen Roosevelt grandchildren turning on me and running all around me. I'd rather have Chequers in the blitz than a weekend in Hyde Park any day."

Churchill's first day in Washington is a black one. Finishing a leisurely breakfast, he seeks out with beaming morning face the President in his study. But there his cheerful mood is swept away. Without a word the President hands him a telegram. It says starkly: TOBRUK HAS SURRENDERED WITH 25,-000 MEN TAKEN PRISONER. All Churchill's hopes of a desert victory lie shattered in an instant.

This fearful reverse has been brought about chiefly by one

man and one weapon—Field Marshal Erwin Rommel, and the
88mm gun from the armories of Herr von Krupp. Rommel
has now been in the desert for more than a year, having
arrived at the very crest of the early British successes that
almost annihilated the Italian Army in North Africa. Boasting at first only two divisions, he now commands the Afrika
Korps, one of the finest instruments of war ever fashioned.
Its training has been Teutonically thorough from the first.
Living and working in overheated barracks, suffering artificial sand storms, and existing on reduced rations of food
and water, Rommel's men have been brought to a peak of
fitness on a sandy Baltic peninsula, and are already desert-
hardened when they step off their troopships in Tripoli. The
British find them formidable opponents, resolute in attack
and tenacious in defense. They are superbly equipped. Their
anti-tank guns in particular, the fabulous long-barreled, high-
velocity 88s, begin to dominate the armored battle.

Back and forth through the wasteland, littering it with
twisted carcasses of tanks and trucks, rolls the battle. Everywhere over the dun and arid plains the flotsam of war—
broken rifles, pierced steel helmets, shreds of uniform, pathetic impromptu crosses—testifies to the savagery of the
campaign. The opposing armies maneuver like fleets through
the sea of sand, forever searching the elusive laurel wreath
of victory. Tobruk is invested, held by the Australians, relieved.

Throughout early spring Churchill has been urging General Sir Claude Auchinleck, Commander-in-Chief in the
Middle East, to attack with the Eighth Army before Rommel
begins an offensive of his own, which he clearly is about to
do. On 26 May 1942 the line between the two armies runs
in a broken curve from a coastal village 36 miles west of
Tobruk southward to the oasis of Bir Hakeim, held by a
Free French brigade. In the moonlight of that night, before

Auchinleck can take the initiative, Rommel lunges forward.

With his two crack panzer divisions and the motorized 90th Light he outflanks the Free French and drives straight for the center of the Eighth Army. For the next four days the fighting is continuous over twelve hundred square miles of desert, with the Germans cannoning from one defensive box to the next, quelling some but rebounding from others. Rommel begins to run short of gasoline and water. But he crushes an attack on his bridgehead, and the tide of battle turns. It centers on an area not inaptly christened the "Cauldron."

A shallow depression in the featureless desert, it is the keystone of the German position and a place of death. As the fighting concentrates around its lip the toll of dead rises with a grim arithmetic—by 7 June the British have lost ten thousand men. Five days later the vast and merciless battle of Gazala is finally decided. By nightfall on 12 June the smoking ruins of the British armor lie deserted on the stricken field. Grants, Stuarts, Crusaders, some with their tracks flung about like steel entrails, others with their sides bulged out by exploding ammunition, many reeking with the sweet stench of burnt flesh, all are pierced or gouged by the twenty-pound solid shot of the 88s and all have been knocked out, long before they could close with the German batteries, at ranges of up to a mile. Rommel has been everywhere. His direction of the fluid battle has amounted to genius, and these shattered hulks pay eloquent tribute to his power.

Grinning through the mask of sand caking his face, the Field Marshal rallies his men and heads for Tobruk. Once more the white walls of that unhappy town are to endure the hammer blows of a siege. But not, it will be seen, for very long.

Withdrawing eastward, Auchinleck leaves behind a garrison of South Africans, with some British and Indian units.

There is no doubt anywhere that Tobruk must be held at all costs. Churchill watches anxiously. As he leaves England for his conference in America he has reason to believe that once more Tobruk will threaten the enemy's flank. Auchinleck is regrouping the Eighth Army, intending to halt the Germans for good in the narrows between the Qattara Depression and the sea, where there nestles a scatter of buildings called El Alamein.

In the midst of these preparations, in the cool air of dawn on 21 June, Rommel's great Mercedes staff car rolls down the Via Balboa, lined with ten thousand sullen prisoners of war, to accept the surrender of General Klopper, South African commander of the garrison of Tobruk. That night, after the austerity of the open desert, the victorious Afrika Korps gorge themselves on pineapple, Irish potatoes, canned beer and pork sausages. They even send home to the Reich parcels of Australian bully beef.

As the Germans are appreciatively sniffing the delicious odor of frying sausages that enriches the air of Tobruk, Churchill is considering the implications of the fortress's fall. The President asks if there is anything he can do to help. At once Churchill replies, "Give us as many Sherman tanks as you can spare, and ship them to the Middle East as quickly as possible." Without question three hundred Shermans and a hundred self-propelled guns are withdrawn from angry divisions to which they have just been issued, loaded into six fast ships and dispatched for Suez. When one of the ships is sunk en route, the Americans quietly send another, carrying seventy more tanks, to overtake the convoy.

Back in England on 26 June, Churchill finds that, as he expected, a vote of censure has been proposed, expressing no confidence in the central direction of the war. It stands in the name of Sir John Wardlaw-Milne, an old guard Tory. He loses the initiative almost immediately by making the curious suggestion that His Royal Highness the Duke of Gloucester be appointed Commander-in-Chief of the Army. But then comes a bitter attack from Leslie Hore-Belisha, a former Secretary of State for War. He concludes: "We may lose Egypt or we may not lose Egypt—I pray God we may not— but when the Prime Minister, who said that we would hold Singapore, that we would hold Crete, that we had smashed the German army in Libya . . . when I read that he has said we are going to hold Egypt, my anxieties become greater. . . . How can one place reliance in judgments that have so repeatedly turned out to be misguided? That is what the House of Commons has to decide. Think what is at stake. In a hundred days we lost our empire in the Far East. What will happen in the next hundred days? Let every Member vote according to his conscience."

On 2 July the House divides for a vote. To nobody's surprise the motion of no confidence is defeated by 475 votes to 25. Churchill wakes next morning to receive a cable from the President. It is quite brief. It reads, GOOD FOR YOU.

Nevertheless it is clear that something must be done about Rommel. He is already across the frontier of Egypt, thirsting still for battle. He is now confident that Cairo and the Nile Delta will fall to his arms. So is Hitler, who writes to Mussolini, pressing him to give all support to Rommel, "The Goddess of Battles visits warriors only once. He who does not grasp her at such a moment never reaches her again." Auchinleck judges it impossible to stand against Rommel at Mersa Matrûh and orders his puzzled men back to the Alamein position a hundred and twenty miles to the rear. A series of desperate delaying actions covers this dangerous retreat. On 4 July, his communications stretched to the limit, his troops exhausted, and all but a dozen of his tanks out of the running, Rommel decides to rest, and begins to prepare his final assault on the Alamein position. Both armies have fought themselves to a standstill.

Churchill decides that he must go to the Middle East at once to settle matters. Providentially, the means for doing so has just arrived—an adapted Liberator bomber piloted by an American, Captain Vanderkloot. Furthermore, since it has now been decided to invade French North Africa, Stalin must be told that the cross-Channel invasion proposed for 1942 has not been preferred, and Churchill feels that this might best be done in person. Accordingly, he arranges to fly to Moscow, stopping over in Cairo on the way.

The outcome of the Cairo meetings is swift. Auchinleck is replaced by General Alexander, veteran of Dunkirk and Burma and once a regimental officer in the Irish Guards. General "Strafer" Gott, a desert commander, is to take over the Eighth Army: when he is shot down by the enemy almost immediately, orders are sent to England to fly out a man who carries Rommel's fate in his hand. His name is Bernard Law Montgomery, and he is a tartar.

A story—not substantiated by Montgomery—is told about this unexpected appointment. On the way to the airfield with General Ismay, Churchill's Chief of Staff, Montgomery falls into a reverie and delivers a monologue on how a soldier devotes his whole energy to his profession, enduring years of discipline, incessant study and perhaps personal danger. He gains eminence in his career, is given command. He wins a great victory. His name becomes a household word, his reputation a thing of glory. Then, in an instant, his fortune may change. Immediately he is classed a failure, and everything he has striven for falls in ruins about him. Ismay tries to comfort the melancholy Montgomery, telling him that after all there is every hope that he may win. Montgomery sits up with a jerk and glares at the friendly Ismay. "What?" he snaps.

"What on earth do you mean? I've been talking about Rommel!"

With Montgomery entering the lists the odds are about to change. A withdrawn figure, lean and loose-limbed, his face severely lined, with a thin mouth and eyes as unflinching as a hawk's, he is restless, shrewd, experienced, a cruel fighting man. Burning with an austere inward fire, he shows the ruthlessness toward an enemy of a Cromwell, the cold calculation of a Wellington, the swift tactical sense of a Marlborough. It is his proud boast that he never sends his men into a battle until he knows it is won. Like the Germans he believes in the big battalions, in the exercise of massive power at a critical point.

Typically, Montgomery assumes command two days early. His first order cancels all arrangements for withdrawal, and to make it stick, all troop-carrying transport is taken away. His next calls all senior officers to a briefing, where they experience for the first time a Montgomery custom: smoking is not allowed. And as they stare at this ascetic new commander there comes another prohibition. "Gentlemen," the high-pitched voice declares crisply, "I will allow one minute for coughing. After that there will be *no* coughing." He then announces his intention to regroup, train, concentrate, and "knock Rommel for six right out of Africa." There are no questions.

Having thus set the cat among the pigeons, Churchill clinches his arrangements on 10 August 1942 with a directive to General Alexander, the new Commander-in-Chief, Middle East:

1. Your prime and main duty will be to take or destroy at the earliest opportunity the German-Italian Army commanded by Field Marshal Rommel, together with all its supplies and establishments in Egypt and Libya.
2. You will discharge or cause to be discharged such other duties as pertain to your Command, without prejudice to the task

> described in paragraph 1, which must be considered para-
> mount in His Majesty's interests.

Satisfied that everything possible is now being done, Churchill boards the Liberator for Teheran. As it approaches the mountains of Kurdistan Captain Vanderkloot, the pilot, observes that Churchill is in high spirits. Never one to deny the benefit of his advice on any subject whatever, the Prime Minister, proud of his status as a lay pilot, steps into the cabin and sits beside the American. *As we drew near to those serrated uplands I asked him at what height he intended to fly them. He said nine thousand feet would do. However, looking at the map I found several peaks of eleven and twelve thousand feet, and there seemed one big one of eighteen or twenty thousand, though that was farther off. So long as you are not suddenly encompassed by clouds, you can wind your way through mountains with safety. Still, I asked for twelve thousand feet, and we began sucking on our oxygen tubes. As we descended about 8:30 A.M. on the Teheran airfield and were already close to the ground I noticed the altimeter registered four thousand five hundred feet, and ignorantly remarked, "You had better get that adjusted before we take off again." But Captain Vanderkloot said, "The Teheran airfield is over four thousand feet above sea level."*

The next day's flight from that romantic city, the last leg of the mission to Moscow, has its own moment of comedy. Churchill has requested the company of Mr. Averell Harriman, who has already had some dealings with Stalin and will help present a united Anglo-American front. Commander "Tommy" Thompson, the Prime Minister's naval aide, is, as usual, responsible for the travel arrangements. It is Churchill's custom when in high spirits to harass him by awarding "black marks," or demerits, for any lapses. A luncheon has been packed by the Embassy in Teheran. Peering suspiciously into the interior of a ham sandwich Churchill demands the mustard. Thompson is forced to admit that there is no mustard. A cloud darkens the Prime Ministerial brow. Glancing at Harriman he announces with awful finality, *No gentleman would eat a ham sandwich without mustard!* and sentences the chastened aide to five black marks. (He graciously lifts them on the return trip when the Russians provide a packed lunch more to his taste, caviar and champagne.)

But once in Moscow the levity is replaced by stern duty. Immediately Churchill, meeting Stalin for the first time, puts the bad news first and explains why there can be no landings in France in 1942. Stalin is silent. As Churchill enlarges on the reasons, he notes a rising anger in the Russian leader, who at last bursts out that the British are afraid of the Germans and will never fight. Churchill swallows his pride and patiently starts an outline of the plans for Operation Torch in North Africa. As he lists its military advantages Stalin grows more and more interested. *To illustrate my point,* Churchill writes, *I had meanwhile drawn a picture of a crocodile, and explained to Stalin with the help of this picture how it was our intention to attack the soft belly of the crocodile as we attacked its hard snout. And Stalin, whose interest was now at high pitch, said, "May God prosper this undertaking."*

Seeming thus in agreement, this first session adjourns amicably. Next day the storm breaks. Stalin again refers to the proposed operations in France, and a second time accuses the British of cowardice. This is really too much for the Prime Minister. Sir Alan Brooke, Chief of the Imperial General Staff, is watching him closely.

He says, "Stalin put plainly what he thought about what

we were stating to him. In fact, a lot of insults poured out of his mouth, about when were we going to start fighting, and why hadn't we started already? He informed us that we wouldn't find it too hard once we did start, and so on. It was definitely intended to be insulting and the reaction on Churchill's part was just exactly what you might expect. He thumped the table and started off on one of those orations of his. I can only remember the starting line, but I remember *that* very well—'If it wasn't for the fighting qualities shown by the Red Army at Stalingrad—' and then it went on to tell him a lot of other things. Stalin's reaction to this flow of language from Winston was very remarkable. He got up at once, still sucking that bent pipe. A slow smile came over his face and as Winston's interpreter started to translate what he had been saying he stopped him, and through his own interpreter he said, 'I don't understand a word of what you're saying, but by God I like your sentiments!' "

So that what remains is to press ahead with Operation Torch. Back in London on 24 August, Churchill sends for its two commanders, the American generals Eisenhower and Clark, who by now have become his close friends. The bond is attributable in no little measure to their liking for Irish stew, a dish of which the Prime Minister is inordinately fond. Another frequent visitor is Eisenhower's Chief of Staff, the indomitable Bedell Smith, a man who works himself so hard that Churchill has to suggest sending him to hospital for rest. After this and further meetings, punctuated by telegrams between President and Prime Minister, the date for Torch is finally settled—8 November 1942.

In the meantime Rommel launches his expected attack on the Alamein positions. And for the first time finds himself in mortal trouble. Montgomery's dispositions are such that the Germans must choose between murderous artillery fire and impossible going that bogs down their tanks. They try both and find them equally unattractive. The British defensive boxes are too powerful to be overcome, and when the panzers try to outflank them they are led into quagmires of fine sand. Though they do not know it, the captured maps they are trusting have been planted on them by Montgomery and are fakes.

Thus thwarted, the wily Rommel resorts to a favorite trick. He withdraws, digs in his deadly 88s, and waits for the British counterattack to smash itself to pieces on them. Unfortunately for the Desert Fox, this time the counterattack never comes. Montgomery will only fight on ground of his own choosing. Rommel tries one more attack, then has to retire, baffled. Immediately the Eighth Army slashes at him, tearing not at his formidable armor, but at his more tender motorized divisions. Bloody and somewhat wiser, the Germans concede the battle of Alam Halfa and drive off to the west. There is no pursuit, for Montgomery's next battle is already planned, and as Rommel has now discovered, nothing—and certainly not the enemy—is allowed to upset that meticulous gentleman's arrangements.

Not even the Prime Minister gets much change out of this determined man. Churchill is forever haranguing General Alexander about the importance of attacking at once. Worn down by the stream of demands, Alexander goes to see his subordinate, who as usual is very busy. As Montgomery tells it: "There are certain moments in war when the commander in the field has to be pretty firm with his Commander-in-Chief. One day General Alexander came down to see me and said, 'I've just received this telegram from Winston Churchill ordering this attack in September. What am I going to say?' 'Well,' I said to my Commander-in-Chief, 'this is how I recommend you answer the telegram: 1. If I attack in September it will fail, or at least will be a very limited success. 2. If I attack in October I guarantee 100% success and we would knock Rommel and his whole setup for six right out of Africa. 3. Am I to attack in September? Only one answer is possible.'" Alexander regards Montgomery with respect. Montgomery looks him straight in the eye, grins wickedly, and turns back to his maps.

About a year before this Churchill had made a prophecy: *Renown awaits the commander who first in this war restores artillery to its prime importance upon the battlefield, from which it has been ousted by heavily armored tanks.* This is precisely what Montgomery proposes to do. Whilst the infantry practice again and again, day after day, their role in the attack, the batteries of squat field guns rumble forward and cautiously, one gun at a time, zero in on their targets. The gun pits are piled high with shells.

On the night of 23 October 1942 the moon rises serene and full, as Montgomery has wished. It throws a gentle glow over the stark landscape of desert, where an unseen army lies poised, seven divisions of infantry, three of armor, supported by a thousand guns. Every man knows his duty, has been told that this battle will go down in history. Alamein establishes the pattern of the Montgomery set-piece battle. It is constructed with all the precision of a great symphony.

At 2140 hours opens the authoritative statement of the theme. Save for a crackle of musketry here and there the desert broods in silence. Then, from the British line, a red flicker spreads right across the horizon. Wheel to wheel in their emplacements the British guns have begun the barrage. A steady rumble makes the air quiver as the German batteries are blanketed by a tornado of exploding shells. A change in the rhythm as the artillery shifts, regiment by regiment, to the Germans' forward positions. From behind, half a dozen bright searchlight beams lance into the gloom, helping the attackers to pick out their objectives. Left and right on the flanks Bofors cannon fire bursts of tracer shell; their winking arcs mark the limits of the assault. Crouched on their starting lines the infantry can distinguish in this man-made dawn a rippling line of flashes as the barrage rips at the German wire and obliterates the forward positions. At his advanced headquarters General Montgomery is asleep.

On the fifth day of the battle the 15th and 21st Panzer Divisions, with a mass of infantry, concentrate for an attack slightly west of a feature called Kidney Ridge, now surrounded by the acrid mist of gunsmoke. This is their last chance; all morning their reconnaissance groups have been probing for weak spots as squadrons and regiments take up their positions in the assembly area. But then from the east, glinting in the late afternoon sky, come RAF bombers. Their sorties last for two and a half hours and when the Germans move in they are already beaten men.

The third phase of Montgomery's plan, called "Supercharge," the breakthrough, is launched at one o'clock in the morning of 2 November. At the height of its fury Rommel receives a message from his Fuehrer: "In the situation in which you find yourself there can be no other thought but to stand fast and throw every gun and every man into the battle. . . . Your enemy, despite his superiority, must also be at the end of his strength. . . . As to your troops, you can show them no other road than that to victory or death." Stunned, Rommel comments bitterly, "This order demanded the impossible. For even the most devoted soldier can be killed by a bomb."

As dawn is breaking on 4 November armored cars of the British yeomanry and cavalry regiments debouch from the gap that has been blasted through, and the armored divisions follow them in long clouds of dust into the open desert in pursuit of the fleeing remnants of the Afrika Korps. Alamein is over. *Before Alamein,* Churchill writes, *we never had a victory. After Alamein we never had a defeat.*

But no victory is won without cost. The field of Alamein broods uneasily under a hideous debris. North and south from horizon to horizon the sand bristles with rifles, their muzzles jammed into the ground, each one marking the spot where a man has fallen wounded or dead. Skeletal trucks, the earth beneath them blackened by fire, wrecked tanks, from which the fat flies already buzz in clouds, bodies sprawled like bloated dolls on the coils of enemy wire—all are littered with the wind-blown letters, snapshots and personal papers that somehow invest battlefields with a pitiful humanity.

Throughout this crucial fight convoys comprising six hundred and fifty ships have been sailing from Great Britain and the United States toward the three main landing zones of Operation Torch, which is considered by some to have been the most complex operation in military history. But the complexity lies less in the military than in the political sphere. In order to clarify matters General Mark Clark has already visited the invasion area on a clandestine mission.

Early in October news comes from Robert Murphy, Counselor in the U.S. Consulate in Algiers, that the French commander there is prepared for a secret discussion about Allied plans for that area. When General Eisenhower delivers this intelligence and suggests that General Clark himself undertake the mission, the Prime Minister agrees with delight and offers the entire transport resources of the British Empire. Sailing in the submarine *Seraph* from Gibraltar, Clark descends like some aquiline angel in the dark of night upon a deserted beach. Meeting General Emmanuel Mast, he secures French co-operation, but has to suffer a few ignominious hours hiding in a wine cellar while a party of police search every room of the villa above. One of the General's aides is suddenly seized with a fit of coughing. Clark passes

him a wad of chewing gum. When the aide grumbles that
the gum seems rather insipid the General explains politely,
"Well, I'd chewed the taste out before I handed it over."

Unfortunately this bold reconnaissance does not wholly
resolve the political problem. For on the very eve of the invasion Admiral Darlan, Vice-Premier of Vichy France and
a leader commanding widespread and fervent loyalty, arrives
unheralded in Algiers to visit his son lying sick with polio.
Just after one o'clock on the morning of 8 November 1942 he
is awakened by Murphy and General Juin, French Military
Commander, and told that the first Allied troops are ashore.
His face purple, he chokes out, "I have known for a long
time that the British were stupid, but I always believed that
the Americans were more intelligent. I begin to believe that
you make as many mistakes as they do."

But as the long lines of landing craft crunch onto the
beaches and the dark streams of assault troops pour inland,
the Admiral bows to *force majeure*. Two days later he orders
a cease-fire and dispatches a signal to the French Fleet to
sail from Toulon before the Germans take it. The Germans
have started Operation Attila—the occupation of Vichy
France—and their columns are headed straight for the port.
The Admiral in Toulon replies indelicately with the single
word *"Merde!"* but later, when the moment of decision is
over, orders the Fleet to scuttle itself and the keels of sixty-
one warships kiss the mud of the harbor.

In North Africa the political situation remains very tense.
After a month of discussions and maneuvers Darlan is shot
in the doorway of his office at the Summer Palace by a
sixteen-year-old boy. *Few men*, says Churchill in obsequy,
*have paid more heavily for errors of judgment and failures
of character than Admiral Darlan. . . . At the time when we
descended on North Africa he was the undoubted heir of
the aged Marshal* [Pétain]. *Now suddenly a cataract of*

amazing events fell upon him. . . . He struck his final blow for us, and it is not for those who benefited enormously from his accession to our side to revile his memory. . . . Probably his sharpest pang was his failure to bring over the Toulon Fleet. Always he had declared it should never fall into German hands. In this undertaking before history he did not fail. Let him rest in peace, and let us all be thankful that we have never had to face the trials under which he broke.

Militarily the operation is a success from the start, though the American troops who play the major part are not yet blooded. One of their commanders, General Matthew B. Ridgway, describes his feelings during this baptism: ". . . for the first time I saw the loneliest and most ominous of all landscapes, a battlefield. And I knew for the first time that strange exhilaration that grips a man when he knows that somewhere out there in the distance hostile eyes are watching him and that at any moment a bullet he may never hear, fired by an enemy he cannot see, may strike him."

Amid such encounters the landings are swiftly consolidated and the invasion forces press inland with resolution. Within twenty-four hours the operation can be counted an unqualified success, and Churchill announces victory. Lunching at the Mansion House with the Lord Mayor of London and the entire majestic bench of aldermen he rises to his feet in answer to a toast, peers about the snowy tables heavy with silver and roundly declares, *Now this is not the end. It is not even the beginning of the end. But it is, perhaps, the end of the beginning.*

EPISODE **11**

CITY
OF STEEL

> *They shall fall by the sword, they shall be a portion for foxes.*
>
> PSALMS 63:10

A BLUE and acrid haze, penetrated now and then by the sour assertiveness of sauerkraut, invests the baroque room, so that its lights filter kindly upon the fat, perspiring faces that cram it like shining pink melons in serried rank on rank. The dark paneled walls speak of a historic past; the floor is worn with the heavy boots of generations of beer drinkers. Now the ceiling re-echoes the raucous laughter of German throats; the thin Munich beer spills over the tables as the steins crash down to emphasize a point or punctuate a *Diktat*. It is a room full of a brute energy. It is the swank Loewenbraukeller, and tonight is the occasion of a sacred Nazi ceremony.

The cropped heads turn one to another in excitement, fat necks swelling over stiff uniform collars, pale popping eyes straining for a first glimpse of tonight's guest. For tonight in this place, which has succeeded to the honor after the

167

destruction of the Buergerbraukeller, will be relived that
magic occasion when Der Fuehrer himself raised the Party
standard on the night of the Beer Hall Putsch—a damp squib
of an event that nevertheless is equated in the perverted
Nazi mind with the Stations of the Cross. This is 8 November
1942, the nineteenth anniversary of that shoddy maneuver
for power, and some of the old guard—the beefy, murderous,
cold-eyed veterans of the SA—are still here, though some of
their fellows have died facing the enemy, or by the black-
gloved hands of the SS.

A stirring, a seething, a guttural animal roar of acclaim.
The dapper Fuehrer smiles. It is like the old days, *nicht
wahr?* He hears echoes of the Nazi myriads in the Sport
Palast, the deep-throated reiteration of the Party war cry:
"*Sieg Heil! Sieg Heil! Sieg Heil!*" It is good to be back among
old comrades. On the rostrum he beams at these simple, unassuming, loyal friends, glances with recognition at their
trusting faces, recognizes his sturdy cronies. Thoroughly at
home, Adolf Hitler, at the turning point of the war, speaks
like a brother to his brothers and explains what is going on.

One of his topics is the campaign in the East, which is
taking a little more time than was expected, though there is
no cause for worry. "I wanted to get to the Volga," he explains in terms simple enough to be comprehended by the
thugs in his audience, "and to do so at a particular point
where stands a certain town. By chance it bears the name of
Stalin himself." He pauses to let the joke sink in. The stone
mugs crash down upon the tables in an ecstatic volley of
applause at this witty sally. Gratified, Hitler continues, "I
wanted to take the place, and do you know, we've pulled
it off, we've got it really, except for a few enemy positions
still holding out. Now people say: 'Why don't they finish the
job more quickly?' Well, the reason is that I don't want another Verdun. I prefer to do the job with quite small assault

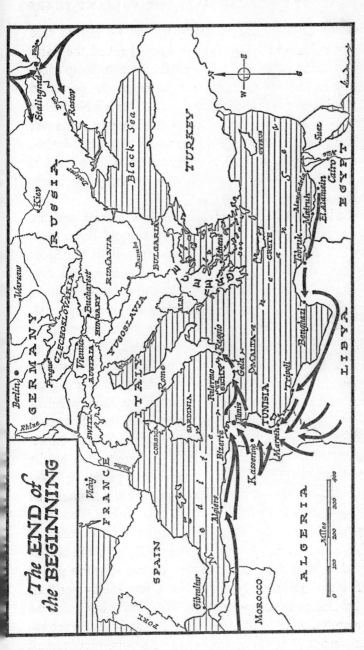

The END of the BEGINNING

From the west, Allied armies strike for Tunis. From the east, the British Eighth Army pushes the Afrika Korps across 1500 miles of desert. On April 7, 1943, the two Allied commands link forces in Tunisia, trapping the German armies. On May 12, the German forces surrender.

groups. Time is of no consequence at all." In a way the Fuehrer is right. Time *is* of no consequence at all to thousands of his soldiers, thrown by a whim into a slaughterhouse, for they lie with flesh and sinews frozen hard as iron in the killing snows of Russia.

An entire German army (von Paulus' 6th) has been committed among the rubble of a once prosperous city, a great manufacturing center and a monument to Russian industry. Every crumbled wall is a frontier, contested for days, every gutted building a fortress, every wrecked hovel a bastion that costs scores of lives. Blood flows in Stalingrad with a prodigality never before seen on earth. Each German attack that succeeds, and success is measured in yards, must assault over a stinking carpet of German dead. It is a battle fought *in extremis* by attackers and defenders alike, a meaningless welter of desperate and heroic sacrifice.

Little by little, because they are ordered to, von Paulus' men claw into their grasp more and more of the shattered city. But, though they do not know it, they are only making a noose for their own necks. The Russians are well aware that there is more than one way of killing a goose. The German line has been weakened by this lunatic concentration on a single spot, and in mid-November two spearheads of Russian armor pierce it with relative ease and speed around the flanks of Stalingrad. On 23 November the pincers close between the Volga and the Don, and Stalingrad is become a cemetery whose tombs, though presently peopled with the living, will soon be inhabited only by memories.

Across the flat snowy fields the Germans begin to hear an ominous message: "Every seven seconds a German soldier dies in Russia. Stalingrad—mass grave." The last three words echo through many a brave German head in that gray hour of the night when all men's courage is at its lowest ebb. They remember the Russians who fought here before the position was reversed, and they gaze with no little sympathy at the blackened, pitted wall that bears the only memorial to their predecessors in this purgatory: "Here Rodintsev's Guards stood to the death."

By holding Stalingrad for so long the Russians have saved the Caucasus and denied to Hitler the oil that is his lifeblood. By blocking Hitler's southern thrust they have redeemed the Middle East and prevented the Germans from realizing that dream of Eastern conquest cherished since the days of the Austrian Empire's policy of the *Drang nach Osten*. To this point the question has been: "Will Hitler conquer the Caucasus and thrust for the Eastern Mediterranean?" Now the question is: "Can Hitler stop the Russians from penetrating into Central and Southern Europe?" The key to both these questions is Stalingrad. The first has been answered, the second is being resolved in agony in the subzero cold of a Russian winter.

Bleeding from this enormous gash in its eastern flank, the Wehrmacht nevertheless can still find the strength to reinforce its threatened units in North Africa. Reacting swiftly and firmly to the successful landings of Operation Torch, by the end of November the Germans have rushed 15,000 men to Tunisia. In another month the total reaches 45,000. In support they have withdrawn four hundred planes from the Russian front. Supplies, meanwhile, build up for the Allies, who are further delighted by the accession of a hundred thousand French soldiers who terminate their allegiance to Vichy and embrace the Allied cause.

Throughout November Eisenhower's troops press toward Tunis, every day meeting with stiffer and stiffer opposition. It becomes clear that the Germans are not beaten yet. By the end of the month the Allies have struggled to within twelve

miles of the city, but the climax has passed. Now the rains
come and in hours the hard earth becomes a morass. Bombers
and fighters stand streaming on useless airfields, tanks flail
about like dislocated monsters, supply trucks sink to their
axles in clinging ooze and the surge forward peters out in
a hissing torrent of water. On Christmas Eve General Eisenhower calls off all attacks and consolidates his line.

During these operations an idea has come to the President.
Confident that the end is in sight in Tunisia, he has decided
that the principal allies should meet, either in Cairo or in
Moscow, to discuss what the next step shall be. Churchill
agrees, but believes that no firm results will be secured unless
the three Heads of State confer in person. As to the site, the
President confesses a liking for warmth, and writes: "I prefer
a comfortable oasis to the raft at Tilsit." Stalin, however,
proves cold. He tells Churchill: "To my great regret . . . I
will not be in a position to leave the Soviet Union. Time
presses us, and it would be impossible for me to be absent
even for a day, as it is just now that important military
operations of our winter campaign are developing. . . . In the
Stalingrad area we are keeping a large group of the German
troops surrounded, and we hope to annihilate them completely."

Faced with this Soviet immobility, President and Prime
Minister decide to go it alone. The President still longs for
the sun: "I asked General Bedell Smith, who left here four
or five days ago, to check up confidentially on some possible
tourist oasis as far from any city or large population as possible. One of the dictionaries says, 'an oasis is never wholly
dry.' Good old dictionary!" Eventually a location is found—
a group of comfortable villas clustered about a hotel in the
outskirts of Casablanca, within earshot of white-topped roll-
ers pounding on the beach. It is an invigorating spot.

One of the consequences of the meeting is an easement of

the explosive political situation between two of the leaders of the Free French, the aggressive General Henri Giraud and the aloof General Charles de Gaulle. Both factions make concessions without engendering much mutual love and are eventually persuaded into a precarious agreement that is symbolized by the most insincere handshake ever recorded by a camera. Of de Gaulle Churchill remarks in a moment of insight, *Certainly I had continuous difficulties and many sharp antagonisms with him. There was however a dominant element in our relationship. I could not regard him as representing captive and prostrate France, nor indeed the France that had a right to decide freely the future for herself. I knew he was no friend of England. But I always recognized in him the spirit and conception which, across the pages of history, the word "France" would ever proclaim. Here he was—a refugee, an exile from his country under sentence of death, in a position entirely dependent on the good will of the British Government, and also now of the United States. The Germans had conquered his country. He had no real foothold anywhere. Never mind; he defied all. Always, even when he was behaving worst, he seemed to express the personality of France—a great nation, with all its pride, authority and ambition.*

On another occasion Churchill sums up his attitude in more typical fashion, or so the popular story goes. *Of all the crosses I have had to bear,* he is said to have complained, *that of Lorraine has been the heaviest.*

The second outcome of the Casablanca Conference is a misleadingly simple expression of two words, and it will later give rise to great issues. Certainly there is a difference of opinion about it in some respects between the two leaders. The term is "unconditional surrender," and it is purposely excluded from the joint communiqué that is to be made public. However, the President lets the words slip out at a press conference, innocently excusing himself for the error thus: "We had so much trouble getting those two French Generals together that I thought to myself that this was as difficult as arranging the meeting of Grant and Lee—and then suddenly the press conference was on, and Winston and I had had no time to prepare for it, and the thought popped into my mind that they had called Grant 'Old Unconditional Surrender,' and the next thing I knew I had said it." An ingenuous and disarming admission, upon which Churchill wryly comments: *I do not feel that this frank statement is in any way weakened by the fact that the phrase occurs in the notes from which he spoke.*

Business over, Churchill will not let his friend leave without seeing Marrakech, which he enthusiastically describes as *"the Paris of the Sahara," where all the caravans have come from Central Africa for centuries, heavily taxed en route by the tribes in the mountains and afterward swindled in the Marrakech markets, but receiving the return, which they greatly valued, of the gay life of the city, including fortunetellers, snake charmers, masses of food and drink, and the largest and most elaborately organized brothels in the African continent. All these institutions were of long and ancient repute.* Within sight of the snows of the high Atlas, with the tumult of a thronged city distantly heard across warm fields, the two men and their entourages enjoy a hilarious dinner party, and the President leaves. Churchill stays on for a couple of days and paints his only wartime picture. He is very happy. Tripoli has fallen to Montgomery's Eighth Army.

Far away in Stalingrad General von Paulus has enough food for only two more days. No respite comes from above. "Where the German soldier sets foot," Hitler has declared, "there he remains." Nothing can persuade him to allow the

6th Army a reprieve. As a Christmas treat the men have been permitted to slaughter four thousand horses. Now the only ones left have been lying frozen in the snow for weeks. Slowly but surely the Russian vise closes on the doomed divisions under their shrouds of snow. On 24 January 1943 von Paulus reports that his perimeter is everywhere disintegrating and, his ammunition almost exhausted, he requests permission to surrender.

The reply is chilling. "Surrender is forbidden. Sixth Army will hold their positions to the last man and the last round and by their heroic endurance will make an unforgettable contribution toward the establishment of a defensive front and the salvation of the Western world." It is signed by Adolf Hitler himself, who shortly is visited by an inspiration. No German Field Marshal has ever surrendered. Here is a way of saving Stalingrad. On 31 January, just before the forlorn garrison destroys its radio equipment because Russian grenades are exploding in the doorway of the bunker, the haggard von Paulus receives the news of his promotion. That day he capitulates.

Among his captured subordinates is one Lieutenant General von Arnim, whose cousin is soon also to fall into Allied hands, in North Africa. There Churchill, fresh from a comfortable series of meetings with the Turks, receives news of this hard-won Russian victory. On 3 February he watches the desert-hardened men of the Eighth Army march in triumph through the streets of Tripoli, headed by massed pipers in the somber tartans of the Highland Regiments. *I have never in my life,* he tells the House of Commons later, *seen troops who march with the style and air of those of the Desert Army. Talk about spit and polish! The Highland and the New Zealand Divisions paraded after their immense ordeal in the desert as if they had come out of Wellington Barracks. There was an air on the face of every private of*

*that just and sober pride which comes from dear-bought
victory and triumph after toil.*

At the end of the parade he calls the troops round him and
pays them his personal tribute: *After the war when a man is
asked what he did it will be quite sufficient for him to say,
"I marched and fought with the Desert Army."*

That Army's forward units have already reached the Tunisian frontier, and as he speaks Churchill is mindful of a
message now rustling in his pocket that has come from General Alexander. Though handwritten on a common message
blank it is couched in somewhat formal terms:

> SIR,
>   The orders you gave me on August 10, 1942,* have been ful-
> filled. His Majesty's enemies, together with their impedimenta,
> have been completely eliminated from Egypt, Cyrenaica, Libya
> and Tripolitania. I now await your further instructions.

Field Marshal Erwin Rommel is now in desperate straits,
penned between two armies. He looks about for a vulnerable
target and, turning to the west, his reconnaissance units find
a green American division in the Kasserine Pass. Rommel
hastens up with his main force and slaughters the valiant but
inexperienced Americans with the weight of his armor. They
fall back, not without some savage delaying actions, and soon
Rommel perceives, incredibly enough, the first glimmer of
a victory. But it is denied him. Rallying, as they always will,
and supported by the crack 1st Guards Brigade and some
British artillery, the Americans push him back inexorably
toward his nemesis.

Now, with an assailant on either side, Rommel must face
about. The coldly methodical Montgomery has reached the
Mareth Line, a series of defenses built by the French and
now improved by the Germans, and is disposing his forces
preparatory to reducing it. He expects an attack by Rommel

* See page 157.

before this, however, and makes arrangements to receive it. Calculating that the Germans will come in at Médenine, he issues the necessary orders and the lethal machinery of the Eighth Army rolls smoothly into place.

Through the early morning mist of 6 March drive all three of Rommel's famous Panzer Divisions, deployed in their familiar attack formation and advancing calmly, precisely, and with murderous intent. Save for the muffled roar of engines and the harsh scream of steel tracks upon rocky ground, the battlefield is quiet. In front of the black squadrons the British line is silent. Nothing moves. Still the low-slung tanks move forward, bucking over boulders and throwing up a spray of earth behind their pounding tracks. They cross an invisible line. Now they are in the killing ground. In an instant they are enveloped in a recurrent flashing storm of shell. Montgomery has been waiting for them with five hundred anti-tank guns dug in, each with its arc of fire registered almost to the inch.

This day the Afrika Korps earns glory with a toll of blood. Before they concede defeat they struggle on four separate times against a concentration of batteries no force on earth could challenge and live. Rommel has fought his last action in North Africa. Already a sick man, he is flown home and von Arnim succeeds him in a doomed command.

When he is quite ready Montgomery moves in for the kill. Hooking around the Mareth Line by dispatching two corps far southward through a sand sea previously thought impassable, he avoids the necessity of a costly frontal assault. The Gurkhas of the 4th Indian Division are loosed in the Matmata Hills. They fight mainly by night, at close quarters, with the wicked curved kukris that once drawn cannot be sheathed until they have drawn blood. (A Gurkha who by mischance does not kill his quarry will cut his own hand to satisfy the sacred tradition.) The night becomes a hideous time for the Germans. One of the Gurkhas' battle reports ends: "Enemy losses ten killed, ours nil. Ammunition expenditure nil."

German resistance in southern Tunisia ends after a one-day fight at Wadi Akarit. On 7 April there is a historic confrontation. Warily approaching over the crest of a hill, where around the gnarled trunks of cork trees curls white and blue convolvulus, an American patrol from II Corps catches sight of friends and calls out in greeting, "Hello, Limey!" The reply is equally cordial: "Bloody Yanks!" At last the two great armies are joined. Tunis falls on 12 May 1943. Waiting at sea for the fleeing remnants of the Afrika Korps, Admiral Cunningham orders all ships to the straits and signals: "Sink, burn and destroy. Let nothing pass."

Shortly after lunch on 13 May General Alexander announces to Churchill: "Sir: It is my duty to report that the Tunisian campaign is over. All enemy resistance has ceased. We are masters of the North African shores." The only Germans left in North Africa are either dead or behind barbed wire. The surrender at Tunis has cost them 248,000 men taken prisoner. Not present among this humiliated gray mass is a party of fanatics from the Hermann Goering division who, having capitulated, seize weapons and fall on their escort. They are shot to a man.

The reckoning in Tunisia has been a hard one for the Wehrmacht. The price of Stalingrad has been even heavier. Of the 330,000 Germans trapped there, more than 200,000 have been killed. A further 91,000, all dazed and famished, most of them frostbitten and many wounded, have been marched off in a temperature of twenty-four below zero toward the Siberian prison camps whence only 5,000 will ever return. They have left behind 400 aircraft, 600 tanks, 1,300 guns, 16,000 rifles and 16,000 trucks.

The toll of this winter has been heavy indeed for the

Fatherland. A German Army report on 30 March sets out the appalling details. On the Eastern Front alone they have lost 1,167,835 men, not including the sick. Of the 162 divisions with which they set out, only 8 are now capable of offensive action. In their 16 armored divisions only 140 tanks are still able to fight. For the moment, in the sand and in the snow, the Wehrmacht has been fought to a standstill.

Yet these dreadful losses at Stalingrad, even with those inflicted in Africa, do not yet constitute a crippling blow. Caught between a Russian onslaught in the east and a threatened Anglo-American invasion in the south, Germany is still a formidable power. It is enough for the moment for the Allies to salute the victory. With Africa redeemed, England celebrates with peals of bells from every steeple in the land. But the Prime Minister cannot hear the carillons chiming and singing over the fields of spring. Winston Spencer Churchill is in a distant city, plotting the next move.

8/6/35

James Holzhaur (Jeopardy)

800 618-3520 Medicor

VISITING ANGELS

1 800 648-4654

Med Core Suppl.

1-800 215-2115

LIFE, LIBERTY & LEVIN

844 LEVIN TV

FOX
NEWS
9 TO 10 PM
NOV 10TH

(1-800) 881-1300

THE ROAD
TO ROME

*Though a man escape every other danger,
he can never wholly escape those who do
not want such a person as he is to exist.*
DEMOSTHENES: *De Falsa Legatione*

IN THE LIFE of a statesman there are few moments of the privacy a common man enjoys. Intruding always are the voracious newsmen, the microphones disseminating cliché and profundity alike into a billion distant ears, the flashbulbs erupting incessantly in their search for an instant of revelation. Forests of eyes and labyrinths of ears follow the statesman's every move, and multitudes of private hopes and fears must wait upon his word. The statesman knows that the future of nations may tremble in a pouting lip, a downcast eye; that history speaks in the posture of a head. It is another burden he must bear atop the weight of ultimate responsibility.

It is therefore pleasurable for great men to escape publicity, and one morning in the middle of May 1943, a Presidential party prepares to leave, for however brief a stay, in a

summery retreat. Deep in the Catoctin Hills of Maryland
President Roosevelt maintains his mountain refuge, Shangri-
La. This morning he is to escort his guest to it for the first
time and the White House seethes with activity. Like all
such preparations it is attended with some differences of
opinion.

At the porch waits the Presidential limousine. Clearly
President Roosevelt must sit in the back. Mrs. Roosevelt
settles into one of the small front seats, leaving room beside
her husband for his guest. There arises a conflict of wills.
But at last President and First Lady are properly aligned and
Mr. Churchill, triumphant in his first battle of the day, arranges his not inconsiderable bulk beside his friend Harry
Hopkins in front. Thus, like any other family, argumentative
and deeply loyal at once, they roll away in holiday mood.

Gazing at the pleasant landscape Mr. Churchill is presently
put in mind—as he is by almost any landscape on the face
of the earth—of times past. Gettysburg he has already visited,
and he would be disposed toward an exposition of tactics
there displayed, were it not that something else engages his
attention. Approaching the town of Frederick he inquires
about the legendary Barbara Frietchie and her house. Innocently rising to this bait Hopkins obligingly quotes from
Whittier's poem:

> "Shoot, if you must, this old gray head,
> But spare your country's flag," she said.

Mr. Churchill continues his bland inspection of the countryside, happily conscious of an uncomfortable silence as his
allies seek to amplify this beginning. Delighted by his own
unfriendly stroke the Prime Minister now discomfits them
further by quotation at length. Line after line, stanza after
thundering stanza, the patriotic narrative rolls out of his
capacious memory, ending nobly:

THE ITALIAN CAMPAIGN

From Tunisia, the Allies cross to Sicily on July 10, 1943, to open the
Italian campaign. On September 3, Allied armies secure a foothold at
Reggio and link with forces landed at Salerno on September 8. At
Cassino, the German Gustav Line in the mountains is almost impreg-
nable. On January 22, 1944, the Allies gain a bloody beachhead at
Anzio, and on two fronts, German resistance holds through the winter.

> So all day long through Frederick's street
> Sounded the tramp of marching feet,
> And all day long that free flag tossed
> Over the heads of the rebel host.

Encouraged by this naughty success (for none of his American companions has been impolite or erudite enough to call attention to his misquotations) the Prime Minister moves on to examine the characters and abilities of Stonewall Jackson and Robert E. Lee.

After a while, he records, *silence and slumber descended upon the company, as we climbed with many a twist and turn up the spurs of the Alleghenies. Soon we arrived at Shangri-La, which was in principle a log cabin, with all modern improvements. In front was a fountain and pool of clear water, in which swam a number of large trout, newly caught in the neighboring stream and awaiting the consummation of their existence.*

The President settles down to a few hours with his stamp collection. But even upon this idyllic spot the somber shadow of war must fall. He is soon interrupted by General Bedell Smith, General Eisenhower's Chief of Staff, who has flown in from North Africa. General Smith's arrival is apt, for Churchill has come to the United States primarily to discuss how the great Allied victories in North Africa shall be exploited. Though the "Trident" Conference is to cover every theater of operations, Churchill is anxious to gain positive support for his major concept. This is no less than to drive Italy out of the war.

The collapse of Italy, he believes, *would cast a chill of loneliness over the German people, and might be the beginning of their doom. . . . Another great effect of the elimination of Italy would be felt in the Balkans, where patriots of various nationalities were with difficulty held in check by large Axis forces, which included twenty-five or more Italian divisions. If these withdrew, the effect would be either that Germany would have to give up the Balkans or else that she would have to withdraw large forces from the Russian front to fill the gap. In no other way could relief be given to the Russian front on so large a scale this year. The third effect would be the elimination of the Italian Fleet. This would immediately release a considerable British squadron of battleships and aircraft carriers to proceed either to the Bay of Bengal or the Pacific to fight Japan.*

It has already been decided at the Casablanca Conference to capture Sicily. The question now is "Where next?" Day after day in Washington's heat the talks continue, ranging over the whole troubled surface of the globe. But beyond stating broad strategic principles they reach few very practical solutions.

At the Speaker's request, Churchill once more addresses Congress in a speech that is broadcast to the world. He begins by reviewing success: *In the north we builded better than we knew. The unexpected came to the aid of the design and multiplied the results. For this we have to thank the military intuition of Corporal Hitler. We may notice . . . the touch of the master hand. The same insensate obstinacy which condemned Field Marshal von Paulus and his army to destruction at Stalingrad has brought this new catastrophe upon our enemies in Tunisia. . . .*

Listing the vast losses in men and matériel the two Axis dictators have incurred in Africa, Churchill continues with a warning, tempering triumph with sagacity: *I was driving the other day not far from the field of Gettysburg, which I knew well, like most of your battlefields. It was the decisive battle of the American Civil War. No one after Gettysburg doubted which way the dread balance of war would incline, yet far more blood was shed after the Union victory at Gettysburg than in all the fighting which went before. It behooves us*

*therefore to search our hearts and brace our sinews and take
the most earnest counsel one with another, in order that the
favorable position which has already been reached both
against Japan and against Hitler and Mussolini in Europe
shall not be let slip.*

By the end of the Trident Conference the strong frame-
work of ultimate victory has been erected, and even a strategy for the ensuing peace is at least tentatively planned. But
when the time comes for Churchill to leave, the Combined
Chiefs of Staff have fulfilled Churchill's hopes only so far as
issuing an order, rather less than incisive, "that the Allied
Commander-in-Chief in North Africa will be instructed, as a
matter of urgency, to plan such operations in exploitation of
"Husky" [the capture of Sicily] as are best calculated to
eliminate Italy from the war and to contain the maximum
number of German forces." Which specific operation is to be
adopted will be decided by the Combined Chiefs of Staff.
Thus whimsically served, Churchill is understandably anxious, and asks that General Marshall accompany him to
Algiers to talk to General Eisenhower. By this device
Churchill might inhibit criticism that he has unduly in-
fluenced events.

In the early morning rain of 26 May the party boards the
clipper *Bristol* at her moorings in the Potomac River. As she
lifts into a high mist, Churchill buries himself in bundles
of drafts and memoranda, emerging only when they land in
Newfoundland to refuel. By now it is dark and shortly after
take-off Churchill stretches out on the great double bed in
his bridal suite, expecting to wake somewhere near Gibraltar.

He falls into a deep sleep, then . . . *All at once there was
a sudden shock and bump. I awoke. Something had happened. There were no consequences, which are after all*

what is important in air journeys. Nevertheless, being thoroughly awake, I put on my zip suit and went forward down the long central gallery of our spacious machine, and climbed the staircase to the navigating controls. I sat in the copilot's seat. It was by now a lovely moonlight night. After a while I asked the pilot what caused the bump. "We were struck by lightning," he said, "but there's nothing wrong." This was good news. . . . I looked down upon the calm ocean, seven thousand feet below; but an ocean always looks calm at that height. Almost underneath us was what looked like a little tramp steamer. I was conscious of a distinct sense of comfort from her presence. Under this reassuring illusion I returned to my bed, and did not wake until just before dawn.

The sun comes up in a majesty of a gold and scarlet behind the black bulk of Gibraltar, but it is midafternoon before the flying boat cuts in past Cape Trafalgar, edges down and slides into harbor on a long white arrow of spray. At her buoy the Governor's launch is waiting. He leads the party ashore for the night, accommodating them in his gubernatorial house, "The Convent." *The nuns,* Churchill is careful to point out, *having been removed two centuries ago.* Next day they are in Algiers, deep in conference with General Eisenhower.

Churchill is well aware that in these talks the British possess a moral advantage. They have three times the troops, four times the warships, and almost as many aircraft in the theater as the Americans. They have suffered grievous losses along these sunburned shores and dared innumerable hazards. In spite of this the British have accepted an American as Supreme Commander and have continued to follow American policy. Churchill can foretell the results: *The American chiefs do not like to be outdone in generosity. No people respond more spontaneously to fair play. If you treat Americans well they always want to treat you better.*

Almost at once General Eisenhower declares that if Sicily falls quickly he will cross the Straits and enter Italy. Though approval is still necessary, Churchill is overjoyed and rushes off to visit his men.

Commander Bill Fairchild remembers one such encounter: "I don't know whether this story about Mr. Churchill is true, but it certainly went the rounds of the naval striking force. It seems that he was discussing with a very senior British naval officer the role that the Navy was going to play in the forthcoming combined operation, and this senior officer felt that the Navy hadn't got enough to do. So he said to Mr. Churchill, 'I don't think the Navy's role is in accordance with its traditions.' 'Oh?' said Mr. Churchill. 'Well, Admiral, have you ever asked yourself what the traditions of the Royal Navy *are?*' And before the Admiral could answer he went on, 'I will tell you in three words—gin, women and the lash!'"

Throughout North Africa the air is vibrant with the pride of conquest. Amid the crumbled palaces of Carthage, now brooding vacantly over the blue Mediterranean where once they held dominion, Churchill calls around him thousands of laughing troops. Into a vast amphitheater they crowd, as tough and crafty in combat as the gladiators whose sandals once raised this same dust. Bronzed, confident and rested, their exuberance informs the gentle evening air. In this place, at such a time, Churchill catches their mood and rockets to a peak of oratory that catches the very distillation of victory. Though afterward he cannot remember what he has actually said, he can still recall his exhilaration for the Chief of the Imperial General Staff. *I was speaking from where the cries of Christian virgins rent the air whilst roaring lions devoured them—and yet,* he confides, *I am no lion and certainly not a virgin.*

*   *   *

Full of confidence, the Prime Minister flies home. And unwittingly causes a tragedy. Aware of his presence in North Africa, the Germans have prepared a trap. Their watchful agents in Lisbon report the departure of a thickset gentleman smoking a big cigar aboard a commercial aircraft leaving on a scheduled flight. Shortly after take-off it is pounced on by a German fighter and shot down with ridiculous ease. Among its fourteen civilian passengers is film star Leslie Howard. The innocent cause of their death is a brilliant accountant and amateur musician called Alfred Chenhalls, whose resemblance to Churchill is superficial merely. An incident without profound effect upon the course of events, it serves nevertheless to illustrate the brutality of which German Intelligence is capable.

These Germans circulating as agents amid the hectic intrigues of Lisbon might better have served their country and their forlorn cause on the beaches of Sicily. For now there point at that parched island the ominous spearheads of invasion. *Soon*, says Churchill, *the German nation was to be alone in Europe, surrounded by an infuriated world in arms.... The hinge had turned.* From the south toward Italy, blotting out the sun, bear the black wings of Nemesis, and as the distant beatings of these mortal pinions whisper closer they stir the echoes of a braggart voice and spell a nation's doom.

Three years before Benito Mussolini made a curiously penetrating remark. "Have you ever seen a lamb become a wolf?" he asked Ciano. "The Italian race is a race of sheep. Eighteen years are not enough to change them. It takes a hundred and eighty, and maybe a hundred and eighty centuries." Whatever the span, Mussolini's sheep are about to turn on their shepherd, for the wolf is outside the fold and racing for Sicily.

The assault forces intended for that island are borne in

and protected by three thousand ships and landing craft—
a hundred sixty thousand men with fourteen thousand vehicles, six hundred tanks, eighteen hundred guns. On 3 July
1943 heavy and medium bombers begin their methodical
demolition of the enemy air power and its installations.
Within six days the only aircraft still able to fly are the
Allies' and they menace the entire sky above the objective.

A fresh wind blows up on 9 July, buffeting the ships on
their way to the beaches. But rough weather alone cannot
stem the press of vessels. Converging stream by stream, they
cohere a few miles offshore into a gray plain of steel tossing
and rolling on the breaking crests. Loud-speakers break out
into a metallic blare of orders and decks clatter under running boots. The parent ships run out the little assault craft
and lower them away while the men of the first wave
clamber clumsily into them down the rope nets, oppressed
by the weight of weapons and ammunition. A wrack of
white wake reaches toward the shingle, where a glowing line
in the darkness marks the edge of land.

Surprised at the ease of his arrival on this hostile shore,
Douglas Grant leads his troops of Commandos through the
night with only minor encounters to differentiate it from
a training exercise. Dawn comes up through a violet mist.
In its growing light, that silences the cicadas' endless chir-
ruping, Grant musters his men and marches forward along a
cliff edge. Here and there are corpses, slain in the swift and
private engagements of the darkness. Gradually the sun's
weight begins to bear down on them in the unnatural silence. . . . "The track widened out again and, where it turned
abruptly inland to run uphill through a vineyard, the body
of one of our own men lay stretched out. His pallid face,
which seemed to have been coated with grease, was emptied
of all expression, and the flies, singing sharply in the rising
heat, crawled as thickly as currants over his skin. A gas cape

had been thrown across his body and we raised it to hide his face, but as we moved it we saw that his bowels had been torn out. We covered his face with a rag and hung his helmet on an upright bayonet to mark his resting place."

From his high point of vantage Grant looks back toward the beaches. Long files of infantry are climbing the narrow tracks that wind up from a shoreline piled high with boxes of supplies. Beyond them landing craft ply to and fro between the beach and the fleet that rides so immutably at anchor. The Allies are firmly ashore. In a few hours they will have such strength in Sicily that nothing will be able to shift them.

Desperately, in the time that remains, the Germans strive against the Americans westward about Gela, and the British in the eastern end of the island. Panzers of the Hermann Goering Division slash through the infantry of the U.S. 1st Division, but these hard and perverse men stay where they are, let the twenty-six-ton Mark IVs roll over their foxholes, and level their machine guns at the spot where they know the Panzer Grenadiers will soon appear. The plains outside Gela swarm with tanks, but now naval gunfire pulverizes them, shattering half their force. A shell from a cruiser, it is found, will quite transform a tank in no time at all. The Germans withdraw eastward toward Mount Etna for what they must recognize, in spite of reinforcement by six battalions of paratroops from the mainland, as their last stand.

For the Germans the summer of 1943 is different from all others. During the past three it was they who launched new offensives. Pressed now from east and west they must begin to think of defense. Their old ally believes, accurately, that he is in even greater danger than the Reich, and for weeks he has been pestering Hitler to sue for peace in the east so as to be able to meet the surging Allied tide in the Mediterranean. When the Allies breach Sicily the Duce nears hysteria. The Fuehrer is not exactly sympathetic. He tells his war council on 17 July: "Only barbaric measures like those applied by Stalin in 1941 or by the French in 1917 can help to save the nation. A sort of tribunal or court martial should be set up in Italy to remove undesirable elements." A tribunal is indeed being set up, though, with a fine irony, for a purpose quite the opposite of that the Fuehrer proposes.

While in a villa near Rimini Hitler is trying to inject some sterner spirit into his former mentor, who is so overwrought that he has to be furnished with notes of the discussions, the principal members of the Fascist Grand Council are plotting the Duce's downfall. This paper Caesar, empty of arrogance and wakened from his dreams of glory into a world of nightmare reality, returns to a Rome still smoldering from her first heavy air attack in daylight.

For the first time in three and a half years the Grand Council assembles on the night of 24 July, in coldly rebellious mood. It's leaders—among them Mussolini's son-in-law, Ciano—divest the dictator of his powers. By so doing they make possible a mortal stroke, for the King and some of his generals have also been plotting. Now they can act. Next day Mussolini is summoned to the Palace.

He suspects nothing. As he stares haggardly at the King in some bewilderment, Victor Emmanuel comes at once to the point. "My dear Duce," he says quietly, "it's no longer any good. Italy has gone to bits. . . . The soldiers don't want to fight any more. . . . At this moment you are the most hated man in Italy."

But the accretion of arrogance built up from years of adulation has not yet so worn away that Mussolini can understand the full meaning of these words. "You are making an extremely grave decision," he replies. Perhaps because of some ultimate lassitude of the heart, he makes no attempt to persuade the King to change his mind. As he leaves the Palace he is summarily arrested by a captain of carabinieri, clapped into an ambulance and carted away to a nearby barracks.

Hitler receives the news with sour aplomb. Already his cynical brain has reached its own conclusion. To his generals he announces: "Undoubtedly, in their treachery, they will proclaim that they will remain loyal to us; but this is treachery. Of course they won't remain loyal. . . . Although that so-and-so Marshal Badoglio declared immediately that the war would be continued, that won't make any difference. They have to say that. But we'll play the same game, while preparing everything to take over the whole area with one stroke, and capture all that riffraff."

The Fuehrer's political intuition is once more pointing to the truth. Badoglio must inevitably seek Allied help, for the Italians cannot turn against the Germans alone. Hastily Hitler makes his plans accordingly. He will rescue Mussolini, occupy Rome and restore the Fascist regime, take into bondage the King and his advisers, grasp Italy in his military control and capture or destroy the Italian Fleet. He believes that he has only hours to set things in motion. In fact he has days, weeks even. For the first overtures of peace are made nine long days after the coup, in Lisbon.

Diplomatic procedures run their leisurely and considered course, and two weeks later the military are called in. General Bedell Smith is ordered to Lisbon to meet Badoglio's representative, General Castellano. Since the Portuguese capital harbors innumerable agents, a high percentage of them German, the General travels in civilian clothes with a false British passport that declares him a hardware merchant of Berkeley Square, London. But nothing is concluded until two more weeks have passed.

By then Sicily has been cleared of the enemy and General Alexander has sent a signal to the Prime Minister announcing: "By 10 A.M. this morning, August 17, 1943, the last German soldier was flung out of Sicily and the whole island is now in our hands." Castellano, having consulted his superiors, meets Bedell Smith for the second time, in an olive grove in Sicily. There, on 3 September 1943, the armistice is signed.

General Castellano, cloistered with his papers and his negotiations, has missed a spectacle. In the Straits of Messina there is a throng of shipping. At dawn that day the Eighth Army has slammed into the toe of Italy, thus marking the fourth anniversary of the outbreak of war by stepping onto the mainland of Europe.

General Montgomery is in command, and he is none too pleased. "If the planning and conduct of the campaign in Sicily were bad, the preparations for the invasion of Italy, and the subsequent conduct of the campaign in that country, were worse still." His Operation Baytown is very much the poor relation of Operation Avalanche, the Fifth Army's descent on Salerno scheduled to follow in five days' time. After a cutting message or two to General Alexander, one of which begins: "I have been ordered to invade the mainland of the continent of Europe on 30 August. In the absence of information to the contrary, I must assume that some resistance will be offered by the enemy . . ." Montgomery carries out his orders and finds that all goes well with the initial landings. Certainly, the Italians are no problem.

Their new government is about to announce the armistice. But they are fearful of the consequences, especially to Rome. The Allies have a plan to drop air-borne troops on the city at the same moment as their invasion fleet stands in for Salerno. General Maxwell D. Taylor, of the 82nd Airborne

Division, is sent secretly to make arrangements with Badoglio.

"I left Palermo with my comrade, Colonel Tudor Gardner, in the middle of the night in a British PT boat," General Taylor remembers. "We rendezvoused at dawn with an Italian corvette north of Palermo, then went up the Tyrrhenian Sea to the port of Gaeta, between Naples and Rome. There the two of us were taken ashore under the guise of being prisoners of war and put into an ambulance. We continued up the Appian Way into Rome itself. We entered Rome just at dusk. The streets seemed normal, although there were many German troops about the streets. Some of them approached our ambulance when it stopped at an intersection. Colonel Gardner and I insisted on being taken in the middle of the night to see Badoglio, the head of the Italian Government. We had a long discussion with Badoglio, who unfortunately showed the same pessimistic attitude as his generals. He emphasized that the Italian divisions were without ammunition and gasoline and were watched closely by a number of German divisions. For these reasons, he opposed the air-borne operation. I therefore contacted Supreme Headquarters in Algiers by clandestine radio and recommended the cancellation of the air-borne attack on Rome and asked that I be allowed to return."

In spite of this lukewarm co-operation on the part of the Italians, Eisenhower decides not to check his main blow, which is directed at Salerno. Once more an Allied invasion fleet steams through the night toward an alien shore. En route comes the Supreme Commander's announcement of the armistice: "The Italian Government has surrendered its armed forces unconditionally. As Allied Commander-in-Chief, I have granted a military armistice, the terms of which have been approved by the Governments of the United Kingdom, the United States and the Union of Soviet Socialist

Republics in the interests of the United Nations. The Italian Government has signed itself to abide by these terms without reservation. The armistice was signed by my representatives and representatives of Marshal Badoglio, and it becomes effective this instant." Tensed with the prospect of imminent battle, the troops are thrown by this unexpected news into an illusion of security.

When the first assault waves storm the beach they have to wade in through withering fire. In the night the Germans have taken over all coastal defenses from the Italians. As dawn breaks they wait with pleasure for the arrival of the Allies. Before the light is full the breakers are already washing the shore with a pink foam, and bodies roll to and fro in the shallows like so much waterlogged flotsam.

But welcome of another sort comes quickly. Forward troops come across friendly leaflets, grossly printed on crude paper. The spelling of their message is bad and the syntax insecure, but no deficiencies of style can mute their warmth. They read:

BROTHERS!
After thirtynine months of war, pains and grieves; after twenty years of tiranny and inhumanity, after have the innocent victims of the most perverce gang at the Government; today, September 8, 1943, we can cry at full voice our joys our enthusiasm for your coming.

We can't express with words our pleasure, but only we kneel ourself to the ground to thank God, who have permit us to see this day.

With you we have divided the sorrow of the war, with you we wish to divide the day of the big victory.

We wish to march with you, until the last days against the enemy N.1.

We will be worth of your expectation, we will be your allied of twentyfive years ago

Hurra the allied

Hurra the free Italy.

The committee of anti-fascist
ex-fighters of the big war

These partisans will shortly be the only Italians left in arms, for that very night the Germans encircle Rome. By 10 September 1943, with sixteen divisions, they have disarmed the Italian regular forces and are masters of the greater part of the country. Fortunately the King and Badoglio are able to escape in time. They settle in Brindisi, where shortly they come under the protection of the Eighth Army.

During these mighty days Mussolini is being held captive in a winter sports center called the Hotel Campo Imperatore, a massive edifice perched six thousand feet in the air on a crag of the Gran Sasso d'Italia, highest range of the Abruzzi Apennines. Hitler is determined that he shall be rescued and chooses as the instrument a young major, an Austrian swashbuckler who has been serving with the Adolf Hitler Regiment of SS. This piratical Aryan is Otto Skorzeny.

In the hesitant early light of 12 September he leads a small force of picked men to a dubious rendezvous. Their gliders curl in along a precipitous valley, check, and slide down like giant ravens onto a lawn twenty yards from the looming walls of the hotel. The carabinieri guarding Mussolini offer no resistance. Skorzeny bundles him into a tiny Fieseler-Storch reconnaissance plane that takes off in a miracle of piloting. In Rome he is transferred to a larger aircraft that carries him to Hitler in his headquarters in East Prussia.

On Hitler's insistence Mussolini creates a new Fascist Republican Party. Guarded by special troops of the SS Liebstandarte he proclaims the birth of the Italian Socialist Republic and sets up a lamentable government beside Lake Garda. There he rules briefly over a nonexistent state by means of imaginary powers. One of the first acts of this grotesque burlesque is the execution, on German orders, of his son-in-law, the honest and unhappy Ciano.

At Salerno the Fifth Army is hard-pressed. For six days the fighting mounts in savagery as fresh German units are thrown against the beachhead. By 12 September elements of six German divisions, with a preponderance of armor, are on the attack. They thrust hard at the center of the Allied perimeter, and pierce it. On 13 September, hacking their way inexorably to the sea, they are stopped by two heroic battalions of American field artillery, the 189th and the 158th. Leaving only skeleton crews to serve the guns, these men dig in right in the path of the German advance. Even a regimental band is armed and dispatched to an anonymous eminence that General Mark Clark christens in their honor Piccolo Peak.

All that day the battle surges beside the Calore River. At its peak every one of the guns is firing eight rounds a minute; at day's end the two battalions have loosed 3,650 rounds at the enemy. Under this frightful weight of shell the Germans withdraw. Next day they try again, this time against the British in the hills about Salerno. Again they fail. On 15 September Kesselring cedes the battle and begins to swing back his whole line, with Salerno as the pivot.

Churchill congratulates Eisenhower by cable: *As the Duke of Wellington said of the Battle of Waterloo, "It was a damn close-run thing," but your policy of running risks has been vindicated. If you think fit, send a message from me on to Clark, who from all I hear has done wonders. We certainly do work together in a way never before seen among allies.*

On 16 September the leading patrols of the Eighth Army, which has advanced 300 miles in seventeen days, reach the southern outposts of the Fifth Army. The victory at Salerno has opened the road to Naples. That smiling port in the shadow of Vesuvius falls on 1 October and within two weeks is handling five thousand tons of supplies a day.

September had been indeed a fruitful month, Churchill

reflects. *The enemy had been defeated in pitched battle and our armies had bitten three hundred miles off Italy's boot ... The Italian enterprise, to launch which we had struggled so hard, had been vindicated beyond the hopes even of its most ardent and persistent advocates.*

Aboard the battleship *Nelson*, guarding the surrendered Italian Fleet in Valletta Harbor, Marshal Badoglio signs the instrument of unconditional surrender. On 13 October 1943, the Royal Italian Government declares war on Germany. The wheel has come full circle and the Axis is broken.

But before peace can come to stricken Italy she will have to pass through purgatory. North of the battle line, where German occupation forces already rule with whip and pistol, little groups of loyal Italians are forming partisan bands to fight a lonely battle. To them Churchill broadcasts a message of hope, welcoming them as allies, and promising succor. *Now is the time for every Italian to strike his blow. The liberating armies are coming to your rescue. The German terror in Italy will not last long. They will be extirpated from your land. ... Take every chance you can. Strike hard and strike home! Have faith in your future. ... March forward with your American and British friends in the great world movement toward freedom, justice and peace.*

EPISODE 13

THE
TRIUMVIRS

*The huntsmen are up in America and they
are already past their first sleep in Persia.*
SIR THOMAS BROWNE: *Garden of Cyrus*

CAIRO is undoubtedly the noisiest city on earth. Down
every broad boulevard ricochets the sharp honking of innumerable dilapidated taxicabs. Streetcars churn and clank
over cobwebs of steel rails, their pounding interrupted by the
rat-tat-tat of frequent intersections. From Kasr el Nil barracks sound the guttural commands of noncoms bawling out
stupid recruits from the Delta farms or from the barren
reaches upriver toward the cataracts. Above the sprawling
market hums the buzzing of a thousand voices, arguing,
cajoling, reviling, always in the ugly tongue of the riverain
peoples.

Shrill from fashionable stores and pleasantly secluded gardens twitter and shriek the inane conversations of the idle
rich of Egypt's ruling class. In every gutter whines a beggar,
twisted hands grasping for baksheesh, hoarse voice calling
interminably on Allah. Urchins along a hundred sidewalks

197

gabble out their treble catalogues of unmentionable vice, all immediately available to the perspicacious traveler. Occasionally there clatters by a lurching camel cart on God knows what mysterious errand, to be followed by the imperious limousine of some heavy pasha whose coming is heralded by an entire keyboard of klaxons.

Form and movement, both express and admirable, are imposed upon this babel by a timely cannon from the Royal Palace, or a flourish of bugles from a parade ground. At regular intervals, from a dozen minarets slim and white against the cerulean blue, wails the slow, high keening of imams calling the faithful to prayer. Then the restless hubbub is threaded for a few moments by the deep-voiced litany of the Koran as congregations of the devout acknowledge their Prophet and abase themselves before their God.

Into this tumultuous and seductive city are about to descend a President, a Prime Minister and a Generalissimo, the first two en route to their rendezvous with the third Tribune of the Allied world. It will be the first meeting of the Big Three, the first Summit.

But before this ultimate consummation it is imperative that Americans and British reach a common understanding on a matter the Russians are bound to bring up—the time and place of the Second Front. To this end Roosevelt and Churchill are to meet first in Cairo. Churchill anticipates that affairs in the Far East can be discussed after the Summit when he and Roosevelt return to Cairo. The presence of Chiang Kai-shek and his formidable wife, however, ruptures this carefully laid plan and a great deal of time is wasted, as the British had foreseen.

All hope of persuading Chiang and his wife to go and see the Pyramids and enjoy themselves till we returned from

Teheran fell to the ground, Churchill laments, *with the result that Chinese business occupied first instead of last place at Cairo.* The most exasperating thing is that the Chinese staffs seem to have no views of their own, meet Anglo-American suggestions for operations in Asia with an inscrutable "We wish only to listen to your deliberations."

At the highest level the meetings are soon dominated by Madame Chiang, who into every discussion interpolates her own mind under the guise of explaining her husband's attitudes. General Alan Brooke finds this infuriating, particularly since he suspects her of mixing politics with sex: "She was the only woman amongst a very large gathering of men and was determined to bring into action all the charms nature has blessed her with. Although not good looking, she certainly has a good figure, which she knew how to display at its best. Gifted with great charm and gracefulness, every small movement of hers arrested and pleased the eye. For instance, at one critical moment her closely clinging dress of black satin with golden chrysanthemums displayed a slit which exposed one of the most shapely of legs. This caused a rustle amongst some of those attending the conference, and I even thought I heard a suppressed neigh come from a group of the younger members!"

Throughout the conference the Generalissimo remains calm and reserved, an aloof figure very conscious of the light in which he is regarded by the Americans. To them he represents the dominant pro-Allied force in Asia and a potent source of help in postwar reconstruction of the East. In November 1943, however, when time presses heavily, he and his staff are an embarrassment to the Cairo Conference and a cause of some discomfort between Americans and British.

These minor clouds are banished on Thanksgiving Day, when the President invites Churchill to a family dinner at his villa. It takes place in an armed camp. Outside Alexandria eight squadrons of British fighters stand at the ready in case of German intruders. All around the Mena enclave where the two leaders and the five hundred members of their staffs are accommodated are disposed a brigade of infantry and more than five hundred anti-aircraft guns. Within the villa the atmosphere is domestic.

Two enormous turkeys are borne in. The President carves for his twenty guests while Churchill watches with growing alarm. The helpings are enormous and it seems that there will be none left when the host comes to serve himself, though those who were helped first have nearly finished. Noticing Churchill's apprehension Hopkins whispers, conscious of a deeper meaning, "We have ample reserves." Dinner over, dancing begins. Churchill's daughter Sarah, the only woman present, is immediately claimed. Making a virtue of necessity, the Prime Minister asks the President's old friend and aide, Pa Watson, for the pleasure of the next dance, greatly to the President's delight.

Then, on the heels of this gay interlude, they leave for Teheran and the brooding figure that awaits them. The conference about to begin there has been accorded the code name "Eureka," an exclamation attributed to the Greek Archimedes that means "I have found it!" Though the Western Allies have in fact found little in Cairo, and scarcely know what to look for in Teheran, the title will shortly prove apt, for this first conference of the Big Three is to record the high-water mark of their friendship and collaboration. Teheran has been chosen only on Stalin's insistence. Not only is it very inconveniently situated for Roosevelt, it is a dangerous city. According to the best authorities it seethes with Axis agents and a rich assortment of Oriental soldiers of fortune and ne'er-do-wells.

Reports have already been received that a force of German paratroops has been dropped in the desert south of the city.

Briefly they threaten the lives of the Allied leaders, but theirs is a forlorn escapade and their inevitable end is shrouded from unofficial eyes. Caught by Stalin's bodyguard of the NKVD they are quickly retired into a permanent obscurity, their only epitaph a casual remark by the NKVD commander to Mike Reilly, the President's personal bodyguard. Telling Reilly that the episode can be considered closed, he says with finality, "We examined the men we caught most thoroughly. . . ."

Even without this sudden shock the evil reputation of the Iranian capital is such that Churchill, normally placid about his personal safety, suffers a twinge or two after landing at the airport. Driving to his quarters, he is conducted along a road lined at intervals of fifty yards or so by single horsemen. Nearer to the city crowds begin to appear, four or five deep behind this inadequate line of cavalry. They gaze without expression at the slowly moving car. At one point it is stopped dead by a traffic jam. It is a perfect opportunity for an assassin. Acutely conscious of his vulnerability, Churchill adopts the best course he can think of. *I grinned at the crowd*, he reports, *and on the whole they grinned at me*. The President is brought in more skillfully, being driven from a secret landing point through back streets, without escort but at some speed. Shortly after their arrival Molotov breaks the news of the assassination plot uncovered by the NKVD. "If anything like that were to happen," he concludes in a triumph of diplomatic language, "it could produce a most unfortunate impression." *This*, Churchill finds himself bound to admit, *could not be denied*.

At the first plenary session, which takes place in the Soviet Embassy at four o'clock in the afternoon on 28 November 1943, there is no set agenda, but the bland air is soon full of honeyed words. The President opens the proceedings with a speech full of warmth, saluting this first friendly gathering of three great allies. Churchill echoes him, with more rhetoric. *This meeting,* I said, *probably represented the greatest concentration of worldly power that had ever been seen in the history of mankind. In our hands lay perhaps the shortening of the war, almost certainly victory, and, beyond any shadow of doubt, the happiness and fortunes of mankind.*

But beneath this apparently harmonious flow of sentiment and high resolve move currents and undertows that have been left unheeded at Cairo. Now they begin to rise and trouble the surface. Sensing an unresolved difference between Prime Minister and President, and inherently suspicious of any British motive, Stalin raises the expected issue and opens an old wound.

Mike Reilly, standing on guard behind the President, watches the swordplay. "The first night of the Teheran Conference Stalin gave a tremendous banquet. I noticed the Prime Minister and Stalin in a very animated conversation. Toward the end of the banquet Stalin got up from his chair and walked out of the room, and Churchill pursued him and backed him into a corner and said, 'Marshal, I want to go up and visit your front.' Stalin coldly turned around and said, 'Mr. Prime Minister, when *you* have a front, you may come and visit *mine.*'"

Churchill accepts this barb with good grace and all is forgotten next evening when he presents the Stalingrad Sword, four feet of tempered steel specially forged and engraved, "To the steel-hearted citizens of Stalingrad the gift of King George VI in token of the homage of the British people." Taking the sword, the Marshal raises it slowly to his lips and kisses it.

The Americans, as well as the Russians, are inclined to believe that Churchill opposes an assault into northern France. In fact, Churchill has been misunderstood. He certainly supports Overlord—the plan to strike across the Channel into France—but equally vehemently protests what he considers the mismanagement of the campaign in the Mediterranean during the two months following the victory at Salerno. He resents, and will continue to do so, any weakening of the armies in Italy, for this is the only terrain on which the Western allies are at present in direct contact with the common foe. In a memorandum to his Chief of Staff he points out, *It is certainly an odd way of helping the Russians, to slow down the fight in the only theater where anything can be done for some months.*

He is even prepared at this time to support the American idea of a landing in the south of France, though his political instinct (with a reasoning that becomes clear only much later) leads him to perceive greater advantage in a thrust through northeastern Italy and into Austria, so as to take Vienna before the Russians and limit their advance into Western Europe. Moreover, he urges an effort in the Eastern Mediterranean, where he believes otherwise idle forces could capture a few German-held islands and thus dominate the Aegean. By this means, with the support of diplomacy, Turkey might well be persuaded into the war. Her entry would insure control of the Black Sea, provide an efficient route for supplying Russia, and afflict German morale with gloom.

All these bubbling plans are misconstrued, particularly by the Americans. They see in this all-embracing concept merely a Balkan adventure, in spite of the fact that Churchill reiterates the balance of forces he thinks these operations would demand: six tenths for the Channel operation, three tenths for Italy, and one tenth for the Eastern Mediterranean. For this there are historical reasons.

British strategy is based upon the full use of sea power. Her wars have been won by her ability to carry relatively small forces at will to the weakest point on the enemy's perimeter and there strike with maximum effect. The result is not, as the Americans believe, a dissipation of force: it is an application of all available strength at the critical spot at the right moment. The Americans, in contrast, have been brought up in the tradition of continental warfare involving the maneuver of massive armies over great spaces of land. They therefore naturally incline toward the single overwhelming thrust with all available power piled together, stabilizing the line outside the point of impact by means of holding actions only.

At Teheran Churchill finds himself unhappily faced by two allies who choose to oppose his arguments, though for quite different reasons. Advised by his military staffs, Roosevelt is not enough of a strategist to comprehend the vision Churchill has sought to reveal. To the Americans, eager to grasp the throat of Nazism and ill contented with tearing off a leg, everything is a question of logistics and inflexible timetables. Stalin's motives are more subtle. Watching him closely, the master-strategist General Alan Brooke concedes him an equal and becomes convinced that he appreciates the wisdom of Churchill's plans. To see them carried out, however, would be quite another matter to Stalin. If, as General Brooke suspects, the Russians feel confidence in their ability to handle the Germans, a great deal of political advantage will accrue in the long run if the Western allies can be kept out of the Eastern Mediterranean, if the advance in Italy (which will threaten Austria and Yugoslavia) can be halted, and if British and American lives can be squandered in France. General Brooke's judgment is cynical, but not without logic.

Moreover, there is yet another factor that influences the Prime Minister's attitude toward Overlord: *The fearful price we had had to pay in human life and blood for the great offensives of the First World War was graven on my mind.*

Memories of the Somme and Passchendaele and many lesser
frontal attacks upon the Germans were not to be blotted out
by time or reflection. It still seemed to me, after a quarter of
a century, that fortifications of concrete and steel armed with
modern firepower, and fully manned by trained, resolute
men, could only be overcome by surprise in time or place,
by turning their flanks, or by some new and mechanical de-
vice like the tank.

By 30 November all these clouds roll away. It is Churchill's sixty-ninth birthday, which he celebrates that evening in
the dining room of the British Legation. Light glints from a
mosaic of tiny mirrors set into the walls, splitting the reflection of a central chandelier into a thousand shards. Sixty-nine
candles gleam fitfully atop a huge birthday cake dominating
the table. The menu comprises oyster patties, consommé,
boiled salmon, roast turkey, ice cream and a cheese savory
soufflé. Behind a thirteenth-century Kashan vase, a present
from Roosevelt, beams the Prime Minister, flanked by the
first gentleman of the United States and the master of Russia.
Together we controlled practically all the naval and three
quarters of all the air forces in the world, and could direct
armies of nearly twenty millions of men, engaged in the most
terrible of wars that had yet occurred in human history. It
is a memorable day for Churchill, less for personal reasons
than because the three Allies find themselves in accord. The
date for Overlord has been set.

The Teheran Conference ends on this optimistic note.
Yet everyone present realizes that there are still grim days
ahead. No one believes that victory can be bought without
great sacrifice of blood. Germany is still as dangerous as ever;
though mauled by the Russians and by the mounting Allied
bomber offensive, Hitler and his satellites still maintain more
than three hundred divisions in the field, supported by seven
thousand aircraft. Confident after the blitzkrieg of 1940 that

the war has been won, Germany is only now, three years later, marshaling her industries and technologies for a full wartime economy. In 1943 her production of vital military gear has doubled. Two thousand Tiger tanks alone have been built, far superior to any armored fighting vehicle in the world and surpassed in the end only by the mighty Stalin tank. She has produced twenty-two thousand aircraft, the majority of them fighters. New weapons are being developed and deployed—jet planes, flying bombs and rockets, acoustic torpedoes, long-range submarines, cheap anti-tank *Panzerfaust*. The road to victory still leads the Allies through the valley of the shadow.

Back in Cairo, Roosevelt and Churchill have little time to discuss the two major conclusions arrived at in Teheran. The first is Overlord, only five months away. The second is Stalin's promise to enter the war against Japan as soon as Germany is beaten. One issue, however, is decided. The Supreme Commander of Overlord is to be General Eisenhower; a British general will succeed him in the Mediterranean.

On their last evening together Churchill takes his friend on a visit to the Sphinx. In the luculent light of a brief Egyptian evening they gaze up at that ancient face worn by desert winds and wise in the knowledge of the centuries. Their twilight shadows stretching long upon the sand, the two statesmen peer intently at that ravaged and ageless head, waiting perhaps for some inspiration that will solve the eternal riddle. At last they turn away. *She told us nothing and maintained her inscrutable smile. There was no use waiting any longer.*

Before going home Churchill has arranged to visit the Italian front, and so flies from Cairo to General Eisenhower's headquarters in Tunis. There, to everybody's consternation but his own, he comes down with pneumonia. It is no surprise to General Brooke, who has been worried about the Prime Minister's health all through the exhausting meetings. The moment they land in Tunis, Churchill goes to bed, and there is tackled by the Chief of the Imperial General Staff, who submits with respect that the Prime Minister has a duty to pay more regard to his own state of health. What is more, he tells Churchill, Lord Moran (Churchill's personal physician) agrees with him. This immediately rouses Churchill from his bed of pain. Shaking his fist at Brooke he bawls, *Don't you side with that bloody old man!*

During the night the Prime Minister runs a fever. For the next few days he hovers between life and death. Deprived of the strength to continue his conduct of the war, Churchill feels that he has lost his *raison d'être*. Visited by intermittent fever, he is confused and lucid by turns, occasionally petulant, always impatient. There is so much to do, and a climax of the war draws daily closer. In the oppressive heat Churchill frets, his agile mind frustrated because it is inhibited and confined by this rebellious body. Such is the power of his will that, aided by expert and devoted medical care, he is back in control by the middle of December. His first concern is Italy, where the fighting has reached a deadlock. He begins in earnest to champion Eisenhower's dream of breaking it by another amphibious landing, thrusting behind the German lines.

Winter has turned Italy into a quaking landscape of mud. The battle has begun to take on the hideous appearance of a war of attrition. Half a million Allied soldiers face a smaller number of Germans, but the latter are admirably sited and know that their backs are to the wall. Among the fighting men in Italy there are no illusions about an easy victory.

General Mark Clark speaks for them when he says, "I'll never forget Mr. Churchill when we met, often at Chequers or 10 Downing Street, standing up at a map of the Mediterranean and pointing to the 'soft underbelly of Europe' as he called it. It later became my job to slit that soft underbelly and I assure you that I found it, instead of being soft, to be a tough old gut." General Clark in the west and General Montgomery in the east have been smashing with their two armies against Kesselring's *Winterstellung* emplacements that straddle Italy from coast to coast.

The Germans are entrenched in hills that overlook the river valleys the Allies must cross. All roads are under direct observation and can be shelled with ease. In this rugged terrain infantry are at a premium and the Allies' preponderance of armor is discounted. The main problem is supplies. In the mountains they have to be carried by human trains of porters, in the lowlands by mules hock-deep in the mud that has bogged down the motor transport of two armies. The campaign becomes as much a fight against the elements as against the enemy.

One soldier at least determines to make the best of the weather. General Montgomery writes home requesting a waterproof suit. A signal comes back to Eighth Army headquarters from the War Office, telling the General that the mission has been entrusted to the Bishop of Southwark, who is on his way to hold confirmations among the troops. It is marked, "Personal for General Montgomery. Following to be read as verse." Deciphered, it reads:

> We've dispatched, *pour la guerre,*
> A mackintosh pair
> Of trousers and jacket, express;
> They are coming by air
> And are sent to you care
> Of the Bishop of Southwark, no less.

                    So wherever you go
                    From Pescara to Po,
            Through mud and morasses and ditches,
                    You undoubtedly ought
                    To be braced by the thought
            That the Church has laid hands on your breeches.

                    We think they'll suffice
                    (As they should at the price)
            To cover your flanks in the melee,
                    And avert the malaise
                    (In the Premier's phrase)
            Of a chill in the soft underbelly.

                    According to Moss
                    (The outfitting Bros.)
            'Twon't matter, so stout is their fiber,
                    If you happen to trip
                    And go arse over tip,
            Like Horatius, into the Tiber.

                    And you'll find—so we hope—
                    When you call on the Pope,
            That his blessing's more readily given
                    On learning the news
                    That your mackintosh trews
            Were brought down by a Bishop from Heaven.

Keystone of the German bastion rooted in the Apennines is
a monastery. Surrounded by a towering massif, it commands
the approaches to Rome and provides the strong point for
the Gustav Line. It is shortly to achieve martyrdom.

Founded by Saint Benedict in the year 529, the Abbey of
Monte Cassino is not only the original home of an order, but
also a symbol of the spread of learning and faith throughout
the kingdoms of Europe. Already it has been destroyed three
times, once by the Lombards, once by the Saracens, and once
by an earthquake. Thrusting down from the mountain mass
of the Abruzzi to the northeast, a heavy spur of hills looms
stark and grim at the point where the Liri and Rapido valleys
meet. At the end of this granite promontory, with an unhindered view in both directions, squats the abbey's venerable

bulk atop the seventeen hundred feet of Monte Cassino. The town of Cassino sprawls at the foot of the mountain.

Four stories high, its broadest outer wall two hundred and twenty yards long, the abbey is built as massively as a fortress and covers the entire mountain peak. The approach to it is slashed by ravines and blocked by ponderous outcroppings of stone. The abbey walls rise sheer from the rock face, a startling white, shaped irregularly about a rich baroque courtyard and four smaller ones. At its very center a colonnaded well, its basin scalloped and its pediment supporting an orb and a cross, bears, down the years, the splendor of a more gracious age. The abbey is a place of learning and of peace. A citadel of the spirit, it is also—viewed with a cynical eye—an appalling place to have to reduce by force of arms. The Battle of Cassino is as savage a siege as any ever fought by desperate men.

It starts in earnest on the night of 17 January 1944 with a British attack across the Garigliano (the lower Liri-Rapido), though to those taking part it is merely a section of a larger operation that has been going on for five days, a major offensive designed to draw down the German reserves before the landings at Anzio. Its unimaginable agony ends only when the Americans drive into Rome months later. The Italian campaign is prodigal of blood. In the past six weeks the eight divisions of the Fifth Army have been able to advance only seven miles, at a cost of 16,000 men. And this in fighting for mere outposts of the winter line.

The master plan is to engage the five German divisions spread along the ten miles of the Cassino sector as heavily as possible with seven Allied divisions, while two more divisions are landed at Anzio. When a few stray shells crump down on Monastery Hill for the first time on 18 January the abbey is inhabited only by the abbot, five monks, a priest, three sick peasant families, a deaf mute, and from time to time the

commander of the Fourteenth Panzer Corps. His name is
General von Senger und Etterlin; he is a former Rhodes
scholar, an Oxford graduate, an anti-Nazi, a superb professional soldier and a lay member of the Benedictine order. His
men, perched in their vantage point, await the Allies struggling toward them through a curtain of shell.

As the British are forcing a crossing of the Garigliano, the
36th (Texas) Division prepares itself for the Rapido. It has
a considerable tactical problem before it. The Rapido itself
is at this point sixty feet wide and nine feet deep; its banks
rise about three feet above water level and the current is
swift. Not, it might seem, too formidable an obstacle. But
this crossing is to be undertaken in the confusion of night,
right into the teeth of a heavily defended locality. The nar-
rowness of the river precludes effective artillery support. The
collapsible boats are cumbersome and unmanageable in the
torrent. The fields are thickly strewn with mines.

For two days and two nights these men batter valiantly
at their objective in an attack so costly that it is afterward
described by one correspondent as the worst disaster for
American arms since Pearl Harbor. This it certainly is not,
but the battle is as primitive and bloody as any in the campaign. It reduces the division to a single regiment, and only
the courage and grit of the 36th Division turn massacre into
victory.

The whole winter line, focused about Cassino, is now red
with battle. The moment is apt for what Churchill calls the
"cat claw" of Anzio. While infantry and artillery strive
grimly to overcome that savage mountain, an invasion fleet
of more than two hundred ships anchors off a beach that in
time of peace is alive with holidaying Italians. At two o'clock
in the morning of 22 January two divisions, one American
and one British, ride a quiet sea into a remarkably peaceful
landing. One of the men there is Pipe Major Roe of the Scots

Guards: "I was a member of the 24th Guards Brigade, who along with the 3rd American Rangers were the assault troops at the Anzio beachhead. And this I'd like to say as a British soldier—I have never found a finer comrade in arms and in action than an American Ranger."

Within twenty-four hours the Allies have landed 36,000 men and 3,000 vehicles. It seems, in this first rush of success, that Rome is theirs for the taking. But the impetus is lost: the invading force spends two crucial days building up within its shallow bridgehead. The Germans have time to commit their reserves from the north, to whose aid are also hastening troops from as far away as France and Yugoslavia. The Germans do not underestimate this new thrust aimed at their vitals. By 30 January elements of eight German divisions are dug in around the Allied perimeter. They begin to counterattack, and Anzio loses all resemblance to a resort. In the entire beachhead there is no single spot that cannot be reached by an enemy shell. Even the tented hospitals receive their daily quota of high explosives. The wounded are dragged back from the miserable swamps of the front line only to perish, together with their gallant nurses, from whizzing fragments of jagged steel.

It is stalemate. Boxed in at Anzio, blunted at Cassino, the Allies are finding the Italian campaign assuming the frightful aspect of a war of attrition. True, they have drawn down great strength upon themselves and thus dragged the Wehrmacht into an imbalance. But in so doing they have turned Italy into a land where the specter of death is a common acquaintance. *The fate of Italy is indeed terrible,* says Churchill. *Here is this beautiful country suffering the worst horrors of war, with a hideous prospect of the red-hot rake of the battle line being drawn from sea to sea right up the whole peninsula.* And the full rigor of the conflict is yet to be felt.

THE FORGOTTEN ARMY

Far other worlds, and other seas,
Annihilating all that's made
To a green thought in a green shade.
ANDREW MARVELL: *The Garden*

WHERE the ground is dry, walking in the jungle is like treading a trampolin; dead leaves and vines and crumbling boughs lie three and four feet deep. Where it is wet, at the foot of mountain ranges or on wooded plateaus, it is like wading through an endless waist-deep lake. The water is dark and brackish and the slightest movement stirs ponderous bubbles of marsh gas that, in a turgid explosion, release the fetid odors of centuries of decay. On the farther bank there must be a pause to burn off with cigarettes the leeches, by now gorged with blood, that are clinging like slick black ribbons to legs and belly.

Earth and sky seem to meet in one impenetrable green.

213

Like giant prison bars the trunks of forest trees rise stark and unbroken for a hundred feet into the dark canopy of leaves that shuts out the sun. Their thick trunks mottled with lichens and fungus, they support trailing sheaves of tangled creepers, glistening and lush with moisture, that fall in green curtains toward the undergrowth. Thickets of bamboo shoot up to meet them, or in rare clearings six-foot stands of elephant grass, each blade as sharp as a sword, bar every vista. Even in the dry season the air is heavy with damp and choked with the earthy smell of rotting vegetation.

Day and night the jungle is filled with the sibilance of leaves and the plash of drops of water. Now and then a heavier sound—the crash of a falling limb perhaps—echoes through the cathedral gloom, hollow, distant and austere. The atmosphere is hushed, for no breeze stirs these still confines and the creatures that inhabit them are silent and watchful. It is a place of stealth and mystery, immemorially dark.

It is a forgotten battleground. Companies, battalions, regiments have disappeared into this sweating wilderness of Burma with few to note their struggle. More familiar fields have provided the focus of attention—the brutal slogging match in Russia, the triumphant seizure of North Africa, the descent upon Italy, the naval actions upon two great oceans —while all the time the war in the jungle has gone unnoticed. And yet in some ways it is the worst war of all.

It is fought against a crafty, ruthless and expert enemy who has adapted himself to the terrain. His uniform is light, his shoes strong and rubber-soled. He lives off the country, carries only a water bottle, a ball of rice and some scraps of dried fish for savor. His weapons are automatics suited to the close-quarters encounters of the jungle, grenades, light machine guns and the flimsy "knee mortars" that fire a two-inch bomb. He does not march along roads if he thinks they are

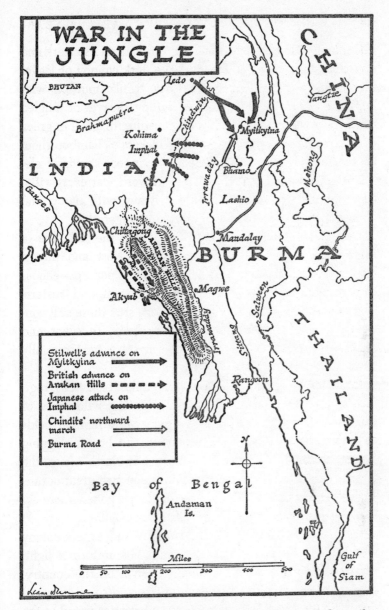

WAR IN THE JUNGLE

BHUTAN

CHINA

Yangtze

Ledo

Brahmaputra

Chindwin

Myitkyina

Kohima
Imphal

INDIA

Irrawaddy

Bhamo

Mekong

Lashio

Salween

Ganges

Chittagong

ARAKAN HILLS

Mandalay

BURMA

Akyab

Magwe

Irrawaddy

Sittang

THAILAND

Stilwell's advance on Myitkyina ⟶

British advance on Arakan Hills ---→

Japanese attack on Imphal ∞∞∞∞→

Chindits' northward march ⟶

Burma Road ═══

Rangoon

N

Bay   of   Bengal

Andaman
Is.

Miles
0   50 100   200   300   400   500

Gulf
of
Siam

Liam Dunne

In January 1944, British forces smash Japanese resistance down the
Arakan coast, and in the spring the jungle brigades and Stilwell's troops
strike toward Myitkyina. In June 1944, British reserves reinforce
Imphal, and Japan's bid for India is virtually over.

defended, but hacks his way through the jungle or follows little-known paths. The first news that the Japanese are attacking comes when defending troops in the forward positions can get no reply from their headquarters in the rear.

When war comes to Southeast Asia at the close of 1941, Siam withstands the Japanese for only twenty-four hours. They are free to swing south to Singapore and north to India. Early in January 1942 they enter Burma with 18,000 men, aiming first for Rangoon. Opposing them are a brigade of tanks and two divisions of British, Indian and Burmese troops, thinly spread and completely unversed in the fatal arts of war. It takes them months of suffering to become proficient.

Willing and ready for pitched battles, the British find their opponents elusive. Constantly outflanked, they are forced to retreat in a series of minor actions. Tied to their transport, they struggle to keep the roads open while the Japanese move swiftly past them on either side. The withdrawal becomes a rearguard battle fought every inch of the way, through ambush after ambush. Armor is of little use against the enemy. They hold command of the air, bombing major towns as if at practice. The only way to fight them is on their own terms, and these the British are slow to accept.

Rangoon is defended by a squadron of Flying Tigers, the skilled mercenaries trained by Major General Claire Chennault to fight in China. Their base is a meager patch of land, their supplies limited and their equipment primitive, but they cause such havoc among the proud bombers of Japan that Rangoon is able to hold out for weeks instead of days. When it falls on 9 March its streets are thick with the debris of looted homes and shops, with here and there the gaunt timbers of a bombed building. Doors swing idly open onto empty interiors, windows are shattered, gardens littered with belongings jettisoned by fleeing residents. Through this plunder and wreckage wander criminal lunatics, dacoits and lepers inexplicably released when the town is evacuated. The rich and pleasant capital of Burma has become a landscape of horror.

Still the British fall back toward India. They are led by one of the greatest soldiers of the war, General William Slim, whose principal facial characteristic is a jaw like a slab of granite. With Rangoon gone, he is fighting in the oil fields to the north. "In mid-April in a fierce attack the Japanese pierced the front of my weakened Burma Division on the banks of the Irrawaddy, and as it withdrew the inevitable happened. It was cut off in the oil fields of Yenangyaung and there, amid the flames and the smoke and the explosions, and the crashing oil derricks and the blazing storage tanks, we fought a nightmare battle. . . . In the last stages of the long retreat from Burma it was a tossup which of our three enemies caught up with us first: starvation through the failure of our rations, immobility caused by the rain of the monsoon, or our fierce pursuing Japanese enemy. Actually—it was the Japanese."

The Burma Division fights its way out of the Japanese trap, but must leave behind a mass of equipment and transport, including a column of ambulances filled with men so gravely wounded that they cannot be carried. Re-forming, the division counterattacks and wins back ground, and a young officer passes through the Japanese lines by night to see what has happened to these wounded. Quietly he crouches beside the narrow track where the ambulances are silhouetted against the sky. All about him at the jungle's edge lies the silence of the grave. The ambulances are still there, and within them are the wounded. Every one of them has had his throat cut or has been disemboweled with the bayonet.

Two days before the monsoon is due the British reach Imphal in Assam, having endured an ordeal unlike any faced by any army before them. They have marched six hundred miles through jungle and over mountains, ill fed and poorly armed, racked by fever and covered with ulcers; limping into India they look like an insane rabble. But now at least they have time. They have beaten the Japanese to Imphal, the devastating rains of the monsoon will give them respite, and help is on the way. *The road to India*, Churchill says, *was barred*. Though they have not won a victory, the forgotten men have certainly avoided a debacle.

While the Japanese enjoy their mastery of a quarter of a million square miles of newly conquered land, the Allies prepare their return and India arms. Though not without pangs. For years the frail and saintly Mahatma Gandhi has been defying the British Raj with his doctrine of nonviolence. Gandhi's protégé, Jawaharlal Nehru, leads the Congress Party in political strife against the British and incidentally against the Moslem League. An extremist, Subhas Bose, organizes a pro-Japanese underground and even begins to raise an Indian National Army to fight alongside the yellow men he sees as India's liberators.

Japan's rapid conquest of Southeast Asia and the swift appearance of her army on India's very frontier, preceded by propaganda describing Japan as the champion of freedom from the white man's oppression, serve to excite these currents of faith, race and politics in India until the clamor reaches an ugly pitch. *Indian politics and the press echoed the rising discords between the Hindu and Moslem communities*, Churchill reports. *It was felt by almost all of my colleagues that an offer of Dominion status after the war must be made in the most impressive manner to the peoples of India*. This is done, but the Congress Party majority demands immediate freedom, believing that if all ties with Britain can be severed the threat of invasion by the Japanese will be removed. Even if the worst happened and India were overrun, it would then be possible to practice passive resistance unhindered by British exhortations to fight.

Like a good ally, Churchill reports all these developments to President Roosevelt, but soon begins to regret it. It is, of course, a problem in which the two men are poles apart. Reared in a great family during the golden years of Empire, blooded as a youngster on the Northwest Frontier, Churchill is steeped in the tradition of British rule in India. He sees her as the proudest domain of the King Emperor, stretching her exotic length from the snows of the Himalayas to the mangrove swamps of Cape Comorin, from the dusty bazaars of Karachi to Calcutta's brawling wharfs. He has tried to understand her problems, knows the appalling poverty of her people, acknowledges a profound depth of gratitude for their past services, can see no easy road to virtue.

Roosevelt's approach, predictably, is much simpler. It causes conflict at once: *The President had first discussed the Indian problem with me, on the usual American lines, during my visit to Washington in December 1941. I reacted so strongly and at such length that he never raised it verbally again.* Correspondence, however, is a different matter, and a good deal of it passes during this crisis.

The President writes: "I still feel that if the component groups in India could be given now the opportunity to set up a Nationalist Government in essence similar to our own form of government under the Articles of Confederation, with the understanding that following the termination of a period of trial and error they would be enabled then to determine upon their own form of constitution and to determine, as you have promised them already, their future relationship with the British Empire, probably a solution could be found."

Churchill explodes. *I was thankful that events had already made such an act of madness impossible. The human race cannot make progress without idealism, but idealism at other people's expense and without regard to the consequences of ruin and slaughter which fall upon millions of humble homes cannot be considered as its highest or noblest form. The President's mind was back in the American War of Independence, and he thought of the Indian problem in terms of the thirteen colonies fighting George III at the end of the eighteenth century. I, on the other hand, was responsible for preserving the peace and safety of the Indian continent, sheltering nearly a fifth of the population of the globe. . . . This was no time for a constitutional experiment . . . It was our bounden duty to send all possible aid to Indian defense, and . . . we should have betrayed not only the Indian peoples but our own soldiers by allowing their base of operations and the gallant Indian Army fighting at their side to disintegrate into a welter of chattering politics and bloody ruin.*

In the event, the British still the political ferment, postpone the major issue, and bend all their efforts toward the rescue of the vast subcontinent and the succor of the Chinese, now left without a supply route since the Japanese have severed the Burma Road. China's coastline is wholly in enemy hands. The only means of access now is by air over the seventeen-thousand-foot peaks of a spur of the Himalayas soon christened "the Hump."

A fantastic operation now begins, the first airlift in history. The dangerous route has already been explored by Chennault's Flying Tigers. Now Colonel Caleb Haynes leads the first flight into the Chinese base at Kunming—four ancient transports packed to overflowing with supplies. The American Air Transport Command that follows these pioneers flies in 763,374 tons in the three years of its operations, a greater weight than ever traversed the Burma Road itself. It costs them 468 planes.

Dissatisfied with even this gigantic contribution, the Americans also begin to build a new road from Ledo into China. Ridiculed as an impossible dream, the road remains a monument to American vision, determination and ingenuity. It clings to the sides of mountains, sustained only by a miracle, plummets down long glissades of rock, spans precipitous chasms, scythes through thick jungle. Thousands of Chinese coolies labor with raw hands to complete it. After two years and twenty-three days it reaches its terminal. It measures 478 miles, every inch won at incalculable cost in effort and sacrifice.

Prime mover of this project is General Joseph W. Stilwell, a legend in his own lifetime. A crusty, experienced foot soldier, "Vinegar Joe" loves the Chinese: he speaks their language, especially the cusswords. He reacts to any criticism of Chinese fighting qualities with instant violence, fears no man, holds firm against all odds. As a diplomat Stilwell may have his critics, but as a leader of fighting men in this dismal wilderness he is the nonpareil. General Slim judges him thus: "Americans, whether they liked him or not—and he had more enemies among Americans than among British—were all scared of him. He had courage to an extent few people have, and determination, which, as he usually concentrated it along narrow lines, had a dynamic force. He was not a great soldier in the highest sense, but he was a real leader in the field; no one else I know could have made his Chinese do what they did. He was, undoubtedly, the most colorful character in Southeast Asia—and I liked him."

Stilwell's summary of the situation of the Allies is typical. "I claim we got a hell of a beating. We got run out of Burma, and it is humiliating as hell. I think we should find out what caused it and go back and retake it." He spends the monsoon season with his two Chinese "armies" of six divisions in the hills above Ledo, with the Chindwin River below him and beyond that the swarming Japanese. With Slim he patiently plans the return.

Until major operations can be mounted there is only one way of fighting the Japanese—by long-range patrols, or raids. The hour fortunately produces the man. A regular officer, he served before the war with an occupation battalion in Palestine and there found his sympathies so strongly with the Jews, for a multitude of reasons, that he embraced their cause with all the ardor of his blazing spirit. For their part, the Zionists thought of him as the potential Commander-in-Chief of the Israeli Army, if ever it should be formed. He has led a force of irregulars in Eritrea and Abyssinia that helped topple the Italian Empire. He is Brigadier Orde C. Wingate, a paradox, a man of the severest discipline and yet rebellious.

Wingate is of medium height, with rigid shoulders and a lean body. His nose is heavy and hooked, his cheekbones high, his mouth firm but not thin drawn. His hair is long and fine and touched with gray, brushed in a flick across a lined forehead. He is a pale man and his eyes burn in their deep sockets with a look of anguish. For Wingate is consumed by a devil: there is never enough time.

By March 1943 Wingate has trained his first long-range penetration groups, mixed units of British, Indian and Gurkha troops. He calls them "Chindits," after the Burmese word for "lion," and leads them out against the Japanese lines of communication on the upper Irrawaddy. His eight columns blow up bridges, destroy supply dumps and ammunition depots, massacre outposts, wreck landing fields and force the Japanese to mount an operation against them. At the end of three months, having been supplied entirely by air, they dissolve into small groups and make their way home through miles of jungle. Of the 3,000 who set out, 2,182 return, but only 600 will ever be fit to fight again. They have undergone privations that can scarcely be imagined.

The Chindits have gained no ground, have struck no mortal blow. But when they stagger back from the rank jungle, racked with fever, emaciated, tormented by the memory of wounded comrades left behind to die because there was no hope of rescue, sick with utter exhaustion of spirit and body, they bring with them a priceless victory. They have proved that the Japanese can be thrashed *in the jungle*.

Churchill is enthralled by this audacious exploit, sends for Wingate and carries him off to Quebec to meet the President. For months the Prime Minister has been complaining about what he considers a lack of vigor in the Burma campaign. In this unorthodox, ascetic and fanatic brigadier, Churchill sees a kindred spirit and backs him to the hilt. He even tells the Chiefs of Staff: *I consider Wingate should command the army against Burma. He is a man of genius and audacity, and has rightly been discerned by all eyes as a figure quite above the ordinary level. The expression "the Clive of Burma" has already gained currency. There is no doubt that in the welter of inefficiency and lassitude which has characterized our operations on the Indian front, this man, his force and his achievements, stand out, and no mere question of seniority must obstruct the advance of real personalities to their proper stations in war.*

In spite of this proselytizing, command remains with the more taciturn but equally determined and aggressive General Slim. In any event, Wingate has only a little time in which to enjoy the fruits of his valor. On 24 March 1944, he dies tragically by fire in the wreck of his aircraft on a jungle hillside. Sadly Churchill writes his epitaph, calling him *a*

*man of genius who might well have become also a man of
destiny. With him a bright flame was extinguished.*

Meanwhile, Wingate's Chindits have been joined by an
equally daring group—the 5307th Composite Unit (Provisional), better known as Merrill's Marauders. They comprise
three thousand volunteers, carefully selected from almost
every unit in the United States Army. In the spring of 1944
Stilwell's Chinese are about to attack Myitkyina as a prelude
to the reclamation of Burma. The Marauders are launched in
three battalions to outflank the Japanese and deny them a
retreat route. For more than two months they engage one
of the finest units in the entire Japanese Imperial Army, the
veteran 18th Division. In that time they fight fifteen major
actions. In the end they are so worn down by disease and
shortage of food and so weakened by losses in killed and
wounded, that they simply cease to exist as a unit. Their sacrifice, however, makes possible Stilwell's long march with his
main force and leads to the reopening of the Burma Road.

The British are marching south with two divisions along
the coast into the Arakan. They are halted, have to bring in
reserves, and are soon so beleaguered by Japanese that they
have to be supplied by air. The fighting is of the most desperate and savage kind, almost always at close quarters and
without exception merciless. A British infantry sergeant describes it: "Although their artillery and mortars were first-rate, our chaps held that the riflemen were poor. At close
quarters, many of them actually looked at the ground when
pressing the trigger. But everyone agreed that the infantrymen were brave to the point of fanaticism. . . . One particular
incident impressed itself upon me—a British officer in the
bayonet charge spared and passed a wounded man, who immediately shot him dead from behind. The man was at once

killed by the officer's batman, who was in turn shot by yet another casualty lying apparently helpless. 'Never pass a wounded Jap,' was now on everybody's lips. 'And one round's no good unless it kills them outright,' I was told. 'The bastards just get up again and come at you.' "

The enemy strength in Burma has now grown from five divisions to eight, which is power enough to launch an attack of their own. All the evidence of its probable location points to the plain in front of Imphal, gateway to India.

By now there is a new Supreme Commander in Southeast Asia, selected with the President's approval at the Quebec Conference. Another protégé of Churchill's, he is junior in rank but acknowledged to be among the most vigorous and able of men.

Lord Louis Mountbatten describes his appointment rather casually. "Mr. Churchill summoned me to the Citadel, where he was living," he says. "He asked me, 'How are you feeling?' He was referring to the fact that I'd had a bad go of influenza a few weeks before.

"I said, 'I'm quite all right, thank you, sir.'

" 'What do you think of the situation in Burma and Southeast Asia?' he asked me next.

" 'Well,' I said, 'I think they're a pretty big mess . . . certainly the biggest I think we've seen in any theater of the war.'

"He agreed, and said, 'Do you think you could go out and put it right?'

"Well, I naturally thought he meant I should go out as one of the Chiefs of Staff on one of those fact-finding tours and give him a report. I said I didn't want to do that, I wanted to get back to the war at sea if possible. So I suggested he might send General Ismay, his own Chief of Staff.

"He said, 'What do you mean? Don't you understand I'm offering you a chance to go out there as Supreme Allied Commander and run the show yourself? What have you got to say to that?'

"Well, it was a pretty big shock to me, but I'm afraid I covered it up with one of my rather cheeky replies. I said to him, 'Well, sir, I've got a congenital weakness for thinking I can do anything. . . .'

"I got the job."

But even the mercurial Mountbatten cannot overwhelm the brute strength of the Japanese with one gentle shove. On 8 March they storm in with three hardy divisions and by the end of the month are hedging in the Imphal plain on three sides. Their attack is held in the north at a village called Kohima—little more than a scattering of thatched huts in the midst of banks of rhododendrons—by a battalion of the Royal West Kent Regiment, a battalion of Gurkhas and a battalion of the Assam Regiment, who find themselves assaulted by the whole force of an entire Japanese division. Slowly the perimeter shrinks until finally, after fifteen days of relentless siege, the defenders are confined on one solitary hilltop, completely surrounded and raked every inch by artillery, mortar and machine-gun fire. Insufferably reduced, the Kohima garrison nevertheless accounts for four thousand Japanese. When they are relieved they leave behind over their dead an inscription:

> When you go home
> Tell them of us and say
> For their tomorrow
> We gave our today.

Anxiously Churchill watches the progress of this protracted and critical battle, signaling to Mountbatten: "In my view nothing matters but the battle. Be sure you win." He has no cause to fear. Of the 80,000 Japanese who raced with sword and grenade for Imphal, 50,000 are dead. The rest are splintered into weary groups of disheartened men. By the end of June Admiral Mountbatten feels able to claim, "The Japanese bid for India was virtually over, and ahead lay the prospect of the first major British victory in Burma."

General Slim's Fourteenth Army have achieved this triumph at a dreadful cost. In the first half of 1944 they have lost 40,000 men. Another 237,000 have gone sick. No bugles sound for the forgotten army, no flags fly. Only the firm voice of their modest commander marks their victory.

"There comes always in every battle against a stout enemy a moment when the General, however clever he has been and no matter what arrangements he has made, must hand over to the soldiers in the ranks and their officers. That moment came early and often in Burma, when men were sick and tired and lonely, and it was only their spirit, their duty and their patriotism that made them carry on. All those men of many races who served in the comradeship of the Fourteenth Army and in the Air Forces which flew over them and fought with them—they were the men who turned defeat into victory."

THE
COUNTER-
ATTACK

For I dipt into the future, far as human eye could see, . . .
Heard the heavens fill with shouting, and there rain'd a ghastly dew
From the nations' airy navies grappling in the central blue.

ALFRED, LORD TENNYSON: *Locksley Hall*

F EW MEN ever really see the sky. Walled about by cliffs of brick and stone, oppressed by a thousand daily cares, their vistas proscribed, directed, inhibited, they have no regard for the endless distances above them. From time to time a man may look briefly up into that void of night and see the glittering patterns of the Hunter and the Bear, see them shimmering immutably above him, and continue on his mundane way. For him the night sky is a series of segments defined by marching lines of chimneys, towers, rooftops, all bordering with a jagged frieze some particular ribbon of darkness sprinkled with anonymous stars.

But to some the sky is a familiar place. These tread the path of Polaris, the North Star, forever circling and forever rising. To these, cold Sirius is an old friend and Aldebaran a neighbor light. These can tell the constellations and their seasons, pick from the stardust Cassiopeia and those far Pleiades that ride upon the shoulder of the Bull. Shining Arcturus and Hydra the Sea-Serpent, Algol the Demon Star so named by Arabian astronomers, Altair the center of the Eagle, Betelgeuse and the red planet Mars are all bright landmarks for those that steer upon the horns of Capricorn. For these are the wayfarers who travel by a map of stars, some over seas and others in the sky.

In time of war the lives of men rest upon a knowledge of these celestial markers, and many men must grow familiar with names and conformations they once did not know existed. By 1943 these men—sailors and airmen—could be numbered by the tens of thousands. In 1943 eyes of every color set in faces of every cast, some haggard and despairing, some hard and confident, some few still innocent, turn upward every night into the heavens and read there either doom or survival.

For during 1943 a great part of that crude force that powers a war effort, at least as far as the Western Allies are concerned, is spent on the sea and in the air. In the east, German and Russian grapple in a welter of blood across a wilderness of war. From the Mediterranean the Allies have reached into Fortress Europe and begun their drive up the grim spine of Italy. In the skies above Germany and on the gray wastes of the Atlantic, two other battles remain to be fought to the climax.

At the end of 1942 the German U-boat fleet numbers nearly two hundred operational vessels, all toughened by constant

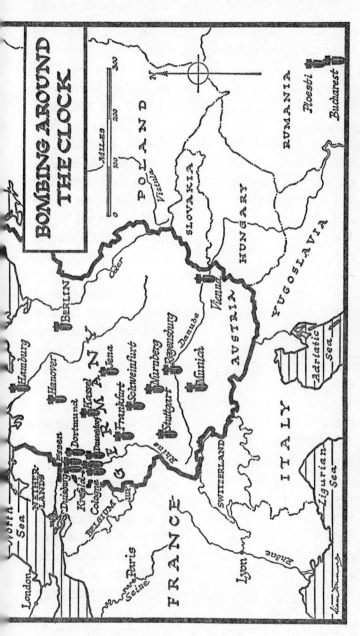

BOMBING AROUND THE CLOCK

By the spring of 1944, Allied air power controls the skies. By day, the U.S. Eighth Air Force in England and the Fifteenth Air Force in Italy strike all the German industrial centers. By night, the Royal Air Force compounds the destruction of the German heartland. No target in Greater Germany is beyond the range of Allied bombers. By summer, the most heavily guarded cities—Berlin, Munich, Vienna—are gutted. Says Winston Churchill, "air superiority became air supremacy."

action and experienced from countless forays. By practice their technique has been fashioned into a deadly efficiency. By now they are lying close inshore off the coast of America from Cape Hatteras to Florida. In the north they pick off ships full of munitions and food; in the south, prowling the Caribbean, they sink tankers carrying oil from the Gulf. Week by week the losses grow, from a trickle to a stream to a torrent. Hardly a torpedo is wasted. In November 1942 the number of ships sunk by submarines is the highest of the whole war, a hundred and seventeen, totaling seven hundred thousand tons. The rate of losses is greater than the speed with which new merchantmen can be built. Something must be done.

Of that, Churchill, remembering the perilous winter of 1917 when U-boats almost brought Britain to her knees, is keenly aware. *The Battle of the Atlantic,* he asserts, *was the dominating factor all through the war. Never for one moment could we forget that everything happening elsewhere, on land, at sea, or in the air, depended ultimately on its outcome. . . . For the individual sailor or airman in the U-boat war there were few moments of exhilarating action to break the monotony of an endless succession of anxious, uneventful days. Vigilance could never be relaxed. Dire crisis might at any moment flash upon the scene with brilliant fortune or glare with mortal tragedy. . . . Our merchant seamen displayed their highest qualities, and the brotherhood of the sea was never more strikingly shown than in their determination to defeat the U-boat.*

The U-boat captains are daring to a degree. They even seek out their targets by cruising on the surface. Blowing their diving tanks constantly so as to ride higher in the water, the U-boats patrol the vital sea lanes in the full light of day. Their crews, not even bothering to don oilskins, mount the conning tower, ardently searching every horizon as the spray lashes their soaking uniforms. Their torpedoes are steered automatically and run in a pattern that spreads over a ship's length by the time they reach the target. The U-boats often close to a thousand meters before firing to make sure there is no escape. At the shuddering impact, as the white mountain of sea rises above the merchantman's side, the U-boat submerges in triumph.

"Everyone has a look through the periscope," Leutnant Heinz Schaeffer reports. "The fine ship before us is sinking into the sea. Emotion overcomes us. The daemonic madness of destruction that becomes law the moment a war breaks out has us in its grip. Under its spell as we are, what else can we do? Lifeboats and rafts are meanwhile being lowered, those aboard saving themselves as best they may. We can't help without running into grave danger, and in any case we've no room aboard—U-boats are built to allow space for the ship's company and no more. The enemy is well equipped with lifesaving gear and these men on the tanker will certainly soon be picked up by a warship."

Some, however, are not. Now and then a lone vessel running with all speed, tiny and defenseless in acres of sea, will be caught and destroyed in a swift agony. Then her lifeboats will ride the great waves of mid-ocean with little hope of succor. Their timber will bleach in the sun and grow rough from the salt spray. Their occupants, husbanding food and water as fearfully as men astray in the desert, will slowly weaken. Days may pass without sight even of a sea bird or a wrack of seaweed to break the gray-green metallic monotony of the water. Slowly the will to live will ebb, though swifter for some who, crazed by thirst, will slash their wrists to drink their own blood, and die of it. When survivors are rescued from such boats they are already old men.

Yet suffering has little bearing on the mechanics of war. The important factor is that the arteries through which the life of the Allies is sustained are being drained. For a time in 1943 it seems to the Germans that they will wrest the victory in a matter of weeks. Admiral Doenitz, the veteran commander of the U-boat fleets, announces exultantly to the German press: "Our submarines are operating close inshore along the coast of the United States, so that bathers and sometimes entire coastal cities are witnesses of that drama of war whose visual climaxes are constituted by the red glorioles of blazing tankers." The extent of his sailors' success might perhaps pardon his exaggeration.

The Allies decide at the Casablanca Conference that their prime object must be to defeat the U-boats. While this decision is being reached, Hitler decrees an ominous change. Grand Admiral Raeder, architect of the new German Navy and its Commander-in-Chief since 1928, is called to the Wolf's Lair, where Hitler in a screaming fury accuses the Navy of cowardice. When Raeder resigns in protest Hitler is glad to name Doenitz his successor. The new Commander-in-Chief knows nothing about surface vessels, having spent his entire career in submarines. The emphasis is clear. The crisis of the U-boat war is approaching fast. It will be kill or be killed.

During March 1943 the U-boats sink well over half a million tons of vitally needed shipping. But in this same month twenty-seven U-boats have been destroyed in the Atlantic alone. For now the Allies are deploying new weapons against them. One of them is a radar device known as "H2S," which operates on ultra short wave and is compact enough to be mounted in aircraft. It can be used not only for picking out land targets, but will also single out a submarine long before it can prepare to dive. Long-range bombers are based in Newfoundland and Iceland, so that at last the air gap in the North Atlantic is closed. The U-boats must now remain under water throughout the daylight hours, so their range is reduced and their potential greatly limited. Above all, they are now constantly vulnerable to attack.

In addition, special warships are fitted out for convoy work, including escort carriers that provide a highly mobile air striking force that moves with the convoy. Even by night the U-boats cannot feel safe, for some of the bombers carry twenty-four-inch searchlights slung in their belly turrets and glaring down out of the darkness like livid Cyclops eyes. So swiftly is this Allied counterattack mounted that in one month the tide begins to turn.

April's total of losses is only half that of March. Churchill points out that this is in spite of the fact that *two hundred and thirty-five U-boats, the greatest number the Germans ever achieved, were in action. But their crews were beginning to waver. They could never feel safe. Their attacks, even when conditions were favorable, were no longer pressed home, and during this month our shipping losses in the Atlantic fell by nearly three hundred thousand tons. In May alone forty U-boats perished in the Atlantic. The German Admiralty watched their charts with strained attention, and at the end of the month Admiral Doenitz recalled the remnants of his fleet from the North Atlantic to rest or to fight in less hazardous waters.* The hunters have become the hunted.

Hitler stamps in fury. "The Atlantic is my first line of defense in the West," he storms at Doenitz. But the Admiral can only confide gloomily to his diary: "The enemy holds every trump card . . . The enemy knows all our secrets and we know none of his."

In June the tonnage sunk amounts to only 21,759 tons, a mere four per cent of the total three months earlier. Significantly, the number of U-boats destroyed also diminishes. The

wolf packs have been called off. With profound relief Churchill notes *the Atlantic supply line was safe.*

This victory at sea not only tears away a deadly strangle-
hold, it makes possible a shift to the offensive in another
element. Churchill has realized this already, telling the
House of Commons on 8 June 1943, *The month of May is,
from every point of view, the best month we have ever had
in the anti-U-boat war. . . . New weapons and new methods . . . have enabled us to inflict casualties which have
surpassed all previous records . . . for the first time our kill-
ings of U-boats substantially outnumbered the U-boat output. . . . I must say I feel confident that the U-boat war will
not stand between the United Nations and their final victory,
while all the time the air war will grow in weight and
severity.*

This is no idle forecast. The prosecution of total warfare
by air against Germany has already begun to take its toll
of life and property and hope. The Royal Air Force is already past the first anniversary of the first thousand-bomber
raid.

The target on that night of 30 May 1942 was Cologne. The
crews were told that even if they missed the primary targets
—the war plants in Cologne's sprawling industrial section—
the ruin of workers' housing would also be effective in breaking Germany's will to fight. One thousand and forty-seven
aircraft took off that night. But fewer than three hundred
were heavy bombers, and some were light training planes.
What mattered was that the RAF could claim its initial massive assault upon a German city.

The raid was a symbol merely, but it raised an issue that
was to become a source of argument between American and
British strategists and tacticians. Having defeated the *Luft-*

waffe's bombers by day, and themselves having suffered
heavily from German fighters on their own daylight raids,
the British turn to the night attack.

And there is a further difference, more basic than a
preference for day or night. The British believe in saturation
bombing which will wipe out whole cities, destroying in
one mortal holocaust factories and civilian population alike,
wrecking vital plants and shattering morale at the same time.
This can be done by night, especially with the Pathfinder
Force to mark the aiming points. The Americans, on the
other hand, believe only in precision attacks on military or
industrial objectives. To achieve this they must fly by day.

The two air forces are therefore pursuing different strategic ends and they must adopt different tactical methods.
They are linked, nevertheless, by a common objective. It has
been clearly enough defined by a directive issuing from the
Casablanca Conference. Addressed to the British and American Bomber Commands operating from the United Kingdom,
it speaks with an awful simplicity: "Your primary object
will be the progressive destruction and dislocation of the
German military, industrial and economic system, and the
undermining of the morale of the German people to a point
where their capacity for armed resistance is fatally weakened.
Within that general concept your primary objectives . . .
will for the present be in the following priority: (a) German
submarine yards; (b) the German aircraft industry; (c)
transportation; (d) oil plants; (e) other targets in enemy
war industry."

The RAF builds up its squadrons of heavy bombers, increases the weight of their bomb-load by three times, and
concentrates on the Ruhr. As dusk falls over England the sky
shakes nightly with the thunder of aircraft, for the first time
in two years. Then the sound came from the palpitating
engines of Heinkels and Dorniers and Junkers; now it is a

steady rising drone as the black four-engined giants lumber
up into their formations, dark shadows massing into streams
and heading away over the North Sea. On the night of 5
March 1943 the ordeal of the Ruhr begins in earnest. In half
an hour 1,000 tons of bombs, high explosive and incendiary mixed, plunge lazily down from the yawning bays
of four hundred bombers and bloom in devilish fury. In this
and two successive raids six hundred acres of the enormous
Krupp armament plant are devastated. No one counts the
modest homes in the meager streets of stricken Essen that
have been blasted to pieces in the same instant.

The pattern is set: fourteen hundred tons in a single raid
on Kiel, a hundred thousand people bereft of their homes
in Dortmund in one night, more than half of Düsseldorf
razed by fire. In July the RAF turns to Hamburg. Bombing
by radar, they find that the waterways and docks of that
city reflect with great clarity on their screens. They carry a
new device, called "Window": bundles of foil in long strips
that when dropped blanket the enemy radar in a sort of elec-
tronic fog and thus blind the flak gunners.

The devastation of Hamburg occupies four separate nights
and reaches its climax in a phenomenon never before seen
in nature and now accomplished by man—a fire-storm. The
first attack is launched on the night of 24 July. Unmolested,
a mass of eight hundred bombers in impeccable formation
crosses the defenses in a stream five miles wide and blankets
the dock area with incendiaries and phosphorus canisters.
There is nothing new to the citizens of Hamburg in the
screech of falling bombs. What *is* new is that the sound is
repeated again and again as wave succeeds wave of bombers.
When the last has roared over, red flames are leaping high

above the rooftops. Next night the bombers return, invisible through the black canopy above the city.

Four nights later they come in for the kill. The whole city is bathed in heat from the fires in the warehouses and factories of the harbor area. Fires are still burning and there is great discomfort merely in walking in the street. In the distance—the drone of death. This time the incendiaries are larded with heavy high-explosive bombs. The effect is a tornado of fire: the blaze started by the incendiaries is lashed like the flame of a blowtorch by the recurrent blasting of the heavy bombs.

People crowded into the deep shelters are safe from the demolitions above, but then an appalling thing happens. Through the air ducts of the ventilating systems, sucked in by fans, flashes living flame. Hundreds die in seconds, their lungs seared to cinders. Within minutes their bodies are reduced to ashes, as if in incinerators. Some, in an extreme of panic, flee the shelters into streets blocked solid by hungry fire. In the intense heat they stagger a few paces and die, dried out like tinder.

Next morning Goebbels takes note of the disaster in his diary: "A city of a million inhabitants has been destroyed in a manner unparalleled in history. We are faced with problems that are almost impossible of solution. Food must be found for this population of a million. Shelter must be secured. The people must be evacuated as far as possible. They must be given clothing. In short, we are facing problems there of which we had no conception even a few weeks ago . . . some eight hundred thousand homeless people who are wandering up and down the streets not knowing what to do."

When the bombers come back for the last time the city has been virtually obliterated. The number of dead (finally accounted for eight years later) is forty thousand. But in this

monstrous total war, the annihilation of Hamburg is of great
benefit to the Allies. "Psychologically the war at that moment
had perhaps reached its most critical point. Stalingrad had
been worse, but Hamburg was not hundreds of miles away
on the Volga, but on the Elbe, right in the heart of Germany.
After Hamburg, in the wide circle of the political and the
military command could be heard the words: 'The war is
lost.'" Thus Colonel Adolf Galland, a fighter ace engaged at
this time against the American Eighth Air Force operating
by day, appraised the results.

This mighty force had been formed by General Ira C.
Eaker, with his headquarters at Wycombe Abbey. Formerly
an exclusive girls' school, the Abbey rises massively from a
green sweep of lawns and commands a lake that supports
a serene congregation of swans not greatly disturbed by this
sudden invasion of strange uniforms and robust accents. The
headquarters is perhaps best remembered for the legend
that describes the peculiar facilities it affords. Moving into
what were once dormitories for the young ladies, the General's staff behold with delight a bell-push beside each bed,
all with the label RING FOR MISTRESS. There is no record of
whether this very pinnacle of hospitality was ever achieved.

The American crews are blooded on 4 July 1942, when
six light bombers make a low-level attack on some airfields
on the Dutch coast. The first major sortie comes on 17
August: twelve B-17s strike Rouen. A year later to the day
they reach the climax of the daylight battle in the skies over
Europe. On 17 August 1943 the Eighth Air Force mounts a
double-pronged attack with one group over Schweinfurt
and another over Regensburg, this latter mission commanded
by Colonel Curtis Le May. The Americans lose fifty-nine
planes. Goering has given orders to his fighter pilots that
the Fortresses must be destroyed "regardless of anything
else." They must no longer attack only stragglers, they must

burst headlong into the main American formations and break them up.

This is easier said than done. For the Fortresses fly in a carefully calculated pattern, so designed as to take advantage of the combined fire-power of the entire group. Each bomber is given a role in the fire-plan. Together they present a formidable target for any fighter. Moreover, the planes are manned by determined and seasoned pilots and bombardiers and aggressive and lively gunners. Day after day, with unshakable resolution, they fly into a zone where every moment carries with it the possibility of death.

Life for these air crews is a continuing paradox. For half the day they are at war, with every second potentially their last, aware that they face extinction, or at best the possibility of being maimed. They return from missions with their friends grievously burned or lying dead in blood-filled turrets. They land among peaceful farms, beside warm villages lulled by sleepy bells. They spend their evenings in country pubs loud with rich country voices, laughing with men who have spent their day at nothing more lethal than plowing. This repetition of strain and relaxation, interminably interchanged, is enough to break the proudest spirit.

Group Captain Leonard Cheshire speaks for all bomber crews when he says of those of the RAF, "They used to fall very largely into two categories. The first category were thinking of what it was going to be like when they got there. They were thinking of the danger . . . the flak, the fighters. You could see them fighting with themselves to hold it down. The other lot were different. All they could think about was the fact that there was a target to attack. They felt the challenge of the opposition. They conjured up pictures of the target and its going up in smoke. It's always those who think of the target and don't think of the danger that do the most spectacular things and appear to achieve the most. But

inwardly it's the others, in my opinion, that have shown
the greatest courage."

The American daylight offensive continues in the face of
growing swarms of fighters and endures more grievous losses.
Over Stuttgart on 6 September, 40 out of 338 Fortresses, and
over Schweinfurt on 14 October, 60 out of 291 are shot down.
This is a policy that is paying no dividends, whatever the
damage may be to the ball-bearing plants that are the target.
The offensive is held until long-range fighters can accompany
the bombers all the way to their objectives. But the night
bombing continues, turning in November upon Berlin.
*If this great industrial center could have been paralyzed
like Hamburg,* Churchill says, *German war production as
well as morale might have been given a mortal blow.*
The onslaught on the German capital, a fat and succulent target, lasts into the following year. The results disappoint the Prime Minister: *We knew from the admis-
sions of the Germans themselves that great destruction
was being caused, but we could not judge the relative success of our sixteen major attacks by comparing the photo-
graphic evidence of each. We had to wait until March 1944
to obtain photographs clear enough for the damage to be
assessed. It fell short of what had been achieved at Hamburg.*
Nevertheless, the statistics are impressive—7,000 tons in December, 9,300 in January, 2,500 in a single raid in February
—and in terms of human suffering they are indescribable.
But this terrible bombardment is winning the war.
In February, guarded by new fighter cover, the Eighth
Air Force re-enters the field, after a preliminary mission with
863 bombers that blasts Frankfurt into ruin in broad daylight. In the last week of the month the Fortresses drop their
loads without a single casualty. Now the Americans range

at will over Occupied Europe and the heartland of the Reich. The Fifteenth Air Force from Italy joins in. By the end of spring in 1944 not one single industrial target on the whole continent remains undamaged. Hitler has not visited a solitary bombed-out city.

The Allies are now bombing around the clock. "The American Air Force went out by day," says Air Marshal Sir Robert Saundby, "and Bomber Command went out by night. It was an excellent plan, because it meant that the German defenses were fully stretched both by day and by night. This great Allied air offensive went on really for only one year—from March 1943 to March 1944. But in that year tremendous destruction was done. When the spring of 1944 arrived the fact that the Americans had beaten the German fighter forces, combined with the damage done to German war industries, created the conditions needed for the invasion of Europe in the summer of that year."

Now we were the masters in the air, Churchill declares. *The bitterness of the struggle had thrown a greater strain on the* Luftwaffe *than it was able to bear. . . . Unbalanced and exhausted, it was henceforth unable to defend either itself or Germany from our grievous blows. For our air superiority, which by the end of 1944 was to become air supremacy, full tribute must be paid to the United States Eighth Air Force, once it gained its long-range fighters.*

But like any other kind of warfare, the issue in the air is not decided merely by machines. Brain and sinew, informed by calculation and endurance and inspired by greatness of spirit, are what count in the last analysis. Men win battles. Those who won the war of the air were among the best. Churchill pays a tribute *of respect and admiration to the officers and men who fought and died in this fearful battle of the air, the like of which had never before been known, or even with any precision imagined. The moral tests to which*

*the crew of a bomber were subjected reached the limits of
human valor and sacrifice. Here chance was carried to its
most extreme and violent degree above all else . . . In the
British and American bombing of Germany and Italy during
the war, the casualties were over a hundred and forty thousand . . . These heroes never flinched or failed. It is to their
devotion that in no small measure we owe our victory.*

By sea and air in the opening of this auspicious year of
1944 the Allied star is in the ascendant. But not clearly so
by land. For on the only terrain where they are in contact
with the Wehrmacht they are finding that the day goes hard
with them. The site of this cruel encounter is the Monastery
of Cassino.

For three months weary Allied troops have been straining, in mud and rain and biting cold, to break the hinge of
the Gustav Line. And still the paratroops of General von
Senger und Etterlin's command resist them.

A cold dawn breaks over the monastery on 15 February 1944. The sky is clearing as the abbot leads his few
remaining companions in their devotions, prescribed in lov-
ing detail centuries before by Saint Benedict, their founder.
Below the ancient walls and all about in the dark hills, the
battlefield lies oddly silent. Mist is clearing from the ridges,
revealing a pitiful debris of temporary crosses and broken
weapons and random articles of clothing. But the mist still
hides the menace that is waiting, dotted in the jagged ruins
of the town at the mountain's foot, deployed in groups and
lines in valleys and on the rocky slopes of the approach. This
area is packed with troops, though none can be seen—nor
the artillery massed behind them.

Inside the abbey, thin but clear, rises the antiphony of a
Mass, echoing through empty cloisters and chambers. A little

before 9:30 there intrudes into this holy ritual a distant but steady skein of sound. It comes from the first wave of a force of 142 heavy and 112 medium bombers whose mission this day is to drop 576 tons of bombs on the abbey. It is the prelude to the final effort to take Cassino and break through to Rome.

From the British lines a war correspondent watches the destruction. "Just before two o'clock in the afternoon a formation of Mitchells passed over. They dipped slightly. A moment later a bright flame, such as a giant might have produced by striking titanic matches on the mountainside, spurted swiftly upward at half-a-dozen points. Then a pillar of smoke five hundred feet high broke upward into the blue. For nearly five minutes it hung around the building, thinning gradually upward into strange, evil-looking arabesques . . . Then the column paled and melted. The abbey became visible again. Its whole outline had changed. The west wall had totally collapsed."

But still the Germans hold their positions. The net gain of bombing the abbey is nil. The Germans now fortify its ruins. The Allies are forced to regroup; it takes them two months to do it, and still their first objective must be the stubborn monastery. At 11 o'clock on the night of 11 May the whole Allied line explodes with the simultaneous concussion of two thousand guns. The infantry set wearily out yet again for the mountains sown with mines and the ravines strewn with dead. Whipped by machine-gun fire and bludgeoned by shells, they inch forward.

The battle continues at its full height for forty-eight bloody hours, with little advantage either way. On the third day the Germans begin to give ground in the west before the Fifth Army. On the fourth the British force a limited advance. On the sixth the Poles claw their way to the very portals of the monastery and on the seventh it falls to them.

The Allied flood pours through the breach and on to the north. From embattled Anzio, General Truscott strikes against Cisterna and on 25 May joins hands with the Fifth Army. General Clark orders him to send three divisions into the Alban Hills on the approaches to Rome. The fighting is still desperate and many Germans have escaped the trap to live and fight again. The final lunge goes in from the Alban Hills. Rome falls on 4 June when at 7:15 P.M. the first American troops march down the Piazza Venezia and into the heart of Rome. They have captured the first of the Axis capitals to prostrate itself before the Allies.

Churchill triumphantly describes it in the House as *a memorable and glorious event, which rewards the intense fighting of the last five months in Italy.* There is a high symbolism in this victory, for on the very morning on which Churchill is speaking, a liberating army has descended on the shores of France in the mightiest enterprise ever seen on earth.

THE SWORD
IS FORGED

Fair stood the wind for France
When we our sails advance,
Nor now to prove our chance,
Longer will tarry.
    MICHAEL DRAYTON: *Ballad of Agincourt*

ACROSS the golden field floats the humming and clacking of the harvester. Behind it an old man patiently gathers the sheaves and methodically arranges them into shocks. The narrow road is quiet and the little boy riding his bicycle along it is dreaming of pistols and birds' eggs and jam and his dog, his mind filled with the serene disorder of the young. Rounding a corner, he swerves suddenly to the left. Thundering down on him is a string of three huge trucks, white stars on their dark bonnets and sides.

Rumbling and swishing past the little boy the troop carriers swing into a side road, slow down and pull up in front of a striped pole that blocks the way. On each side of it stand notices, crimson and white. In bold letters they spell out DANGER: HIGH EXPLOSIVES, adding with authority

244

WAR DEPARTMENT PROPERTY. The trucks ease through the gate and behind them the bar swings down again. More slowly now, they advance.

From the gloom beneath their canopies the troops stare out into the bright afternoon. Now and then a boot grates on the steel floor. Rifles bump uncomfortably against cramped limbs. The faces are relaxed, unsurprised, patient. Whatever is happening is all part of the great incomprehensible military scheme. With the stolid indifference of infantrymen they wait for something to happen. Sitting beside the driver, the young lieutenant glances about at a landscape unlike anything he has seen before. It is as though the gate has brought him to another world. There are farmhouses, like those outside, but these are smashed and scorched. There are copses of oak and ash, but the treetops are splintered and frayed. There are pastures, but they are fitted with shallow holes whose perimeters of raw earth are oddly blackened. This wounded countryside is a battleground and these green troops have come to learn the last refinements of the arts of war. This is a battle school.

A few miles farther and they come to a ruined hamlet. Brusque young officers gather about the trucks. The infantry clamber down, hitching up their packs, ambling into some form of order, and stand quietly in rank. A lean major walks toward them, assesses them slowly with steady eyes and begins to talk. They are here, he tells them, to practice an attack with artillery support. Behind them, over there, are the batteries of Polish field artillery. In front of them, over there, is the objective. It is vital, he says, to stay as close to the barrage as possible. As it moves forward they must walk behind it, not more than two hundred yards from the shell bursts. But not less. The Polish gunners, he assures them, are extremely accurate. The infantry move off to their baptism.

A hundred miles away other men are walking waist-deep in the sea toward a crescent of sand. They are a different kind of men. On the average they are bigger; they are certainly more talkative. Yelling, they swarm onto the beach, throw themselves flat on its landward edge and begin to crawl. Left and right of them machine guns start to clatter, and at once the air a few feet above the men is filled with a chirping, whispering agitation. Cursing, they drag themselves under strands of wire, aware of nothing but the mortal streams above them and the dry earth beneath them where every tuft of salt grass becomes a landmark. This too is a battle school.

British or American, the troops destined for France are being tempered by fire. The tougher the training, say the generals, the fewer the casualties when the battle opens. They are right. All through the fall of 1943 the divisions destined for the assault on Fortress Europe grow harder, more experienced and more confident.

The plans are already laid and the Chiefs of Staff have reported, "We have approved the outline plan of General Morgan for Operation Overlord, and have authorized him to proceed with the detailed planning and with full preparations." On 14 January 1944 General Eisenhower arrives from the Mediterranean to assume supreme command and sets up his headquarters, known as SHAEF (Supreme Headquarters Allied Expeditionary Forces), at Bushey Park, just outside London. His deputy in command is Air Chief Marshal Sir Arthur Tedder, his chief of staff, General Walter Bedell Smith, and the commander of his ground forces for the invasion, General Sir Bernard Law Montgomery. At once they study General Morgan's plans and immediately expand them.

The operation calls for an initial assault of five divisions borne in by sea with two more following up, and three parachute divisions to be dropped inland. In the first two days 176,000 men must be put ashore with 20,000 tanks and vehicles. During the first ninety days three-quarters of a million more must be sent in with all their impedimenta. Twelve thousand tons of cargo a day must be landed to support them and the second million who will follow in preparation for the final thrust into Germany. This vast concourse has been assembling in England for months while a thousand things are done to insure success.

Already the invasion beaches have been selected. They stretch along the Norman coast north of Caen between the mouth of the River Orne and the Cherbourg peninsula. They are relatively close to the south coast of England and well within reach of fighter cover. They are reasonably sheltered from storm and their configurations lend themselves to the Allies' plans for landing supplies. They have been examined and mapped from the air from every angle; each additional fortification has been noted as it appears. Even the soil has been sampled by frogmen of the Combined Operations Pilotage Parties swimming in by night from small craft or canoes.

Churchill plunges into the details of the operation, the difficulties of which he has never underestimated. *Across the Channel the whole front bristled with obstacles; defenses had been built and manned. The enemy expected us, but did they know where or when or how? They had no flanks that could be turned, at any rate within range of our fighter air-cover. Ships were more vulnerable than ever to shore batteries which could aim by radar. Once our troops were lanced, they still had to be supplied and the evening's air and tank counterattacks beaten off. I never ceased to search for means to overcome the perils which lay before us.*

One of the perils is the absence of a large harbor within the sixty-mile crescent of beaches. The Americans landing on the western flank are expected to capture Cherbourg, but not for some time after the assault, and there is no guarantee that its port installations will not have been destroyed by the German garrison. Some means must be found of maintaining the huge flow of supplies, for clearly it cannot be done with safety across open beaches. In an inspired moment, the planners find the answer. The Allies must take their ports with them.

There are to be two of these artificial harbors, christened "Mulberry," one off the American beaches and one off the British. They are to consist of an outer breakwater (a "Gooseberry") formed by sinking blockships along the edge of the Calvados Reef. In all there will be five Gooseberries, one for each divisional assault area; two of them will later become the outer rings of the artificial harbors. Seventy old merchant ships and four obsolete warships are set aside for the purpose.

Once in position the line of ships will be strengthened by concrete caissons ("Phoenixes"), towed across the Channel by tugs. Within this security the supply ships will discharge their stores onto long piers stretching out a mile from the shore. They are called "Whales" and there will be three to each harbor. The technical problems they present are enormous, but Churchill makes the principle quite clear. At the bottom of a Top Secret paper on the subject from the Chief of Combined Operations, he writes in his small, precise hand: *They must float up and down with the tide. The anchor problem must be mastered. The ships must have a side flap in them, and a drawbridge long enough to overreach the moorings of the piers. Let me have the best solution worked out. Don't argue the matter. The difficulties will argue for themselves.*

In some areas the whole British war effort is redirected to this new task. Churchill points out, *The whole project involved the construction in Britain of great masses of special equipment, amounting in the aggregate to over a million tons of steel and concrete. This work, undertaken with the highest priority, would impinge heavily on our already hard-pressed engineering and ship-repairing industries. All this equipment would have to be transported by sea to the scene of action, and there erected with the utmost expedition in the face of enemy attack and the vagaries of the weather.*

Alongside the Port of London the Surrey Docks and the East India Docks begin to sprout a weird tangle of girders and steel plates, and the Cockney riveters begin to look puzzled at the strange monsters they are asked to fashion. Downriver, bulldozers tear at deep excavations, each big enough to accommodate a five-story building. Concrete is poured in by the scores of tons. Then channels are dug, the river rushes into the basin and another Phoenix is born, to be floated past the flat marshes of the Thames mouth and towed to the assembly area at Southampton.

Week after week the preparations mount in intensity, and week after week the problems become more diverse. Papers by the hundred arrive in the Prime Minister's office; memoranda, orders, inquiries, exhortations, warnings issue from it in a blizzard. To the Secretary of State for the Dominions he observes on 25 January, *It is to my mind very unwise to make plans on the basis of Hitler being defeated in 1944. The possibility of his gaining a victory in France cannot be excluded. The hazards of battle are very great....* He takes issue with Montgomery on an old theme: *Two hundred thousand vehicles seem a vast outfit to attach to an army which ... would only have 600,500 men.... One hopes there will be enough infantry with rifles and bayonets to protect the great mass of vehicles from falling into enemy hands.*

To the English watching this concentration with awe, it
seems there will be plenty. It looks as though the entire
southern part of the country has been taken over by the
Americans. They are crossing the Atlantic at the rate of two
divisions a month. Cities of quonset huts and whole metrop-
olises of khaki tents spring up to house them. Their supplies
occupy twenty million square feet of covered storage space
and forty-four million square feet more in the open. Their
giant machines flatten a quarter of a million acres to provide
airfields. They lay a hundred and seventy miles of railroad
track. On the sidings are drawn up a thousand locomotives
and twenty thousand railroad cars. Tree-lined roads are
piled high with crates of shells for the guns and howitzers
that lie in vast parks, wheel to wheel. Tanks by the hundred,
trucks and jeeps and cars and armored half-tracks by the
thousand crowd beside the guns. Everything is there, from
pills to explosive bullets to boots and portable altars and
snipers' sights. It is as though the entire output of a mighty
nation were set out for display.

From time to time the Prime Minister emerges from his
paperwork and bustles away to watch the troops at their
training. General Horrocks, one of Montgomery's corps commanders, arranges some entertainment for him. "I knew that
he liked tanks," the General says, "and so I laid on a full-
scale attack by all my tanks, a whole armored division, all
firing live ammunition and backed up by artillery. I also knew
that he had to be up in the front line. He would never stay
back. So I had a small stand made about two hundred yards
from where the shells were to land. I can tell you that I
spent a very anxious day, because it only wanted one single
shell just slightly off target and the Prime Minister might
have been killed. He absolutely loved it."

Visiting the Americans, he is allowed to fire a carbine. Welcoming him to his crack 9th Division, General Manton S. Eddy sets out three targets, one for General Omar Bradley at 75 yards, one for General Eisenhower at 50 and the third for the Prime Minister at 25 yards, and issues clips of ammunition. Jamming his derby firmly on his head, Churchill hands his cigar to an aide and adopts a warlike stance. Fifteen rounds from each carbine rip into the targets, but before the hits can be counted, the diplomatic General Eddy ushers his guests away to new attractions.

Despite these diversions, the strain is beginning to tell. Field Marshal Alanbrooke, who meets him daily, notices that he is growing tired. On 7 May, a Sunday, he dines with the Prime Minister at Chequers, and afterward notes in his diary: "Dinner was followed by the usual film, after which Winston took me down to the little study where the secretaries work. There he sat by the fire and drank soup. He looked very old and very tired. He said Roosevelt was not well and that he was no longer the man he had been; this, he said, also applied to himself. He said he could always sleep well, eat well, and especially drink well, but that he no longer jumped out of bed the way he used to, and felt as if he would be quite content to spend the whole day in bed. I have never yet heard him admit that he was beginning to fail. He then said some very nice things about the excellent opinion that the whole Defense Committee and War Cabinet had of me, and that they had said that we could not have a better C.I.G.S."

Later Alanbrooke adds a footnote to this entry: "Considering the difficult times I had had recently with Winston, I appreciated tremendously his kindness in passing on these remarks to me at the end of our talk. I did not often get any form of appreciation of my work from him and therefore treasured it all the more on these rare occasions. He was an astounding mixture, could drive you to complete desperation and to the brink of despair for weeks on end, and then he would ask you to spend a couple of hours or so alone with him and would produce the most homely and attractive personality. All that unrelenting tension was temporarily relaxed, he ceased to work himself into one fury or another, and you left him with the feeling that you would do anything within your power to help him to carry the stupendous burden he had shouldered."

Weariness is not confined to the Allied leaders. Peering out onto a bleak future, Hitler declares, "The attack will come; there's no doubt about that any more. . . . If they attack in the west, that attack will decide the war. If this attack is repulsed the whole business is over. Then we can withdraw troops right away." Already he and his intimates are beginning to wonder, faced by the bête noire of German military policy, the war on two fronts, whether East or West would be more receptive to overtures of peace. Will Stalin be more approachable than Churchill; when the moment comes, to which side shall they incline?

Though the Germans are now certain that invasion will come, none knows just where the blow will fall. The Allies have undertaken an enormous cover operation. The flamboyant General Patton is publicized as the commander of a new army group forming in southeastern England. He establishes a headquarters near Dover, within sight of the Calais coast. In fact, no such army group exists. But a facsimile does. Hundreds of paper tanks are scattered in badly camouflaged lagers; fake landing craft are massed in the Thames and the Medway; acres of deserted tents are erected in East Anglia and visited from time to time by troops instructed to lend them some semblance of life. German reconnaissance planes photograph this vast preparation and the High Command draws the wished-for conclusion. The

invasion will be directed at the Pas de Calais. They persist
in this mistake even after the assault has descended on
Normandy.

In addition the British institute an implacable security
system. The entire coast from Wales to Land's End, in a strip
ten miles deep, is closed to all but residents, their relatives
if emergencies require it, and people authorized to enter it
on business. On 17 April they close the whole country. Not
even foreign diplomats, save those of the United States or
Russia, may leave or enter. They may not even dispatch
coded messages. The use of diplomatic pouches is forbidden.
All communication by letter, cable or telephone with Eire
is cut off. On 27 April *all* travel outside is stopped, even of
generals wishing to visit the Italian front. England is sealed
off.

The final briefings begin with a meeting of all general
officers in Montgomery's headquarters, St. Paul's School,
where the General as a boy had undergone the rigors of a
sound education. One of the halls has been converted into
an arena circled by tiers of benches that surround a huge
relief map of the invasion area. Meticulously the General
explains his plans, pointing out features, outlining methods,
expounding principles, never halting the lucid flow of his
thought, utterly concentrated. When he has finished everyone is, as he is fond of putting it, "in the picture."

For the troops there are two full-scale rehearsals as a
climax to their amphibious training. The men embark in
the same ships that will carry them to France, assemble in
the Channel and land on British beaches as similar as possible to those they will actually attack. During one of the
rehearsals the landing ships are surprised by nine fast
E-boats slashing in with torpedoes. Two landing ships are

sunk in the flurry and 638 men are drowned. Among them
are ten officers who carry secret knowledge about the time
and place of Overlord. There is no way of knowing if they
are dead or have been taken prisoner. Several days later,
however, their bodies are washed ashore; their secrets have
died with them.

On 28 May all subordinate commanders are told the date
of the attack, 5 June. From that moment every man committed to the operation is isolated from the outside world.
Their mail is impounded, they cannot reach telephones and
their camps and barracks are hemmed in with barbed wire
patrolled by service police. They settle down to the most
thorough briefing from maps and models and aerial photographs and intelligence reports ever received by an army.
It is so detailed that when some of the men actually see the
objective they feel certain they have been there before.

As in all things military a great effort is made to ensure
that nothing is left to chance. The over-all plan settled and
explained, the British Army plunges with relief into the
minutae that have been the principal form of its interest
since the first general issue arrow flew toward the startled
chivalry of France on Crecy field. In huts and barracks and
tent-lines men stand rigidly rank on rank for inspection
after inspection. The number and exact placing of the hobnails on the spare pair of boots, the state of readiness of the
razor and its single accompanying blade, the number of
needles in the sewing-kit, the alignment of the tines of the
fork, the wording of the Soldier's Last Will and Testament
at the end of the paybook, the degree of flexibility in the
suspenders, khakis, packs; one and all are checked and re-
checked in the majestic ritual that makes battle an in-
trusion and war an impertinence. More men suffer the rod of
justice for losing a pin than for having dust on their rifles.
Which is just as it should be.

Meanwhile the Allied air forces are isolating the whole of northwestern France by destroying all rail communications. Their design is to drop some 66,000 tons of bombs on locomotive sheds, tracks, repair shops, bridges and marshaling yards. In particular they are to smash ninety-three key rail centers on the approaches to Normandy. Careful as they are, the bombers take a mounting toll of civilians in Belgium and France. Distressed and anxious, Churchill and Eisenhower wonder whether the destruction is justified. They realize, however, that in the end it will save many more Allied lives than it is costing now, and may well mean the difference between success and failure.

General Eisenhower has moved his Advanced Headquarters to the coast, joining the headquarters of his naval forces at Southwich House, a mansion set graciously in extensive parkland outside Portsmouth. On one of the immaculate lawns rests General Montgomery's caravan, looking very workmanlike. Not a soul in this congress of staffs knows that Mr. Churchill proposes to accompany the invasion forces to view the show at first hand. No one, that is, but Admiral Ramsay, who has been required to make the arrangements. He assigns a cruiser to pick up the Prime Minister in Weymouth Bay before sailing at full speed to join her squadron in one of the bombardment groups; after the dawn attack the Prime Minister desires to make a short tour of the beaches before transferring to a destroyer homeward bound for more ammunition. But the Admiral is beset by doubts. He feels it his duty to tell General Eisenhower what is afoot.

The Supreme Commander protests at once. The Prime Minister retorts that though the General is accepted as Supreme Commander of the British forces involved this does not give him the right to determine the membership of the crews of ships of His Britannic Majesty's Navy. The Supreme Commander agrees, but stresses that the venture will add greatly to his anxieties by imposing a heavy responsibility. The Prime Minister points out with some truth that he too carries responsibilities, and now feels that the matter is settled.

However, he later notes, *a complication occurred which I have His Majesty's permission to recount. When I attended my weekly luncheon with the King on the Tuesday before D-Day, his Majesty asked me where I intended to be on D-Day. I replied that I proposed to witness the bombardment from one of the cruiser squadrons. His Majesty immediately said he would like to come too. He had not been under fire except in air raids since the Battle of Jutland, and eagerly welcomed the prospect of renewing the experiences of his youth.* Churchill promises, as he must, to consult Admiral Ramsay, and later the Cabinet.

But next day the King has second thoughts, and writes to ask his First Minister to reconsider the whole matter. He arrives in person on the heels of his letter, accompanied by the redoubtable Sir Alan Lascelles, his Private Secretary. Unaware of what has been proposed for the King, Admiral Ramsay describes the itinerary he has prepared for Mr. Churchill. When asked what he thinks of His Majesty's joining in he hurriedly declares himself not in favor. The Prime Minister gives it as his opinion that in that case he doubts whether the Cabinet will recommend that His Majesty sail. Sensing trouble, the Admiral leaves.

What is sauce for the goose is sauce for the gander. The King says that if it is not right that he should go, neither is it right for the Prime Minister. The Prime Minister has foreseen this gambit, and cheerfully replies with respect that he is traveling in his capacity as Minister of Defense. Sir Alan, ignoring this side step, remarks gloomily, "His Majesty's anxieties would be increased if he heard his Prime

Minister was at the bottom of the English Channel." According to Mr. Churchill's best information the risk is negligible. Sir Alan rallies. He has always understood that no Minister of the Crown may leave the country without the Sovereign's permission. Mr. Churchill considers the point. He offers that the rule can have no force since he will be aboard one of His Majesty's ships. Sir Alan makes a deadly riposte: The ship, he points out, will be well outside territorial waters. "The King," Mr. Churchill records, "then returned to Buckingham Palace."

But victory is not yet won. A letter from the Palace reaches the Prime Minister's train as it draws up close to Supreme Headquarters. Once more the King appeals to him not to go to sea. The letter ends: "I ask you most earnestly to consider the whole question again, and not let your personal wishes, which I very well understand, lead you to depart from your own high standard of duty to the State. Believe me, your very sincere friend, George R.I." Harassed by several telephone calls, the Prime Minister at last is forced to furnish his answer. In the small hours of the morning he points out that while the Cabinet would not advise the King to go, they cannot by any means restrict the peregrinations of the Prime Minister. He writes firmly, "I must most earnestly ask Your Majesty that no principle shall be laid down which inhibits my freedom of movement . . ." but eventually gracefully acknowledges defeat.

Since Your Majesty does me the honor to be so much concerned about my personal safety on this occasion, I must defer to Your Majesty's wishes, and indeed commands. It is a great comfort to me to know that they arise from Your Majesty's desire to continue me in your service. Though I regret that I cannot go, I am deeply grateful to Your Majesty for the motives which have guided Your Majesty in respect of

Your Majesty's humble and devoted servant and subject,
                                                    Winston S. Churchill

Writing long after the event, Churchill adds, *The cruiser squadron concerned was, as I had justly estimated, not exposed to any undue danger. In fact, it did not sustain a single casualty. I should not have referred to this matter if it had not been publicized in a friendly but unwittingly inaccurate form by General Eisenhower.*

This reply is dated 3 June 1944. The wheels are already turning. The southern counties of England are crammed with 2,800,000 men. Thirty-nine divisions, with all their weapons and supplies and waterproofed vehicles, are held incommunicado in the concentration areas. Three air-borne divisions are at readiness beside their airfields. Components for the Mulberry harbors are at sea, heading for their assembly points. Ships of the bombardment squadrons, including six battleships, two monitors and twenty-two cruisers, are on their way to join the host of destroyers, torpedo boats, rocket ships, mine sweepers and other small craft that make up the naval task forces. The number of air strikes builds up to its crescendo. Everything now depends upon the weather.

D-Day has been fixed for 5 June because that is the first of three days which fulfill most of the requirements of the operation as regards moonlight and tides. The air-borne troops need a moon, the sea-borne forces need a short interval of daylight between their arrival offshore and the first moment of the assault. The tide must not be so high as to cover the lines of underwater obstacles strung along the sea's edge, nor so low as to expose the assault waves to a long dash across open beaches. The weather must be promising enough to give time for a lodgment and the erection of the synthetic harbors.

If the weather is bad on 5 June and on the two days following, the operation will have to be postponed for two weeks, perhaps even for a month. Such delay might well prove disastrous. The Russians have promised to synchronize their own new offensive with Overlord. Postponement will shatter the morale of troops already too long confined. Security is bound to be broken. All eyes turn therefore with anxiety to the sky.

Disappointed that he cannot join them, Churchill watches the first troops embarking on 3 June and takes a launch from ship to ship as they ride at anchor in the Solent. The sea is beginning to chop and whiten as a cool wind freshens from the west. The sky is gray with clouds that seem to be thickening. Things do not look at all promising. Full of foreboding, Churchill boards his train and at the last minute receives a message that the weather is growing worse. Overlord may have to be postponed for twenty-four hours. Aboard their tiny ships, now being battered by heavy seas, the assault troops are beginning to get seasick.

At four o'clock in the morning of 4 June General Eisenhower calls in his commanders and his Meteorological Committee. Its head, Group Captain J. M. Stagg, predicts that 5 June will bring low clouds, high winds and rough seas along the Normandy coast. Eisenhower postpones the operation for twenty-four hours and recalls those elements that are already on their way across the Channel. They pitch back to port under squalls of deadening rain.

This is a black prospect indeed. But then there comes a gleam of hope. "Late that Sunday afternoon," Group Captain Stagg recalls, "reports from the Atlantic suggested that unforeseen developments were taking place very rapidly, much more rapidly than we could have expected. We saw that if those developments continued they could bring a brief but improved interval of weather into the Channel which might just allow the Supreme Commander to get the operation going again. We knew that. But we also knew that if the Supreme Commander decided that way, then there could be no further halting and no turning back. The whole fate of the operation would be sealed."

At 3:30 A.M. on that Monday morning General Eisenhower hurries to a meeting through winds that have reached almost hurricane force and which are hurling heavy rain in savage sheets the length and breadth of the Channel. The weathermen were right. Will they be right again? The oak-paneled conference room is silent as they announce a break in the storm the following morning and the certainty of thirty-six hours of good weather.

Stagg's quiet voice is muted by the battering and howling of the gale outside. Eisenhower hears him to the end, glances around at his deputies, the sea, land and air commanders, and finds affirmation. He looks down at the polished table, absolutely still. His hands lie in his lap. His sensitive eyes are large and bright with anxiety. He debates the safety of a hundred thousand men, measures the future of the Allied cause. His head lifts and he gives the word. "O.K.," he says, "we'll go." It is 4:15 on the morning of 5 June.

What Churchill calls "the supreme climax of the war" has been reached. *The immense cross-Channel enterprise for liberation of France had begun,* he continues. *All the ships were at sea. We had the mastery of the oceans and of the air. The Hitler tyranny was doomed. Here, then, we might pause in thankfulness and take hope, not only for victory on all fronts and in all three elements, but also for a safe and happy future for mankind.*

D-DAY: THE GREAT ASSAULT

I don't know what effect these men will have upon the enemy, but, by God, they terrify me.
ARTHUR WELLESLEY, DUKE OF WELLINGTON

TROOPER George Preston is aware of a sense of unusual well-being and yet, lurking somewhere deep down in his consciousness there is the little devil doubt. Trooper Preston is a large man, an expansive man, a brute of a man. He could break a back with one wrench of knee and arms or cut a throat in a single, clean, powerful slash. He has been fully trained to strangle by any one of several grips, to rip, gouge, stun, emasculate, garrote, stab, shoot to wound or to kill, and in all ways to overcome the foe. There is little doubt that Trooper Preston will do just that.

He is not without confidence. In fact, the question does not arise, for to Trooper Preston his Commando training has been an apprenticeship to a trade, just as before that he was apprenticed to a fishmonger and was taught to fillet, decapitate, eviscerate and skin with the greatest possible expedition. He does not feel in the least insecure. Nor does he look it. Sitting back at his ease in the driver's seat of his jeep, his brawny shoulders supported by an ammunition box, he is wholly occupied in trimming his fingernails with a very large knife which, by some idiosyncrasy, he keeps in a sheath inside his left sleeve.

But still within this menacing bulk there stirs a tiny qualm. Trooper Preston glances about. It cannot be his companion, equally large and equally taciturn: they have no need of conversation and thus no quarrels can arise. It cannot be his surroundings: they are drab, it is true, but not displeasing to a casual eye. It cannot be his mission: he has been through all that a score of times—no problem there. The weather perhaps? Trooper Preston observes that the sky is bright, if cloudy; the wind is invigorating; the waves splash against the side of his landing craft with sufficient sprightliness to make him feel he is at sea, which he has enjoyed ever since he sailed in holiday high spirits on that paddle steamer as a small boy.

Suddenly he realizes what it is. Instinctively he lifts a stubby hand to his head. His beret . . . his beautiful green beret. That pompous gunner colonel had wanted to take it away. He had told Trooper Preston to take it off and wear a steel helmet. Patiently Trooper Preston had explained that his orders were to wear a green beret. The colonel insisted. Indeed, Trooper Preston had become involved in a stiff intellectual skirmish. He smiles. After all, he has won. All he had to do was tell the colonel the truth. He had not brought his steel helmet. War is very simple, really, Trooper Preston finds. He continues his manicure.

He has reason to believe that he will soon have to do some work. Not far ahead there is a very impressive noise indeed.

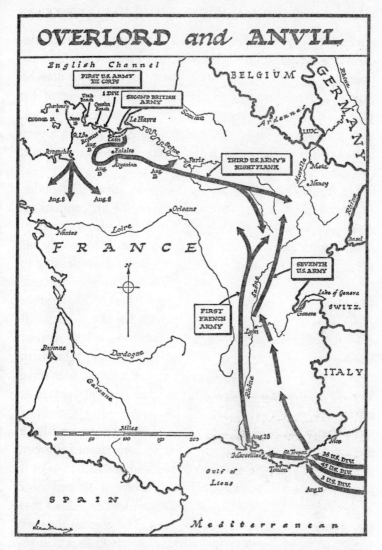

OVERLORD and ANVIL

English Channel

BELGIUM

GERMANY

FIRST U.S. ARMY
XII CORPS

1 DIV.

SECOND BRITISH
ARMY

Utah
Beach
Omaha
Beach

Cherbourg

CHANNEL IS.

June 13

St. Lô

Bayeux
Aug. 13

Caen

Le Havre

Somme

Ardennes

LUX.

Avranches

Falaise

Seine

Moselle

Metz

Aug. 13

Argentan
Aug. 13

Aug. 13

Paris

THIRD U.S. ARMY'S
RIGHT FLANK

Nancy

Aug. 8

Aug. 8

Orleans

Rhine

Nantes

Loire

Basel

F R A N C E

Saône

SEVENTH
U.S. ARMY

Lake of Geneva

Geneva

SWITZ.

N

FIRST
FRENCH
ARMY

Lyon

Bayonne

Dordogne

Rhône

ITALY

Garonne

Miles
0   50   100   150   200

Aug. 23

Nice

Marseilles

St. Tropez

36 U.S. DIV.

Toulon

45 U.S. DIV.

Gulf of
Lions

3 U.S. DIV.

Aug. 15

S P A I N

M e d i t e r r a n e a n

D-Day of "Operation Overlord," the Allied invasion of the Normandy coast of France, begins at dawn on June 6, 1944. Over 5,000 ships, carrying Allied troops across the English Channel, participate in the assault. The battle is bloodiest on Omaha Beach, but everywhere on the coast the Allies achieve their objectives and swiftly move inland. On August 23, Paris is liberated by the "Overlord" armies as the "Anvil" forces move northward up the Rhone Valley.

It sounds like battleships. Still, it is a very nice day and no doubt that is all part of the plan. The craft lurches onward. The fussy colonel is bobbing about among his men. Trooper Preston regards him with disgust. The bows of the craft clang down within feet of the beach. Trooper Preston presses the starter. The engine roars at once. He looks at his colleague. The colleague nods. Trooper Preston speaks. "Right!" he says. The jeep bounds down the iron deck, passes at great speed through the water so as not to drench their uniforms, and touches the sand. Trooper Preston gives her the gun, reflecting that it is nice to be back once more on the shores of France. The jeep surges away with her half ton of high explosives.

Not all men landing on this June morning are as phlegmatic, or as fortunate. Some drift the last few yards to the beach in landing craft that have suddenly become slaughterhouses under the German batteries. Others step off the clanging ramps into deep water and drown without a sound, carried under by the weight of ammunition and equipment. Yet others, scrambling over the tideline, find the beaches swept with a concentration of machine-gun fire they could not have thought possible. The lucky ones reach the landward edge of the beach stunned and shaking, and scrabble in the shingle to find some small protection. Over the entire coast there hangs an acrid haze, scarcely penetrated yet by the early sun.

Inland, other men have been fighting all night. Or getting ready to. Three divisions of paratroops have been dropped in an arc covering the landing bridges. Their object is to destroy what enemy they find, to seize bridges, to silence certain gun emplacements, and in the west to take the causeways that form the only path over the marshes between the American beaches and the open country beyond. One of the first men into Normandy is General Maxwell D. Taylor, commander of the 101st American Airborne Division.

He arrives unobserved: "The only witnesses of my landing were a herd of Norman cows. In anticipation of the difficulties of assembling the troops in the dark, we were all equipped with a little toy, one that made a clicking sound. They called it a cricket. With my pistol in one hand and my cricket in the other, I cautiously edged my way down the Norman hedgerow. Eventually, I heard someone moving on the other side and anxiously sounded my cricket. To my joy, a friendly cricket responded. I jumped around the hedgerow and there saw the most reassuring sight in the world—an American parachutist. He had lost his helmet, but he had his M-1 with his bayonet fixed and he looked ready to go. He was the finest soldier I ever saw. We embraced each other and then set out to reassemble the 101st Airborne Division.

"It took us several hours in the darkness to assemble as many as seventy of our parachutists. Unfortunately they were the wrong kind; they were cooks and KPs and typists. Only too few carried the M-1 rifle. Also, there were lots of officers. We had a couple of generals, a colonel or two, and an indefinite number of majors. As daylight came we headed toward the coast to discharge our mission of helping ashore the amphibious landing. The thought occurred to me, which I've often expressed, that never in the history of human conflict were so few commanded by so many."

Two very much smaller groups have been on the scene even longer than the paratroops. They are the crews of the midget submarines X-20 and X-23. As General Taylor's men are floating down over the rich pastures of Normandy, these two tiny craft are lying submerged, one at each flank of the invasion area. Their crews are wondering just what is going on. The invasion is a day late. Their duty is to surface just before dawn and show lights to seaward to guide the invasion fleet. They have done that once already, then when it grew too light they had to submerge again. One of them stayed at periscope height and for a few minutes watched some German troops innocently playing football on the beach.

Acting on his orders, Lieutenant George Honour, skipper of X-23, orders his tank blown and emerges into the darkness of 6 June. "We surfaced just before dawn," he recounts, "set up our marking beacons and waited for the invasion to arrive. As dawn broke, we saw the invasion forces coming toward us in the distance. This was a great relief but also a very frightening sight, and I can imagine the Germans' feelings at that moment."

The Germans' feelings are mixed. Predominant is a sense of surprise. Their meteorological experts had assured them that there was no possibility of suitable weather on 5 or 6 June. Their superior commanders expect the assault in the Pas de Calais; they are so far from anticipating this descent that Field Marshal Rommel himself has gone home for a brief rest. Even the paratroop landings are interpreted as a diversion. The heavy bombing of the night is taken as merely another of the raids that have been going on for weeks.

Nevertheless, in his discreet villa at 28 Rue Alexandre Dumas in St. Germain-en-Laye, a suburb of Paris, the last of Germany's Black Knights is awakened. Field Marshal Gerd von Rundstedt, Commander-in-Chief West, rises slowly and with pain, for he is an old man. He leaves his home by a private corridor that leads him directly to Oberbefehlshaber West, a huge concrete-shielded emplacement dug into a hillside, with an outer wall a hundred yards long and three stories high.

At first Rundstedt is not unduly worried, for he has just been forwarded a report from Rommel's Army Group B that reads "The systematic and distinct increase of air attacks indicates that the enemy has reached a high degree of readiness. The probable invasion front still remains the sector from the Scheldt to Normandy . . . and it is not impossible that the north front of Brittany might be included. . . . It is still not clear where the enemy will invade within this total area. Concentrated air attacks on the coast defenses between Dunkirk and Dieppe may mean that the main Allied invasion effort will be made there. . . . But the imminence of invasion is not recognizable." Field Marshal Rundstedt places great confidence in the judgment of his field commander. He cannot yet know that this time Rommel has guessed wrong.

As an insurance, however, Rundstedt orders two armored divisions, the 12th SS and the Panzer Lehr, to stand by. In doing so he is acting against orders, for both these formidable units, which could well decide the battle, belong to the OKW reserve. They can move only on Hitler's orders. When Rundstedt later seeks confirmation of his order from OKW it is withheld. The forward troops are left to fight it out in their concrete gun positions and strong-points.

The seascape visible through the slits of these defenses is not pleasant to behold. Low on the horizon ride lines of capital ships, shrouded intermittently by gouts of smoke through which there lance and flash great spurts of flame. Hove to, or cruising slowly, they are firing broadside after heavy broadside. On their flanks and closer inshore are the white wakes of destroyers racing from position to position, but all adding to the ceaseless barrage. Inshore the landing ships lie at anchor, and from them stream small craft bearing men and tanks and guns ashore. Here and there among them a rocket ship looses its shrieking broadside in a livid belt of flame.

During the night the German gun emplacements have been attacked by the RAF's heavy bombers and blasted by five thousand and two hundred tons of bombs. Now, in the gray dawn, the United States Air Force takes over with medium and fighter bombers, raking every defended area with high explosives. During this day Allied planes will fly a total of 14,600 sorties. As the Germans stare out from their embrasures not yet blocked by crumbled masonry they begin to recognize their fate. Yet still they fight, denying every inch of ground until resistance is no longer possible.

To the east the British and Canadians are already established on their three beaches, Sword, Juno and Gold. The Americans, too, are ashore in the west, but they are having a far stiffer fight. On Utah Beach, a third of the way up the Cotentin Peninsula, Brigadier Theodore Roosevelt is able to walk about flourishing his cane and encouraging his men through the danger zones. But on Omaha nobody can walk.

There the battle is frightening. The beach itself is overshadowed by towering cliffs; parties of Rangers have been detailed to scale them by means of ladders and ropes. But as quickly as grapnels can be fired to the top they are dislodged by the Germans. The ladders cannot be climbed because the defenders are hanging over the cliff edge firing down them with machine pistols.

There is little enough sign of movement on Omaha Beach when one of the Beach Commanders, Lieutenant Commander Henry Watts, rides into it through a squadron of swimming tanks. "I was assigned to a section there designated Easy Red," he recalls. "Once upon the beach we worked our way up under machine-gun fire through the obstacles. Men were falling to the right and left of me and it was very difficult to crawl on our hands and knees up to our first shelter. There was a bank of stones at the highwater mark which protected us from small-arms fire. Much to our surprise, on reaching it we found the bank covered with American assault troops. These were the fellows who were supposed to take the cliffs that commanded the beach. One of my outfit shouted to the sergeant, 'Why the hell don't you go up and take the cliff?' The sergeant shouted back, 'Why the hell don't *you?*' "

General Omar Bradley watches anxiously aboard his command ship. An identification is sent through. His men have come up against one of the best infantry divisions in the whole Wehrmacht, the 352nd, which has been caught in the middle of an anti-invasion exercise. General Bradley is relieved that First U.S. Division is fighting them: a less experienced one might get nowhere. Patiently he studies the battle.

At one minute past nine o'clock the first official news breaks, in the form of Communiqué Number 1. It states "Under the command of General Eisenhower, Allied Naval Forces supported by strong Air Forces began landing Allied Armies this morning on the northern coast of France." Its very plainness is a comfort to those waiting in fear at home.

Fuller information is given to the House of Commons by the Prime Minister. The Debating Chamber is crowded and electric with excitement. Mr. Churchill opens his speech with ten minutes on the Italian campaign. When he is quite sure his colleagues on both sides of the House have been teased enough he continues: *I have also to announce to the House that during the night and the early hours of this morning the first of the series of landings in force upon the European continent has taken place. In this case the liberating assault fell upon the coast of France. An immense armada of upward of 4,000 ships, together with several thousand smaller craft, crossed the Channel. Massed air-borne landings have*

been successfully effected behind the enemy lines, and land-
ings on the beaches are proceeding at various points at the
present time. The fire of the shore batteries has been largely
quelled. The obstacles that were constructed in the sea have
not proved so difficult as was apprehended. The Anglo-Amer-
ican Allies are sustained by about 11,000 first-line aircraft,
which can be drawn upon or may be needed for the purpose
of the battle. . . . Reports are coming in rapid succession.
So far the commanders who are engaged report that every-
thing is proceeding according to plan. And what a plan! This
vast operation is undoubtedly the most complicated and
difficult that has ever taken place.

King George VI broadcasts a message of hope to his people. His usually diffident voice is clear and warm. He says,
"The Queen joins me in sending you this message. She well
understands the anxieties and cares of our womenfolk at this
time and she knows that many of them will find, as she does
herself, fresh strength in such waiting upon God. She feels
that many women will be glad in this way to keep vigil with
their menfolk as they man the ships, storm the beaches, fill
the skies."

In the United States the President too speaks of prayer.
"My fellow Americans! Last night when I spoke with you
about the fall of Rome I knew at that moment that troops of
the United States and our Allies were crossing the Channel
in another great operation. It has come to pass with success
thus far, and so in this poignant hour, I ask you to join with
me in prayer." To a silent nation he goes on: "Almighty
God: Our sons, pride of our nation, this day have set upon
a mighty endeavor, a struggle to preserve our Republic, our
religion and our civilization and to set free a suffering
humanity. Lead them straight and true; give strength to
their arms, stoutness to their hearts, steadfastness in their
faith . . ."

The New York Stock Exchange suspends its activities while its members stand silently for two minutes amid the usual litter of paper and tape. Bearded patriarchs in prayer shawls walk through Brooklyn's streets sounding the shofar. In Philadelphia the Liberty Bell is rung.

General Bradley, red-eyed now from the smoke of his batteries, is beginning to feel happier. "The going on Omaha Beach was very rough," he reports, "and since we had some follow-up units to go in over that beach we began to think of other places to put them ashore. It wasn't till 1:30 that the troops on Omaha began to get up the cliffs and clear the beach for the follow-up units." The last obstacle is being overcome.

Some days later Montgomery writes of this decisive action to Field Marshal Alanbrooke: "The first vital moment in the battle was, I think, on the afternoon and evening of D-Day when the left American Corps had a beachhead of only 1,000 yards after fighting all day. Other parts of the lodgment area were not linked up, and we were liable to defeat in detail. The answer to invasion across the sea is a strong counterattack on the afternoon of D-Day when the invading force has not proper communications and has lost certain cohesion. That was Rommel's chance. It was not taken, and we were given time to recover—thank goodness! If you saw Omaha Beach you would wonder how the Americans ever got ashore."

But Rommel only arrives on this disastrous scene from Germany late that afternoon. And even then he cannot act with full vigor, for the force needed to drive the Allies back into the sea is still held in OKW reserve and cannot be deployed without Hitler's personal permission. When that finally arrives the decisive moment has already passed. But the Fuehrer is still optimistic: at five minutes before five o'clock von Rundstedt's headquarters passes on his directive to all units. "Chief of Staff Western Command emphasized the desire of the Supreme Command to have the enemy in the bridgehead annihilated by the evening of June 6 since there exists the danger of additional sea- and air-borne landings for support . . . the beachhead must be cleared up by not later than tonight."

What at first glance seems blind optimism is not absolutely without some foundation. The Germans are still enormously powerful in the west, and though on this first day the British are already five miles inland, they have not yet met the full weight of the Wehrmacht.

Churchill surveys the enemy strength. *Marshal Rundstedt, with sixty divisions, was in command of the whole Atlantic Wall, from the Low Countries to the Bay of Biscay, and thence along the southern French shore. Under him Rommel held the coast from Holland to the Loire. His Fifteenth Army with nineteen divisions held the sector about Calais and Boulogne, and his Seventh Army and nine infantry and one Panzer division were at hand in Normandy. The ten Panzer divisions on the whole Western Front were spread-eagled from Belgium to Bordeaux. How strange that the Germans, now on the defensive, made the same mistake as the French in 1940 and dispersed their most powerful weapon of counterattack!*

But now the vaunted Atlantic Wall has been breached within a few hours by an irresistible force of men and machines. By nightfall 70,500 men have passed over the American beaches and 83,115 over the British; inland are close on 20,000 paratroops. Of these devoted men 10,724 have become casualties, and 2,132 are dead. What the German losses have been on this day no man can say; the report from Rommel's Army Group B at the end of the month puts them thus far at a quarter of a million men and twenty-eight of their generals.

By D+4 (10 June) all the beaches have been joined together and the Allies enjoy a lodgment area sixty miles long and twelve miles to eight miles deep. It is firmly held. German reinforcements hurrying toward it are being blasted off the roads by strafing fighters, and men, ammunition and supplies are pouring in as the synthetic harbors receive their lines of ships.

Churchill decides it is time to take a trip and arranges an invitation from Montgomery. Dressed in his dark-blue uniform of an Elder of Trinity House, surmounted by a black-peaked yachting cap, the Prime Minister boards a destroyer at Portsmouth and is carried across the Channel. Montgomery, all smiles, greets him on the busy beach.

There was very little firing or activity. The weather was brilliant. We drove through our limited but fertile domain in Normandy. It was pleasant to see the prosperity of the countryside. The fields were full of lovely red and white cows basking or parading in the sunshine.* The inhabitants seemed quite buoyant and well nourished and waved enthusiastically. Montgomery's headquarters, about five miles inland, were in a château with lawns and lakes around it. We lunched in a tent looking toward the enemy. The General was in the highest spirits. I asked him how far away was the actual front. He said about three miles. I asked him if he had a continuous line. He said "No."

"What is there then to prevent an incursion of German armor breaking up our luncheon?" He said he did not think they would come.

---

* Churchill remarks to Alanbrooke beside him, "We are surrounded by fat cattle lying in luscious pastures with their paws crossed!"

Waving his walking stick and his cigar, raising his little cap and beaming with unconcealed pleasure, the Prime Minister hastens about the bridgehead among the laboring troops. Everywhere are signs of growing might. Churchill and his party leave on a British destroyer, where the Prime Minister meets an old friend. Admiral Vian is in command of the flotillas protecting the artificial harbor at Arromanches. Churchill seizes his opportunity. It is not difficult to persuade the Admiral to take part in an evening bombardment.

The little destroyer cuts between two battleships thundering away with broadsides, through a cruiser squadron whose firing gongs can be heard as a brazen clamor in the lulls of their cannonade, and closes to within six thousand yards of the wooded shore. Churchill looks at the Admiral. The Admiral issues his orders. The destroyer bears away, looses every gun she has, and departs with all speed. *This is the only time I have ever been on board one of His Majesty's ships when she fired "in anger"—if it can be so called,* Churchill records. Somewhat cast down not to have drawn fire in retaliation, he adds nevertheless, *I slept soundly on the four-hour voyage to Portsmouth. Altogether it had been a most interesting and enjoyable day.*

Back in London, correspondence awaits him. First is a telegram of congratulation from Stalin, to whom Churchill has meticulously reported in detail. It is remarkable for its warmth, if not for its command of the language.

As is evident, the landing, conceived on a grandiose scale, has succeeded completely. My colleagues and I cannot but admit that the history of warfare knows no other like undertaking from the point of view of its scale, its vast conception, and its masterly execution. As is well known, Napoleon in his time failed ignominiously in his plan to force the Channel. The hysterical Hitler, who boasted for two years that he would effect a forcing of the Channel, was unable to make up his mind even to hint at attempting to carry out his threat. Only our Allies have succeeded in realizing with honor the grandiose plan of the forcing of the Channel. History will record this deed as an achievement of the highest order.

To this in explanation Churchill adds the footnote: *The word "grandiose" is the translation from the Russian text which was given me. I think that "majestic" was probably what Stalin meant. At any rate, harmony was complete.*

Everything now depends on the speed of the buildup. At the close of the eleventh day of the operation the Allies have put ashore nearly six hundred thousand men and ninety thousand vehicles. On the twentieth day they can boast a vast host of a million men. But the last battle has yet to be fought. The Germans are hard men and ruthless. The terrain is ideal for defense and evil for attacking troops. Much blood will yet be spilled on the fat fields of Normandy, and it will not all be German.

LIBERATION

You must either conquer and rule or
serve and lose, suffer or triumph, be
the anvil or the hammer.
JOHANN WOLFGANG VON GOETHE: *Der Gross-Cophta*

DUST, a thin and ubiquitous dust, paints every hedgerow a pale brown. Even the sharp spears of grass by the roadside are covered with its gritty film. High banks shelter the road, which winds and twists illogically through hamlets and villages garish with military signs announcing the location of a hundred different units. On each side orchards and open fields alternate; here and there a low farmhouse, curiously Elizabethan with its dark timbers and its lath-and-plaster walls, provides shelter for a tank recovery unit or a workshop.

The orchards are places of cool shade, havens for marching troops. Their grass is cropped by geese. The trunks are gnarled and twisted into anguished shapes, like trees in a bewitched wood. The apples are small and sour, fit only for the thin and smoky cider of Normandy, or for the Calvados applejack for which the region is famous. Some of the troops find this fiery liquor ideal for fueling their spirit stoves.

Others, more bibulous, use it to dispel for a while the realities of war.

Normandy is a rich province, spread with fruitful farms. The butter is yellow with summer, and flavorsome, the cream thick and sweet. Her people are sturdy, thickset and self-sufficient. They are not ungrateful, but on the other hand they are not too enthusiastic about this liberation by such hordes of men and machines. The Germans, after all, were "correct," and could be duped. These newcomers are more demanding. But one can say this (the stolid farmers nod to one another)—they pay well for what they take.

Toward the sea the road is heavy with traffic, day and night, and vast dumps of crates and boxes rear on either side. Trucks and tractors and bulldozers are busy along the road between the beaches and the depots, piling up the supplies that must arm and sustain this great army of liberation. Shambling toward the bustling scene from the south come gray prisoners in single file, lightly guarded. These are exhausted men, smashed by too great a weight of shellfire, their eyes wide and dull, their brains deadened by the shock of battle. Among them, in twos here and there, are a few men of strange appearance: these are Tartars from the southern wastes of Russia, captured on the Eastern Front and pressed into the Wehrmacht to fight at pistol point. Slowly the defeated men wind their way toward the cages that await them atop the ridges that survey the sea. Already the cages are a mass of men, clotted into groups and crowds, all in gray field uniforms save for a small and separate group of a score or so. This group is dressed in black, and is the sum total of SS men who have been captured.

Farther inland, the road's traffic changes its character. It becomes harder, leaner, more warlike. Tanks lie beside the tethered cattle. Here and there an open field is lined with long-barreled medium guns. An ambulance or two comes

racing back toward the tented hospitals near the sea. A mile
or two farther on, the road is given over to jeeps and ugly
armored half-tracks. A little farther still and the traffic ceases,
except for an occasional carrier clanking hurriedly by.

Here all that moves does so at speed, or by stealth, and
always with caution. For this is the battle line. Here the
fields are dotted with little mounds of earth, topped with cut
turf, from which peer grimy and wary faces. This is the
world of the infantry. The road is deserted, except for a body
here and there, cut down by shell fragment or bullet. These
are the casualties, lying grotesquely as if dropped from the
sky, and still, still as abandoned luggage. In the hot sun they
are already beginning to rot.

This is the terminal. The road stretches on, still narrow
and dusty, but somehow featureless. It is going to—nowhere.
It has no use from this point forward. One cannot walk along
it except toward death. No man will approach by it save one
who wishes to die. From here onward the road is dead. Per-
raps eventually it will reach some happy bourn, but here
and now it is a ghost of a road, silent, deserted, uninviting.

This is the country of the *bocage,* a checkerboard of fields
and narrow streams and thick woods. It is deadly country to
fight in because every hedgerow can become a strong-point.
Every road is sunk between high banks; they cannot be used
as approach routes, because troops caught on them cannot
escape when the bullets come whipping down. There is no
choice for the infantry but to advance through the parceled
fields alongside. This is a murderous game, for the line of
march is cut every few hundred yards by a deep bank of
earth flanked with trees and bushes. Each of these is an
ambush.

The Germans dig through the bases of these banks and
flank their machine guns to fire in lines that intersect at the
center of the field. Troops caught in the open have a choice:

they can charge, or they can run away and die. Tanks are useless because the Germans also use bazookas in the hedgerows, and at this range could not miss. For the infantry the panorama of war narrows itself to a single field and a single hedgerow. It is costly ground and hateful.

But by now, in high summer, the bridgehead is long established. The time has come for the breakout. So far everything has happened as Montgomery planned it. The main weight of the German armor, sadly battered on its way to the fighting by strafing aircraft, is deployed against the eastern portion of the Allied perimeter. Canadians and British fight a series of limited actions against it, inching forward, keeping it engaged, pressing hard enough to prevent its moving to the western flank, where the Americans are preparing the vital thrust.

In the east the British and Canadians grind southward for Caen through a Golgotha of bomb craters. In the west the Americans swing up the Cotentin Peninsula and invest Cherbourg. The German garrison, afraid of its fanatic SS commander, holds out for four days. When the Americans finally reach the quayside they find only ruins. The Germans have dynamited every installation, blocked every dock with a tangle of metal and machinery, and sown the wreckage with mines and ingenious booby traps. American engineers begin the delicate task of reopening the port.

As they begin this precarious labor the next phase of the campaign opens. Churchill describes the attack: *The hour of the great American breakout under General Omar Bradley came at last . . . the bombardment by the United States Air Force had been devastating, and infantry assault prospered. Then the armor leaped through and swept on to the key point of Coutances. The German escape route down the coast of Normandy was cut, and the whole German defense west of the Vire was in jeopardy and chaos. The roads were jammed with retreating troops and the Allied bombers and fighter bombers took a destructive toll of men and vehicles.*

General Patton's Third Army sweeps westward across the Breton Peninsula and overruns it. His major effort is a hook to the south and east, aimed at the Seine, and designed to close in the German Seventh Army with a tightening ring of tanks and guns.

Patton treats his divisions like cavalry, leads them with tremendous élan. There is a threatening moment when his flank is struck, on Hitler's personal orders, by a determined group of five Panzer divisions and two infantry divisions at Mortain. But a single, dogged U.S. division halts them dead. Their counterattack a failure, the Germans disengage and withdraw in the direction of Falaise. Patton's forward troops are already far away: they have traveled so fast that they run off their maps and have to signal urgently for new ones showing the unfamiliar terrain in which they find themselves.

Much slower, but against more compact and sterner resistance, the British batter their bloody way down to Falaise. Montgomery arranges one of the set-piece battles that are his chef d'oeuvre, by night south of Caen. The infantry line up between guiding lines of tracer shell, their ears stuffed with cotton wool lest their eardrums be blown in by the bombardment that is about to open. A thousand heavy bombers roar over, their bomb line a mile ahead. When they are done the guns open up like hammers and the infantry drive forward. At dawn the Polish Armored Division is loosed. Its dark-green tanks roll off to seek revenge in the ravaged country about Falaise. The trap is closing.

Churchill is much relieved at these successes. If the German Seventh Army can be destroyed at Falaise, or even badly mauled, the Allies can swing across the Seine and into the Pas de Calais. For this is where the first of Hitler's secret weapons is located. London is under heavy bombardment.

The first of the flying bombs—the V-1s—plummets down in the darkness of June 12/13, 1944, followed two days later by 200 more. They are vicious weapons. Their fastest speed is four hundred miles an hour. They carry a ton of high explosives, and unlike bombers they can fly day and night through the most powerful anti-aircraft guns, and the fastest fighters are hard-pressed to catch them. Moreover, their small size means that the fighters must close in to make sure of a hit; yet a fighter opening up at less than two hundred yards will fly straight into the explosion. Their engines are disagreeably loud, but when they stop the silence is even more ominous, for it means that the bomb is gliding down. The silence invariably lasts seven seconds. When the bombs strike the blast is prodigious, for they explode at ground level.

London, only now beginning to recover from the blitz, finds old wounds reopened. A mood of chilling uncertainty grips the city, for these unmanned missiles are quite impersonal and none can predict their random fall. The strain is continuous and great detonations rumble over miles and miles of streets whatever the hour and whatever the weather.

The defenses are set up along the coast and anti-aircraft guns claim a total of 232 of the intruders. Three thousand reach their target. Six thousand Londoners are killed and eighteen thousand wounded. Many more civilians would have suffered but for the American Eighth Air Force and the RAF, whose heavy bombers blast the launching sites in France and the rocket pads at Peenemünde, where the V-2 is being prepared. On 6 July Churchill reports to the House of Commons: *The total weight of bombs so far dropped by us on flying bomb and rocket targets in France and Germany, including Peenemünde, has now reached about fifty thousand tons,*

*and the number of reconnaissance flights totals many thou-
sands.... Quite a considerable portion of our flying power has
been diverted for months past from other forms of offensive
activity. The Germans for their part have sacrificed a great
deal of manufacturing strength which would have increased
their fighter and bomber forces working with their hard-
pressed armies on every front. ... This invisible battle has
now flashed into the open, and we shall be able, and indeed
obliged, to watch its progress at fairly close quarters.*

He ends on a stern note: *There can be no question of allowing the slightest weakening of the battle in order to
diminish in scale injuries, which, though they may inflict
grievous suffering on many people and change to some extent
the normal life and industry of London, will never stand between the British nation and their duty in the van of a victorious and avenging world. It may be a comfort to some to
feel that they are sharing in no small degree the perils of
our soldiers overseas, and that the blows which fall on them
diminish those which in other forms would have smitten our
fighting men and their allies. But I am sure of one thing, that
London will never be conquered and will never fail, and that
her renown, triumphing over every ordeal, will long shine
among men.*

What buoys up the spirits of the British is the Allied advance in France. There, the decisive thrust across the Channel is about to be supported by an operation in the south,
code-named Anvil, by troops withdrawn from Italy. Unfortunately, the strategic concept is a source of discord. Churchill
notes: *Decisions had now to be taken about our next move in
the Mediterranean and it must be recorded that these occa-
sioned the first important divergence between ourselves and
our American friends.*

•   •   •

The British point of view, conceived and prosecuted by Churchill, is that the thrust at the spine of Italy should continue with all expedition. The most urgent reason is that such a maneuver is likely to draw down from France a greater force of Germans than would a landing in the South of France. The second is the outcome of penetrating political insight, as General Sir Oliver Leese, commander of the Eighth Army in Italy, explains. He is visited by the Prime Minister: "It was fascinating to hear Winston talk. Eventually we spoke of the South of France. I think it had been a bitter blow to him that the Combined Chiefs of Staff in Washington had decided to denude us of so many of our troops and make it impossible for us to break into the mountains. And the more I listened to him talk, the more it became confirmed in my mind that if only we'd been left as we were and I had been allowed to sweep over the plains of Venezia with my five great armored divisions, we would have been able to get into Austria and capture Vienna long before the Russians got there."

For their part, the Americans are determined to attack the entire western frontier of Germany from top to bottom and across the whole breadth of Europe. Preparations for Anvil go ahead. To the very last moment Churchill argues against it. Visiting Normandy in August he tries once more to turn General Eisenhower to his own point of view. The answer is an unequivocal no. Guilefully, Churchill motors to General Bradley's headquarters; though Bradley does not know it, Churchill hopes to convert him, then use his opinion as a lever on the Supreme Commander.

But Bradley is a tricky fish to hook. When Churchill arrives at his headquarters he is in the middle of a battle: "On August 7, about the time when the battle at Mortain was shaping up, Mr. Churchill came to my 12th Army Group command post. After some discussion of the situation he began to ask questions about the invasion that was scheduled to come up in Southern France on August 15. I listened, but didn't comment, and I found out afterward that he had suggested to General Eisenhower that the attack in Southern France be called off and those troops be brought around to the beaches already established in Normandy. I suspect that he came to me hoping that I would be on his side and that he would enlist my aid in getting General Eisenhower to make such a change." Had General Bradley accepted his point, Mr. Churchill would presumably then have gone back to the Supreme Commander, have agreed that the Normandy beachhead could not maintain additional divisions, and suggested that they therefore stay where they were—in Italy.

The military has overcome the political, and Churchill must accept defeat. He does so with grace, wasting no precious energy in striving against the immutable. He hastens away to watch the assault on the French Riviera. At daylight on 15 August he sails in the destroyer *Kimberly*, accompanied by Captain Allen of the Royal Navy, who is charged with the delicate and difficult duty of seeing that the Prime Minister does not land with the assault forces. Every one of *Kimberly's* boats is battened down and firmly secured.

Churchill suspects nothing until later: *Captain Allen . . . was sent by the Admiral to see that we did not get into trouble. We had five hours sailing before we reached the line of battleships bombarding at about fifteen thousand yards. I now learned from Captain Allen that we were not supposed to go beyond the ten-thousand-yard limit for fear of mines. If I had known this when we passed the* Ramillies, *which was firing at intervals, I could have asked for a picket boat and gone ashore. As it was we did not go nearer than about seven thousand yards. Here we saw the long rows of boats filled with American storm troops steaming in continuously to the*

Bay of St. Tropez. As far as I could see or hear not a shot was fired either at the approaching flotillas or on the beaches. The battleships had now stopped firing, as there seemed to be nobody there. We then returned to Ajaccio. . . . On the way back I found a lively novel, Grand Hotel, *in the captain's cabin, and this kept me in good temper till I got back to the Supreme Commander and the Naval Commander-in-Chief, who had passed an equally dull day sitting in the stern cabin.*

Shortly after this pleasant excursion, far to the north the iron jaws close about the Falaise pocket. Along the single road that leads from that ancient town to the Seine every yard bears a testament of death. Fleeing from the threat of encirclement and extinction, German tanks and trucks have been caught by the rockets and machine guns of low-flying Typhoons. Many of them lie belly up by the roadside, ripped open like sardine cans, their crews shredded to pieces inside them. Falaise itself is filled with dead, so many that they have to be shifted by bulldozers to avoid the possibility of epidemic. Every field beside the river contained its quota of horses, turned loose by their German drivers when they reached the water.

For miles before the river every telegraph pole has been cut down to make rafts. On these clumsy craft Germans by the score and by the hundred splash and swim to the far bank and what they hope is safety. The Seine at this point is a gentle stream, but there is a hazard of fire. The British have reached the wooded bluffs that command the river. Setting up medium machine guns, they begin to divide the ill-formed, struggling refugee mass below as an anatomist will dissect a cadaver. They fire until the water in their coolers boils into steam. Rommel's Seventh Army is no more.

*   *   *

Rommel himself is lying in a *Luftwaffe* hospital, slowly recovering from multiple wounds. He has been caught on the open road in his staff car by three Allied fighters looking for prey—anything that moves. The bones of his head fractured and his left eye almost destroyed, he is still unconscious when an amazing plot in which he is implicated comes to light.

Its object is no less than the assassination of Hitler. Though Rommel does not know it, he has been selected by the conspirators as Hitler's successor as leader of the Third Reich. But he does know some details of the plot against the Fuehrer's life. A group of German generals, dismayed by Hitler's megalomania and, more important, anxious to avoid the descent into the abyss to which they are being led and in which Germany will be extinguished, have been arranging his demise by violent means. Their leader is General Ludwig Beck and their instrument a young and brilliant staff officer, Lieutenant Colonel Count Klaus Philip Schenk von Stauffenberg, an officer of the finest lineage and a man of great personal courage.

On 20 July 1944 Hitler calls a conference at the Wolf's Lair in East Prussia which von Stauffenberg must attend as Chief of Staff of the Reserve Army. He arrives carrying a leather brief case. It contains a quantity of plastic explosive attached to a timing device which von Stauffenberg has that moment activated before stepping into the conference room. The Count edges as close to the Fuehrer as he can and casually slides his brief case under the heavy oak table. One of Hitler's generals is briefing the meeting on the latest situation on the Russian Front. Murmuring some excuse, von Stauffenberg quits the room. Another officer, assuming his place, kicks something under the table and shifts it behind a stout bar. A few seconds later the bomb explodes, killing four men and wounding twenty more. Hitler is trapped by a fallen beam: his right arm is paralyzed, his right ear deafened and his legs are scorched. But he is still alive.

He moves to a dreadful revenge, an act as hideous as any perpetrated in the concentration camps, though on a less ambitious scale. The conspirators are hunted down by the Gestapo. Hitler announces, "It is my wish that they be hanged like cattle." He is taken literally. In a bare room in the Plotzensee Prison eight meat hooks are fixed to the ceiling. On them, one by one, stripped naked, are hung the leaders of the plot, to die by slow strangulation. The occasion is filmed to provide Hitler with a record which he watches over and over again.

Rommel is not among these vicitims, being still unconscious in the hospital. But he is suspect, and that is enough. Three months later, convalescing at home, he is visited by two fellow officers, creatures of Hitler. He sees that his house is surrounded by SS behind machine guns. It is suggested that he seek an "honorable course." Joining the two men in their car, Rommel is driven away and is forced to poison himself as soon as he is out of sight of his home. His funeral oration, by personal order of the Fuehrer, is read by Field Marshal Gerd von Rundstedt. It is the final degradation of the Officer Corps and the Junker class.

But a surer hand than the assassin's is deciding Hitler's fate in the west. During August the Allies are drawing closer to Paris. General Patton's Shermans are racing in an arc through the old, beautiful cities of Chartres and Orléans and on 19 August twenty thousand of the maquis within the French capital rise against the uneasy garrison. Once more the barricades are raised. The broad boulevards echo the reverberations of grenades, and narrow alleys crackle with the stutter of machine guns. Cafés become strong-points and salons dressing stations for the wounded.

On orders, Patton stops short of Paris and gallantly hands

the honor of its seizure to a junior commander. It is fitting that the French 2nd Armored Division liberate the city. The Division is commanded by General Philippe Leclerc who three years before had earned his fame by marching with a column from Lake Chad across the Sahara to join the Allies in North Africa.

General Leclerc advances from Rambouillet and on the evening of 24 August the tip of his spearhead reaches the capital. In the gathering dusk his leading tanks, the Cross of Lorraine bright on their iron sides, rumble through Porte d'Italie and grind to a stop on the cobblestones in front of the Hôtel de Ville. Next afternoon the Germans surrender to the somewhat phlegmatic Leclerc, who after his immense journey, merely murmurs, "*Maintenant, ça y est!*" and issues a few brief but precise orders. The tumult breaks out.

Churchill reports the rejoicing: *The city was given over to a rapturous demonstration. German prisoners were spat at, collaborators dragged through the streets, and the liberating troops fêted. On this scene of long-delayed triumph there arrived General de Gaulle. At 5 P.M. he reached the Rue St. Dominique, and set up his headquarters in the Ministry of War. Two hours later, at the Hôtel de Ville, he appeared for the first time as the leader of Free France before the jubilant population. . . . Next afternoon, on August 26, de Gaulle made his formal entry on foot down the Champs Elysées to the Place de la Concorde, and then in a file of cars to Notre Dame. There was one fusillade from the rooftops by hidden collaborators. The crowd scattered, but after a short moment of panic the solemn dedication of the liberation of Paris proceeded to its end.*

The Allies have freed the first of the occupied capitals. But the taking of Paris is more than that. In the tall, withdrawn and difficult figure walking in the front rank of a phalanx of fighting men, the French see the instrument of their rebirth. With Paris liberated, a nation's honor is redeemed and a center of Western civilization rescued from the black grip of a perverted race.

EPISODE **19**

CLANDESTINE COMBAT

A little rebellion now and then
is a good thing.
THOMAS JEFFERSON: *Letter to James Madison*

PRIMLY the confidential secretary sits on the edge of a large wicker basket, his notebook neatly folded, his pencil poised. His spectacles are faintly misted with steam and his attitude is apprehensive, and perhaps disapproving. The ciphers he has written on the page that is now growing soft with damp are fading into blurs. He gazes pensively at the huge bath beside him. From it come occasional sentences and, more rarely, paragraphs of high rhetoric that are punctuated by puffings and bubblings. The confidential secretary peers over the edge of the bath. His Britannic Majesty's First Minister, the Right Honorable Winston Spencer Churchill, has totally submerged.

At length Mr. Churchill clambers reluctantly from the water and is enveloped in a large Turkish towel. Thus costumed in Roman fashion he walks down the White House landing to his bedroom. There he strides about, still declaim-

289

ing. As the vigor of his oratory intensifies, the towel slides off his shoulders, and finally, at some mighty peroration, is discarded altogether. At that moment there is a knock at the door. President Roosevelt is wheeled in. The Prime Minister, pink as the day he was born, turns to face him. "Ah, Mr. President," he beams. "You see, I have nothing to conceal from you!"

The President has come to discuss the draft of the United Nations Pact, completed that morning. It marks the birth of the United Nations and the future world organization they expect to found on the conclusion of the war. But that day is still far away. Many of these United Nations exist as combatants in name only, their exiled governments living on charity, their peoples yoked to the Nazi plow and subjected to a ruthless foreign tyranny. The only warfare possible is clandestine.

Arrangements for waging this secret war are made shortly after Mr. Churchill comes to power and forms his national government of all parties. One of the Labor Party members appointed to high office is Hugh Dalton, son of a former chaplain to Queen Victoria and blessed, like his father, with a stentorian voice. He becomes Minister for Economic Warfare. On one of his spheres of duty, one that seems to have little to do with economics, the Prime Minister is explicit. Mr. Dalton's office will be in charge of all secret operations; he will wage war against the Germans with every underhand means at his disposal. The Prime Minister growls his final instruction: "Set Europe ablaze!"

One of the agencies set up to stimulate this conflagration is the Special Operations Executive, quartered in Norgeby House and Michael House in Baker Street. Its members soon become known by the sobriquet "The Baker Street Irregulars"; they themselves refer to their group as "The Firm."

Their training is painstaking in the extreme. Recruits are

first screened in Baker Street, then given code names and posted to "the school of lost identities," where for ten weeks they are taught to submerge their own personalities in new ones more suited to the tasks they will have to perform. It is a sort of brainwashing, but gently and voluntarily done. Then they proceed to their professional training, usually at a spacious house deep in the country. Here they are taught map reading, survival drill in remote or inhospitable areas, wireless telegraphy, how to handle explosives, and the use and maintenance of various weapons, as well as a few useful criminal arts like forgery, lock picking and one or two confidence tricks. Every moment they are being watched and tested to prove their emotional stability, the swiftness of their reactions and the depth of their discretion.

Those who survive this preliminary course are then sent to the Scottish Highlands to sweat off their spare poundage and learn a few more tricks. For sixteen hours a day they are exercised to the limit of endurance over all kinds of country in all descriptions of weather. They are shown how to kill with the bare hands alone. Then comes parachute training at an airfield near Manchester. The graduation course is held in the New Forest, near the popular summertime resort of Bournemouth: secret codes are learned, proficiency in foreign languages is brought to a peak, cover stories are tested, broken, built up again and tested yet again. Clothes and false papers are issued, and finally the agents are briefed.

Their last few hours in England are spent at Gibraltar Farm, in Bedfordshire, a few miles outside London. By day, laborers plod along its carefully tended fields of kale and beet, or walk through its poultry houses to collect the eggs, or in the evening drive its small herd of cows back to their byre. By night it is transformed. During the hours of darkness Gibraltar Farm operates as the airfield for the Moon Squadron.

This is a Special Duty Squadron of the Royal Air Force, trained and equipped primarily to drop agents and supplies over Occupied Europe. In the four years of its existence the Squadron flies 2,562 sorties, drops 995 agents, 29,000 large containers of arms and ammunition, and 10,000 smaller packages. It loses a total of seventy aircraft in the process.

In March 1942 a second Moon Squadron is formed, intended to perform a different duty. Its aircraft are Lysanders, little artillery spotting planes that can land and take off in a confined space. Its job is to bring agents back. Its commander is a former pilot to the Prince of Wales who subsequently becomes Captain of the King's Flight to King George VI and then Captain of the Queen's Flight.

While all these preparations are afoot, Churchill seeks to encourage the peoples of Europe not to lose heart. *All over Europe,* he says, *races and states whose culture and history made them a part of the general life of Christendom in centuries when the Prussians were no better than a barbarous tribe, and the German Empire no better than an agglomeration of pumpernickel principalities, are now prostrate under the dark, cruel yoke of Hitler and his Nazi gang. Every week his firing parties are busy in a dozen lands. Monday he shoots Dutchmen; Tuesday, Norwegians; Wednesday, French or Belgians stand against the wall; Thursday it is the Czechs who must suffer and fill his repulsive bill of executions.*

He broadcasts from the BBC to the four hundred millions engulfed by the Nazi tide, and for whom the possession of a radio set tuned to London is a capital offense: *Do not despair, brave Norwegians; your land shall be cleansed . . . Be strong in your souls, Czechs; your independence shall be restored. Poles, the heroism of your people, standing up to cruel oppressors, shall not be forgotten. Your country shall live again. Lift up your heads, gallant Frenchmen . . . Stouthearted Dutch, Belgians, Luxemburgers, tormented, mishan-*

*dled, shamefully cast-away people of Yugoslavia, glorious
Greece, yield not an inch! ... Help is coming! Mighty forces
are arming in your behalf. Have faith! Have hope! Deliverance is sure!*

The most active department of the Special Operations Executive is "F" Section, headed by Colonel Maurice Buckmas-
ter. It is responsible for all clandestine operations in France
and for sustaining the resistance movement there. It is purely
British. Another department, "RF" Section, works with de
Gaulle's intelligence and underground network. The first
mission to France is carried out in March 1941. By the beginning of 1942, ten agents a month are being dropped; seventeen sabotage teams are established along the Mediterranean
coast alone.

Among these agents is a pretty young woman who has got
into the game by chance. A Frenchwoman married to an
Englishman, she is living contentedly in the West Country
with her three young daughters when in 1942 the War Office
asks the public for any snapshots they might own of places
on the Continent, particularly of coastal areas. Just before
the war she and her family spent a holiday in Brittany, so
she gathers her photographs and sends them off to London.
They have been dispatched to the wrong address, though it
is some time before she learns this. As a result of this minor
error she is to become one of the most famous women of this
or any war. Her name is Odette.

After a little while Odette is summoned to the War Office.
Puzzled, she keeps her appointment, and after a curious in-
terview returns home. She has been examined by a number
of officers, but her own questions have received no replies.
A few weeks later she is called again. This time she is angry.
But at this second interview the purpose of her interrogators

becomes clear. She is asked whether she would like to serve her country as an agent. Couriers are needed to carry messages between the groups already operating in France, and women are more suitable for the duty because they can move about more freely. At once, though without any real sense of purpose yet, Odette volunteers for this hazardous task.

That sense comes later. At the end of the year she is landed on the coast of France. A curious thing happens as she approaches shore in the darkness. She *smells* her native soil. She knows at once why she is here.

For some months she circulates in the underground resistance. Her commander is Captain Peter Churchill, an experienced agent who is in charge of organizing resistance in southeastern France. Odette is happy and confident. She cannot know that every move is being watched by a German agent, an expert in counterespionage. His name is Heinrich Bleicher. He is a pleasant enough fellow, but utterly devoted to his profession, and ruthless and talented in the execution of his duties. Bleicher does not act at once: he prefers to wait until the whole network is in his grasp. Then he strikes.

Odette and Peter Churchill are arrested together and begin a period of the most intense suffering. Churchill escapes death because his captors mistakenly believe him a nephew of the Prime Minister and thus potentially a valuable hostage. He does nothing to disabuse them of this notion. Odette also avoids extinction.

Soon after her capture she is sentenced to death. She has already been tortured in various ways. The nails of her fingers and toes have been twisted, burned and torn away. Various parts of her body bear scars, almost all of it is blackened by the bruises of incessant beatings. Her teeth have been pulled out. Yet she has not talked. Her appearance belies her strength: she is a small, attractive woman, with a sensuous body. Her large dark eyes are set in a delicate heart-shaped face; it would be gay and smiling if she did not always hold her lips so oddly pressed together.

The Gestapo hold Odette in solitary confinement for twenty-three months. Her tiny cell is perpetually dark and hot as an oven. Her sanity is saved because as a young girl she was blind and so the darkness holds no terrors, and also because she forces her mind to concentrate on the things she loves. In her imagination she sews dresses for her daughters, savoring each stitch. They become so real to her that when eventually she returns to her children she cannot understand why they are not wearing the dresses. She is not afraid of death after the first shock of capture; she learns to accept its presence.

The Germans send her to Ravensbruck concentration camp, and she is still there at the end of the war. At that time the commandant of the camp realizes she is a valuable bargaining instrument and delivers her to the Americans in the hope of saving his own skin. She is flown back to England, dead-white from her imprisonment, wasted with hunger and fever, lamed by the sores on her feet and tormented by an ulcer in her toothless mouth. Her one thought is to get to a dentist.

That is the first thing she says to the SOE people waiting for her at the airport. They drive her to their own very discreet dentist, whose surgery is in fashionable Wimpole Street. Odette is astonished when an elegant young man opens the door; he is the handsomest man she has ever seen. Surely he cannot be a dentist? But he settles her in the chair and examines her mouth. "I believe," he says tentatively, "I believe you have been a prisoner of the Germans?" Odette nods. There is a pause. Then he murmurs, "How very tiresome for a woman!"

"Then," says Odette, "I *knew* I was safe. Only an English-man could have said so little and meant so much."

It is relatively simple to pass agents in and out of France by air, sea or land. In other occupied countries the difficulties are immeasurably greater, yet it is in one of these that the SOE's most daring coup succeeds. This is the execution of one of the top half-dozen leaders of Nazi Germany.

Abandoned by England and France in 1938 and overrun by the Germans without a pitched battle, the Czechs have nevertheless carried on the lonely struggle by means of sabotage and isolated acts of bravery. So stubborn are the Czechs, so dangerous are the flames they are constantly fanning, that in the fall of 1941 Hitler dispatches Reichsprotector Reinhard Heydrich to Prague to quell all insurrection and bring the Czechs to heel. His first action is to clap six thousand people in jail.

Heydrich is a supercilious young man, but talented. He is handsome, blond, tall, a ladies' man. He is intelligent, able and ruthless. From his long narrow face stare eyes that are empty of everything but contempt. A founder-member of the SS, Himmler's heir-apparent, a patron of Dachau, a past-master of torture and mass-murder, he has earned his title. Throughout Europe he is known as "Hangman" Heydrich.

His fate is decided. Six tough young Czechs have been training hard in Scotland for a single purpose. Two of them, Jan Kubis and Joseph Gabcik, are dropped in a little field east of Pilzen on 28 December 1941. They are soon in touch with the regular underground. For four months the two executioners make their plans, watching Heydrich's every move, observing every moment of his daily routine. On 27 May they cycle to the village of Brezany, a few miles outside Prague, lean their bicycles against a streetcar stop and stand idly at the corner of the street. As they have calculated, Heydrich approaches in an open Mercedes Benz. The car rounds the curve and Gabcik presses the trigger of his submachine gun. It jams. Kubis throws a heavy grenade into the car and it is blasted off the road.

For eight days Heydrich lingers at the threshold of death. When he slips over it the Germans begin their reprisals. Not least of these is the annihilation of Lidice. A village of twelve hundred people, it is to become a symbol of martyrdom. At dawn on 10 June the SS close it off from the world. All the men of the village are shot in batches of ten. The women are loaded into trucks and driven away to concentration camps. The children are scattered anonymously to foster homes all over Germany. Then the village is razed with dynamite and set afire. By the next morning Lidice is level with the ground.

Heydrich's evil body has lain in state in its dapper black uniform for four days while the hunt for his killers intensifies. On 18 June Gabcik and Kubis and a tiny party of men of the resistance are run to earth in the crypt beneath the Church of Saints Cyril and Methodius. The German garrison of Prague tries to drive them out with firearms and grenades. When these fail they mobilize the fire service to pump in water. By nightfall the heroic handful are dead.

All over Europe the flame is kindled by such men, and begins to roar. One of the first to nourish it in Yugoslavia is Brigadier Fitzroy Maclean, who is sent as Churchill's personal envoy to a shadowy figure. Soon conquered by Hitler's invasion in the spring of 1941, the Yugoslavs have now settled upon guerrilla warfare as their only means of carrying on the fight. Their first leader is General Mihailović, whose followers are known as *Chetniks*. He struggles on for a while in the mountains, but then begins to lose the initiative, and even to come to terms with some of the German and Italian troops of occupation.

Into this void now steps Tito. It is to Tito that Fitzroy Maclean flies one moonlit night. Dangling on the end of his parachute over an extremely inhospitable bit of countryside, Maclean has time to reflect on the delicacy of his mission. As yet no one knows who or what Tito might be. Some say it is a committee, others that it is a man of singular ferocity and sullenness of disposition. Yet others believe Tito to be a young woman of incomparable beauty and generosity. Maclean considers this latter conjecture the least probable.

Tito's nature is soon clear, however. His battle against the Germans in the barren highlands of Yugoslavia is among the most savage and successful in Europe. Churchill describes it: *A wild and furious war for existence against the Germans broke into flame among the partisans. Among these Tito stood forth, pre-eminent and soon dominant. Tito, as he called himself, was a Soviet-trained Communist who, until Russia was invaded by Hitler, and after Yugoslavia had been assailed, had fomented political strikes along the Dalmatian coast, in accordance with the general Comintern policy. But once he united in his breast and brain his Communist doctrine with his burning ardor for his native land in her extreme torment, he became a leader, with adherents who had little to lose but their lives, who were ready to die, and if to die to kill. This confronted the Germans with a problem which could not be solved by the mass executions of notables or persons of substance. They found themselves confronted by desperate men who had to be hunted down in their lairs. The partisans under Tito wrested weapons from German hands. They grew rapidly in numbers. No reprisals, however bloody, upon hostages or villages deterred them. For them it was death or freedom. Soon they began to inflict heavy injury upon the Germans and became masters of wide regions.*

The cost is high. Yugoslavia's casualties at the end of the war represent 30 per cent of the grand total of the Allies' losses. She loses 1,706,000 killed, and 3,741,000 people are sent to concentration camps. The damage to land and property is assessed at forty-seven billion dollars. Of all the Allies only Russia and Poland sustain more grievous hurt.

After 1939 Poland becomes a wasteland. *The atrocities committed by Hitler upon the Poles,* Churchill declares, *exceed in severity and in scale the villainies perpetrated by Hitler in any other conquered land.* Poland becomes part of that empire in the east which Germany will first wipe clean of her native population, then fill with lusty young members of the Master Race and so absorb it into the Fatherland. The Germans announce, "We do not admit the right of Poles to life in any form." Through the years of occupation six million Poles are exterminated. A few die gallantly in the opening battles of the war, and some under the torrent of bombs that herald the first blitzkrieg of all. But in the first year of occupation the total of men, women and children slain by the Germans is five times that of the onslaught of 1939. By 1944 only a few hundred thousand out of Poland's population of four and a half million Jews (the largest in Europe) are left alive.

Jews and Gentiles alike are killed like cattle by the *Einsatzgruppen* of the SD. Auschwitz, Treblinka, Oswiecim consume their quotas of flesh and blood. People disappear—families at a time, by the score, by the hundred, sometimes entire populations of villages at once. And still the Poles can fight.

The Polish underground is organized like an army. In fact, it is called The Polish Home Army. Its commander is General Bor Komorowski. By 1944 its strength stands at 280,000 men, armed by the British from the air in 488 sorties. In July of

that year General Bor is alerted to proclaim a general insurrection when he judges the time has come. The Russians are
advancing, and Warsaw could be liberated from within to
coincide with their arrival. As the Russians approach the
Vistula, Bor issues an Order of the Day:

Soldiers of the Capital!
Today I have issued the order so long awaited by all of you,
the order for an open fight against the German invader. After
nearly five years of unceasing underground struggle, today you are
taking up arms openly to restore the freedom of our country and
to punish the German criminals for the terror and bestialities they
have committed within our frontiers.

All over Warsaw at five o'clock that afternoon the Poles
open fire. A hundred streets become battlefields. Caught un-
awares, the Germans are cut down by the score and the Poles
seize their weapons. But the German reaction is swift: three
fresh divisions are moved into the capital to reinforce the
five already there. By now the Russians are swarming on the
far bank of the Vistula and their planes are patrolling
the sky above Warsaw. The Poles can hear the thudding of
the Russian artillery. They believe that help is near. But soon
after the Warsaw Rising begins, all signs of aid from the east
vanish and the front along the river falls into silence. The
population of Warsaw has been left to fight alone: they cannot even be supplied in any quantity from the air, for Stalin
will not allow American or British planes to operate from
his bases.

German pressure tightens street by street. *The battle
raged literally underground,* Churchill records. *The only
means of communication held by the Poles lay through the
sewers. . . . Battles developed in pitch-darkness between men
waist-deep in excrement, fighting hand to hand at times with
knives, or drowning their opponents in the slime.* In their
agony the women of Warsaw beseech the Pope to bless them,
as if taking the last rites. The radio station broadcasts a mes-

sage of farewell: "Your heroes are the soldiers whose only weapons against tanks, planes and guns were their revolvers and bottles filled with petrol. Your heroes are the women who tended the wounded and carried messages under fire, who cooked in bombed and ruined cellars to feed children and adults, and who soothed and comforted the dying. Your heroes are the children who went on quietly playing among the smoldering ruins. These are the people of Warsaw."

On 13 September American planes are allowed to use the Poltava airfield, and Fortresses drop supplies over Warsaw. Next day the Russians resume their advance. It is all too late. On 3 October General Bor signals to London "Having exhausted all means of fighting . . . Warsaw has fallen on the sixty-third day of the heroic struggle against crushing odds." One quarter of her million inhabitants are dead among the ruins. Of the remainder, half are deported to slavery or death in Germany within days of the capitulation. *When the Russians entered the city three months later,* Churchill records, *they found little but shattered streets and the unburied dead. Such was their liberation of Poland, where now they rule.*

AIRBORNE
ARMY

*We will now discuss in a little more
detail the struggle for existence.*
CHARLES DARWIN: *The Origin of Species*

IN HER wartime drab, the brave scarlet of her three smoke-stacks obscured by a hideous coat of neutral buff, her tall sides patched and mottled and her gleaming white super-structure camouflaged in the interests of self-protection, the great ship looks more like a monster tramp than a queen of the ocean. Yet that is normally her claim.

Taking the pleasant summer air on his favorite deck, for-ward of the wide curved window of his dining room, sits an informal figure. He has just lunched most excellently on one of his favorite dishes, which the ship's First Chef prepares with surpassing skill. It has been served as he wishes it—that is, at his elbow in the iron casserole in which it has been cooked. There is nothing, Churchill reflects, quite as deli-cious as Irish stew as they make it on the *Queen Mary.*

High above him a V of aircraft approaches, followed by another, and another. Reclining at his ease, Churchill counts them. There are sixty-five in all. As they dive in salute, screaming in formation over *Queen Mary*'s beam, he notices they are fighters. Churchill is moved. They have been dispatched by a passing aircraft carrier to greet him on his voyage to Halifax for the great conference at Quebec. He remembers that not so very long ago the sight of so many aircraft in the sky would have been ominous.

Now there are other worries. He has spent a good deal of the summer smelling powder in France and Italy; he has heard the thunder of the attack beating at his ears. Now he must turn to politics. Victory is in sight. What now must be done about the world that will emerge from all this devastation?

Two matters are uppermost in Churchill's thoughts, each an anxious problem. The first concerns his closest ally: *What I feared most at this stage of the war was that the United States would say in after years, "We came to your help in Europe and you left us alone to finish off Japan." We had to regain on the field of battle our rightful possessions in the Far East, and not have them handed back to us at the peace table.* The second, a more enigmatic ally: *Another matter lay heavy on my mind. I was very anxious to forestall the Russians in certain areas of Central Europe. The Hungarians, for instance, had expressed their intention of resisting the Soviet advance, but would surrender to a British force if it could arrive in time.*

On 10 September 1944 Churchill reaches Quebec, where Roosevelt is waiting at the station, and is soon established at the Citadel. At their first meeting Churchill summarizes the latest developments in the war: *Everything we had touched had turned to gold, and during the last seven weeks there had been an unbroken run of military success.* He offers the British main fleet, no small instrument of war, to serve in the Pacific under American command. Admiral King gruffly turns it down, but the President overrides him. Churchill adds a force of the RAF's heavy bombers and between six and twelve divisions to supplement the sixteen already fighting in Southeast Asia. *Our key word,* he concludes, *should be to engage the largest number of our own forces against the largest number of the enemy at the earliest possible moment.*

In this amicable fashion the discussions continue. Until one day the talk turns to the treatment of Germany after the war. The President has brought with him Henry Morgenthau, Secretary of the Treasury, whom Churchill is rather surprised to see. The two American leaders begin to expound the Morgenthau Plan. Its thesis is that since Germany's military power rests on her industrial strength, her factories and plants should be broken and removed. Germany would then be transformed into an agricultural—and tractable—community. Churchill is appalled: the idea is not only questionable ethically, it is patently impracticable. But he must at least promise to consider it for the sake of his debt to the United States. He is much relieved when the British War Cabinet later rejects it out of hand.

The second Quebec Conference ends with a report from the Combined Chiefs of Staff. It approves General Eisenhower's plans for breeching the Siegfried Line and seizing crossings over the Rhine. (The Supreme Commander has now taken personal control of the campaign, as of 1 September, with Montgomery and Bradley as his lieutenants.) Following the capture of Antwerp and Rotterdam the report favors the northern line of approach into Germany and hopes for it before bad weather sets in. It recommends doing nothing against the German forces left in the Balkans, since it seems likely they will soon be marooned anyhow, and in any case there are no forces available to send against them. Thus doubly rational, it concludes with the prediction, for plan-

In September 1944, the Allies drive north across Belgium and west through Luxembourg toward Germany's natural barrier—the Rhine River. On September 17, in a bold attempt to cross the lower Rhine, airborne troops are dropped at Nijmegen and Arnhem to seize bridge-heads behind the German lines. Nijmegen is taken but the Arnhem paratroopers are cut off and forced to struggle back to the Allied lines with heavy losses. The Rhine is finally crossed on March 7, 1945 by the U.S. First Army, which captures the Remagen railway bridge intact.

ning purposes, that Japan will fall eighteen months after
the defeat of Germany.

Next day, a Sunday, Churchill and his wife and daughter
leave Quebec by train for Hyde Park and a few pleasant
hours with the Roosevelts. It is Sunday, 17 September. Their
train rumbles through peaceful whistle stops, across quiet
farmland. Over other fields far away, more hazardous, are
blossoming a thousand parachutes. Operation *Market Garden* has begun.

In Europe the campaign has begun to develop its awful
strength in full. By the time of Churchill's embarkation for
Canada, Patton's vigorous Third Army, already thick with
battle honors, has crossed the Meuse. On 5 September they
take Nancy and ready themselves to cross the Moselle between that city and Metz. General Devers' southern group
of armies, driving up from the Riviera, joins hands with them
west of Dijon six days later. On 13 September General
Hodges' First Army reaches Patton's left at Aachen on the
edge of the Siegfried Line.

This is exactly the situation in which the Supreme Commander delights. Everybody is fighting hard, all along the
front, all the time. But German resistance, pressed back into
the sacred Fatherland, is beginning to stiffen. The Allies
have supply problems. A greater weight of shell is needed to
smash the Wehrmacht out of its grimly held defenses; the
stream of reinforcements makes extra mouths; more supplies
mean more trucks, more gasoline. The shortage spirals. A
major port is needed, and fast.

To the north Montgomery's armies have entered Antwerp.
But the installations have been dynamited and the ap-
proaches to the port are still commanded by eager German
gunners who command every inch of the Scheldt estuary.
Moreover, Montgomery's grip on the port is none too secure.
He wishes uneasily that he had stronger defenses between

Antwerp and the German border. A counterattack in force could make things very sticky.

Between Montgomery and his Supreme Commander there now arises a difference of opinion. Montgomery wants a single massive thrust with all concentrated power at the heart of the Ruhr. He believes it will be mortal, that it can end the war in the winter of 1944. Eisenhower will not shift from his concept. He wants a broad front and continual attack in every sector. The difference is solved only when the Supreme Commander issues an order. Still dissenting, Montgomery obeys.

One outcome of the controversy and this complex situation is Operation Market Garden, a by-product of Montgomery's main plan. He thinks he can seize a bridgehead over the Rhine at Arnhem. Eisenhower agrees, and gives the venture priority over clearing the Scheldt estuary. The design is to launch a massive air-borne drop ahead of the British XXXth Corps, now fighting in a murderous salient across the Meuse-Escant Canal on the Dutch border. Montgomery's 21st Army Group can then follow through and burst across the Rhine.

Apart from its tactical advantage, the operation will bear a second fruit. During late summer the first of the enormous V-2s has fallen on London. At first this new hazard is kept secret and the huge detonations are referred to officially as exploding gas mains. But now they are hurtling down upon wounded London with increasing regularity. A good hard blow to the north will clear at least some of the rocket bases.

The plan involves a whole air-borne army, waiting in England and anxious to come to grips while there is still an enemy left. Well-trained, experienced, they are exceedingly battleworthy. The spearhead will be the British 1st Airborne Division with the Polish Airborne Brigade in support. Dropping on the north bank of the lower Rhine, they will seize the little town of Arnhem and its vital bridge. Behind them

the American 82nd Airborne Division will land on Nijmegen
and Grave and secure the two bridges there. Between them
and the ground forces, the American 101st Airborne Division
will fall upon Eindhoven and clear the main road for the
general advance that will follow. Led by the Guards Armored Division, XXXth Corps will then break out of its
bridgehead, force through to Eindhoven, and sweep on to
the relief of the paratroopers and their captured bridges.

There is one snag to this bold idea. Even the Allies cannot
produce the number of aircraft needed for a simultaneous
drop. The operation must be spread over three days, with
a consequent dilution of its force. The necessity for speed on
the part of XXXth Corps becomes more vital.

The limiting factor is accepted. Just after dawn on 17
September the leading elements of the three divisions float
down onto their landing zones, mark them, establish their
perimeters, and wait for the gliders and the succeeding
waves. Southward they can hear the opening barrage of
XXXth Corps.

With Typhoons scoring the roads ahead with rockets the
Guards Armored Division's tanks lance out of the bridgehead, with two more corps behind them to push out the
flanks. The Germans fight like men possessed. It takes the
Guards twenty-four hours to reach the outlying paratroops of
101st Airborne Division. The Americans have just captured
Eindhoven, having been delayed by a blown bridge, by
means of a desperate charge.

South of the town there is now a salient. It is far too narrow for safety. Next day the Germans counterattack with
fury. The salient's only feature is a single road bordered by
pine woods. Forming up under this convenient cover the
enemy are able to attack repeatedly and still achieve surprise. Again and again the road is cut. It is jammed with
soft-skinned supply vehicles and troop carriers nose to tail.

At times this transport comes under such a weight of fire from 88s and heavy mortars that the drivers must leave their trucks in bottom gear, climb down and walk in the ditch, jumping up now and then to adjust the wheel. The column crawls at a snail's pace.

Sudden forays by marauding tanks halt the entire convoy. Trucks are set on fire and shattered by armor-piercing shot. As the day wears on a few Tiger tanks appear, cruise up and down the column, arrogant and invulnerable, and turn havoc into chaos. Again and again the paratroops attack in an attempt to keep the salient open. They succeed, but they cannot win time.

On the morning of 19 September 1944 the Guards set out for Grave and 82nd Airborne Division. The Americans have taken the bridge at Grave, but possession of the one at Nijmegen is still a matter of dispute. Next day Americans and British attack shoulder to shoulder. The air-borne troops cross the river west of Nijmegen (in itself a feat of arms), swing right and capture the far end of the railway bridge. The Grenadiers, point regiment of the Guards Armored Division, charge like cavalry across the road bridge, annihilate its defenders in minutes and storm down the far ramp. Their rush has been so sudden that the Germans have not even had time to fire their demolition charges.

Success begins to glimmer. Only a few miles of dead-flat land between the Rhine proper and the lower Rhine separate the troops at Nijmegen from their friends in Arnhem. If only the main body would come up. But the main body is toiling far behind along its devastated road.

In Arnhem things are not going too well. At first it seemed as though it could not fail. Stanley Maxted, a BBC War Correspondent, flies in by glider with the first wave on that fateful morning: "The side door slid up and I jumped, landing in soft ground among young turnips. I started to run.

Looking up, I saw another fleet of planes without gliders. Wisps of something started to stream from them and suddenly the sky blossomed into many-colored flowers that tilted downward, tiny dolls of men swinging below them. Four times it happened. Our team was back unloading the vehicles from the gliders. I ran back to help. Everyone knew what they were doing but me, but I waded in anyway. Meantime, machine-gun and rifle fire seemed to be all around. I didn't know where from, or who was being fired on, and there was no time to find out. Air-borne troops don't fool, they don't wait, they're trouble-hunters."

The German Area Commander is at his breakfast, enjoying his cup of excellent coffee, when the drone of what is unmistakably an armada of aircraft begins to reverberate through the tall windows of his stately residence. Somewhat at a loss the General crosses to the window, wiping his lips as he walks with a fine linen napkin. Then, before his very eyes, a white mushroom floats down in an adjacent field. Dropping his napkin, and not delaying to seize his cap, he dashes out, bellowing for his car. The General has had a nasty shock.

It is nothing, however, to the shock the paratroops are about to get. Brigadier Hicks, commander of the Air Landing Brigade, explains it: "What we didn't know was that there were two Panzer Divisions refitting in the Arnhem area. They were alerted straightaway and they reacted quickly. By the time the 1st Parachute Brigade got to the outskirts of Arnhem they were in touch with tanks, self-propelled guns and armored cars, and heavy fighting developed." One of the divisions is at full strength and completely ready for battle; it has only been held in the town by coincidence. The other is only a little less powerful. Both belong to the SS, both have been mauled in Normandy, and both are lusting for revenge. They attack with speed and ferocity. They are certain they can crush the lightly armed paratroops in a matter of hours.

But little parties of air-borne men occupy scattered groups of buildings and hold off all comers, supported and comforted by Arnhem's gallant citizens. A forward group has managed to close in to the approaches of the bridge, but is too weak to take it. These pockets of men, out of touch with their headquarters most of the time, are still resilient enough to hang on to their game as long as is necessary.

Their friends are still far away, except for those now fighting for Nijmegen. The main body is finding it a hard road, for a reason which R. M. Wingfield describes with grim humor: "We slowed down to a stop and the wireless crackled. The tank commander stuck his head out—'Royal Tiger Tanks a mile ahead. Get under cover. Planes have been called.' His calm words were immediately drowned by the scream of aircraft engines as our Typhoon fighter 'cab-rank' peeled off from their constant circling above our heads. They skimmed overhead, steadied themselves by the huge bulk of the Philips works and let fly with their rockets. They banked and let fly again. The projectiles, like foreshortened lamp-posts with plumes of smoke bursting from the back, vanished behind the works. Seconds later came a dull explosion and a dirty plume of black smoke jetted up. A black object sailed lazily upward and disappeared into the smoke. It was a tank turret, complete with gun. Our tank commander swallowed hard. We moved on."

In Arnhem the German ring is tightening. Through their stubble the faces of the paratroops are grimy and drawn, blackened by the smoke of their guns. But their eyes are still calm and confident. They have received no supplies for a couple of days. The weather is too bad to fly them in. They solve their ammunition problem by using German weapons, with which they are very pleased. They take shelter below ground, popping up now and then to see that the Germans do not come too close. They are beginning to feel very hungry. General Urquhart, the Division's commander, finds food scarce. "In the cellar of the Hartenstein, the sergeant-major was going round with a mess tin. He had appointed himself guardian of the rations for the duration and was making absolutely sure that there was a fair and equal distribution of whatever was going. When he reached me, he said, 'Two this time, sir.' I collected my ration of two boiled sweets."

At the end of the seventh day of siege, without sign of rescue or relief, General Urquhart sends a still unruffled signal to Montgomery, setting out his condition: "Must warn you unless physical contact is made with us early 25 September consider it unlikely we can hold out long enough. All ranks now exhausted. Lack of rations, water, ammunition and weapons with high officer casualty rate. . . . Even slight enemy offensive action may cause complete disintegration. If this happens all will be ordered toward bridgehead if anything rather than surrender. Any movement at present in face of enemy is not possible. Have attempted our best and will do so as long as possible." The message does not mention the fact that the Division now has two thousand wounded and no medical supplies.

Montgomery orders a withdrawal the next night. The river runs deep and fast here between banks thirty feet high, forming a trying obstacle even to well-rested men. In the darkness the paratroops begin to scramble down into the icy water. That night, and for a few following, they dribble back in stolen boats or on improvised rafts; some by a miracle swim across. At last a total of 2,400 of the original 10,000 are recovered. All their battalion commanders but one have been lost, and only three senior officers remain. Neither a victory nor a defeat, the eight-day Battle of Arnhem has made honor for their names.

The Germans make determined counterattacks in an attempt to recover Nijmegen. The bridge itself is bombed and damaged, but not destroyed. Frogmen with high explosives swim downstream, but are discovered in the darkness as they are struggling with numbed fingers to attach their demolition charges to its piers. By day the bridge is under direct observation, and batteries of 88s upriver snipe at anything that moves across it. Trucks and jeeps heading for the front line near Arnhem are forced to run the gauntlet. They are warned at the southern approach by an enormous sign that admonishes them, somewhat redundantly: FAST ACROSS THE BRIDGE. Hurtling over at top speed they are greeted at the other end by a much smaller notice. It says simply—JESUS SAVES.

With Arnhem unachieved, the main effort turns to the Scheldt estuary. The task falls to the Canadians, and it is not an easy one. The Germans are well placed on a series of islands. They are experienced and tough, and they are cornered. The Canadians have to fight waist-deep in water, without a scrap of cover. It is cruel work. By the end of October they have captured 12,500 Germans, few of whom were in the least anxious to surrender. Their last obstacle is the island of Walcheren, which they take after a vicious battle. They have freed the port of Antwerp.

Though greatly comforted by these successes, Churchill is worried by a threat that only he can at the moment see. The Russian juggernaut is beginning to gather speed. *The Russian armies,* he says, *were now pressing heavily upon the Balkan scene, and Rumania and Bulgaria were in their power. As the victory of the Grand Alliance became only a matter of time it was natural that Russian ambitions should grow. Communism raised its head behind the thundering*

Russian battlefront. Russia was the Deliverer, and Communism the gospel she brought. He feels it is time for a personal meeting with Stalin. The Marshal responds with a warm invitation to Moscow.

Flying via Naples, Cairo and the Crimea, he descends on Moscow on 8 October 1944. At the airport, Churchill makes an optimistic speech: *I come here on a tide of hope, on a tide of assurance that victory will be won. . . . And of hope that when it is won we shall all of us make the world a better place for the great masses of human beings to live in.*

At ten o'clock the next morning Churchill and Stalin hold their first conference. The Prime Minister comes to the main point. What shall be done about the proportion of influence in the Balkans? While his preamble is being translated he scribbles on a half-sheet of paper a rough design:

Rumania	
Russia	90%
The others	10%
Greece	
Great Britain	90%
(In accord with the U.S.A.)	
Russia	10%
Yugoslavia	50%–50%
Hungary	50%–50%
Bulgaria	
Russia	75%
The others	25%

He pushes the paper across the polished table. Stalin stares at it without expression, but then with a blue pencil endorses it with a large tick. *After this,* Churchill records, *there was a long silence. The penciled paper lay in the center of the table. At length I said, "Might it not be thought rather cynical if it seemed we had disposed of these issues, so fate-*

ful to millions of people, in such an offhand manner? Let us burn the paper." "No, you keep it," said Stalin.

Part way through these cordial discussions Churchill develops a high temperature and must take to his bed. He lies propped up by pillows, with a black velvet bandage placed lightly across his eyes, listening to Elizabeth Nel, his secretary, reading a Russian book. It is entitled *A Primer of the Coming World* and deals, so far as Miss Nel can make out, with the guilt capitalism must accept for causing wars. Churchill alternately urges her to speed up or slow down. With this as the sole entertainment his convalescence is not long delayed. He recovers in twenty-four hours.

The British party is entertained one evening at a Command Performance of the Bolshoi. It consists of the first act of *Giselle*, some opera, and songs and dances of the Red Army. Standing together in their box, all rich red and gold, the two leaders smilingly shake hands. The audience clap their hands and cheer wildly at this. It is Stalin's first public appearance of this kind since the outbreak of war.

Afterward there is an intimate party, which Field Marshal Alanbrooke attends: "The ballet lasted about an hour. It was perfectly lovely as usual. Then we withdrew to a small antechamber behind the box, where a banquet was laid out. It lasted approximately an hour, with the usual many speeches. Stalin got up very soon after we arrived and proposed the health of Maisky, who had been Ambassador in London. Maisky was sitting on my right. This toast to Maisky was received with wonderful applause and laughter by the audience. Unfortunately it was one of the few toasts that were not translated into English. So when finally we had drunk the toast and Maisky sat down alongside me, I turned to him and said, 'Well, what's the joke?' He hadn't been laughing very much at it himself, as a matter of fact. He said, 'The joke is that the Marshal referred to me as the poet-diplomat, because I wrote some poetry when I was Ambassador in London. But that's not the joke, that's not the joke. The joke is that the last poet-diplomat was liquidated.' "

From Churchill's point of view the series of meetings has been highly successful. He sums up: *There is no doubt that in our narrow circle we talked with an ease, freedom and cordiality never before attained between our two countries. Stalin made several expressions of personal regard which I feel sure were sincere. But I said to my colleagues at home, "Behind the horseman sits black care."*

The Prime Minister's next mission is to France, where he arrives on 10 November, and is conducted in state to the Quai d'Orsay. *The building had long been occupied by the Germans,* he notes, *and I was assured I should sleep in the same bed and use the same bathroom as had Goering.*

At eleven o'clock the next morning, Armistice Day, very dapper in the blue uniform of an Air Commodore, Churchill drives with General de Gaulle through the Place de la Concorde and down the cheering Champs Elysées to the Arc de Triomphe. A single gun booms out and silence falls. Another, and they lay their dark wreaths on the tomb of the Unknown Warrior, where a small flame of memory burns eternally. Later, Churchill lays another wreath on the base of the statue of the Old Tiger Clemenceau, his idol, whom he thinks of always with respect and deep affection.

He visits the French Army fighting in deep snow near Besançon, then goes on to General Eisenhower's headquarters.

Thanksgiving Day arrives, the last, as everyone hopes, of the war. Churchill celebrates it with his American friends and toasts the future in a mood of hope. *We are moving forward in this struggle which spreads over the lands and all the oceans. We are moving forward surely, steadily, irresistibly, and perhaps, with God's aid, swiftly, toward vic-*

torious peace. This is a subject for profound thanksgiving. There is a greater Thanksgiving Day which still shines ahead, which beckons the bold and loyal and warmhearted, and that is when this union of action which has been forced upon us by our common hatred of tyranny, which we have maintained during these dark and fearful days, shall become a lasting union of sympathy and good feeling and loyalty and hope. Then, indeed, there will be a Day of Thanksgiving, and one in which all the world will share.

THE LAST
CHRISTMAS

Times go by turns, and chances change by course,
From foul to fair, from better hap to worse.
ROBERT SOUTHWELL: *Times Go By Turns*

SWEETLY down broad corridors echo the voices of children singing in unison. The bare brick walls turn and intersect on a complicated and depressing geometry. But the pleasant melodies eddy clearly through their ramifications, coming now from this direction, now from that. The cold, scrubbed formality of the place is softened by this gentle benediction of music. The clear voices sing of dignity and joy. Lilting, delicate, pure as spring water, they fill the austere air with innocence.

All through the rambling building the children walk in a demure procession, passing from time to time a niche from which the faces of saints and martyrs gaze in holy calm. Coming at last to a great double door the children form into a group, shepherded and fussed over by the nuns in charge of them. They begin the slow, majestic national hymn of Holland, "A Prince of Orange . . ." Ponderously the doors

317

swing open. The babel inside is stilled. The sweet sound of the choir rises through the hall, changing now into a Latin carol to the glory of the newborn Christ.

There is a pause. The nuns bend toward each other, whispering. When they look up they are smiling. At their signal the children burst out into a rousing tune. This time they are singing in English, beaming with pleasure at their own proficiency in this outlandish tongue. There is a rustle of recognition from the men crowding the hall. "God rest you merry, gentlemen," carol the children. "Let nothing you dismay . . ." When they come merrily to an end they are wildly applauded. A sergeant major steps forward, gestures to the nuns, and leads the diminutive choir into the hall. They are lost at once in a horde of grinning, shouting soldiers. They are the guests of a battalion of infantry at their traditional Christmas Day dinner. For once, in this wilderness of war, the children of the convent of 's Hertogenbosch will be well fed.

For a few hours no one thinks of the battle. Many of the men are glad to have an excuse to forget. For they have seen a hideous thing in the pine woods outside the town. There, in a great clearing, they have encountered for the first time the full evidence of Nazi bestiality. Coming away from the route that runs northward from the town is a narrower road that cuts through tall stands of fir and pine, dark green and wintry and silent. To one side there suddenly appears an iron gate guarded by a sentry post from which march high fences of wire and steel.

The first building inside the encampment is a stark barracks, smart with paint and clean as a hospital. It is built about a gigantic dining hall with one broad wall decorated with an astonishing mural. Its theme is victory and the triumph of youth. But there is something more, a deeper meaning. At its center stands a young athlete, head raised, blond hair streaming, a demigod bathed in the full light of day and grasping with an appalling certainty at the future. Slightly behind him, touched equally with this strange divinity, stands his young and wholesome mate. She too is blonde. But their purity is flawed, like Lucifer's before the Fall. For theirs is a spurious godhead, and what lies beyond the wall makes it a mockery.

This is the dining room of the SS guards of a concentration camp. The hall and the rest of the barracks are airy, light, hygienic. And they represent, perverted as they are, the last remnant of civilization in the camp. The next construction past the barracks is a gallows. Equipped with an iron pulley slung from a heavy beam, it is a sturdy instrument, built to last. Beside it, conveniently placed, is a small furnace. Its doors are open now, its iron sides cold. Ashes lie beneath it, and a few pieces of calcined bone. Nothing human.

The Allied troops who first came to this camp could not imagine what had happened there. The sickening evidence they found pointed to nothing within their experience or imagination. But when the full meaning of that Aryan mural and these degraded remains bore down upon them they closed the accounts with bullets, quickly and in anger, as though they could, by dispatching thus mercifully a few young Nazis, expunge the memory of a nation's sin.

So now, in the convent, they make much of the little Dutch children, calling for more turkey, deluging them with chocolates and miraculous pungent orbs some of the children have never seen before, except in picture books—oranges. As is the custom, the troops are served by their officers, and make the most of it. Now and then, licensed for a day, they call out familiarly to their colonel, who is at pains to give as good as he gets. He stands at the door, watching with wise eyes these men who have fought so hard and so long from the golden fields of Normandy to the dank meadows of Holland.

His adjutant walks in from an office down the corridor, a message in his hand. The colonel can read the message's contents from the younger man's eyes. Almost reluctantly he takes the paper. Those nearest him fall silent, and quite suddenly the room is hushed, waiting. The colonel looks up. "We have half an hour to finish our dinner," he announces quietly. "I have a message from the General. The Americans are surrounded in Bastogne. We are to go down to help them. We shall be ready to move off in two hours."

As he turns away the men are already concentrating on their food. "Cor!" says a stocky little lance corporal, inspecting the remains of a turkey leg. "Bloody Yanks. Trust them." He finishes his meal at top speed and gets up. He is ready. The last time he saw the Americans they were outside Nijmegen; they gave him a pair of GI gloves and thus became his lifelong friends, though he would die rather than admit it.

Inside white-clad Bastogne, General Anthony McAuliffe is not in the least worried. He has been touring his snowy perimeter all morning as usual, and his men are in great spirits. He has become famous, though he is not yet aware of it, as the author of a classic message.

Three days before, as the General tells it, "Four German emissaries with a great white sheet on a stick approached our lines in the south. There was a lull in the battle. Well, our people blindfolded these fellows and took them to the command post of Colonel Harper. There the Germans delivered an envelope which Colonel Harper brought to me at my command post inside the town."

The envelope is inscribed "To the U.S.A. Commander of

the encircled town of Bastogne" and is dated 22 December
1944. Somewhat distracted, General McAuliffe opens it and,
still thinking about the dispositions of his men, begins to read.
He wonders vaguely why Colonel Harper should be writing
him a letter at a time like this. The single sheet bears an
exhortation. It declares:

> The fortune of war is changing. This time the U.S.A. forces in
> and near Bastogne have been encircled by strong German armored
> units. More German armored units have crossed the River Our
> near Ortheuville, have taken Marche and reached St. Hubert by
> passing through Honores-Sibret-Tillet. Libriment is in German
> hands. There is only one possibility of saving the encircled U.S.A.
> troops from total annihilation: that is the honorable surrender of
> the encircled town. In order to think it over, a period of two hours
> will be granted, beginning with the presentation of this note. If
> this proposal should be rejected, one German artillery corps and
> six heavy anti-aircraft battalions are ready to annihilate the U.S.A.
> troops in and near Bastogne. The order for firing will be given
> immediately after this two-hour period. All the serious civilian
> losses caused by this artillery fire would not correspond with the
> well-known American humanity.
>
> The German Commander,
> General von Luttwitz, G.O.C.
> XLVII Panzer Corps

After the first few lines it becomes clear to General Mc-
Auliffe that the letter is not from Colonel Harper after all.
He stops reading. Time is valuable. Puzzled, he inquires of
his staff, "What is this thing?" They tell him it is a demand
for surrender. The General utters a mild expletive and
hustles away.

"I went out then," he says, "and visited other troops of the
command. I had a second call from Harper, who told me
the Germans were still sitting there blindfolded in his headquarters. They said they'd submitted a formal, official communication and they felt they were entitled to a formal,
official reply. I turned to my staff. 'What shall I tell them?'
I asked. Thereupon Colonel Kinnard, my brilliant G-3, said,
'That first crack of yours would be just the ticket.' 'Okay,' I

322]   WINSTON CHURCHILL: THE VALIANT YEARS

said, 'write it up!' So they brought me a formal communication, just like the German one. It was addressed to the German Commander and signed by the American Commander—me—and the message was the single word 'Nuts!' I gave it to Colonel Harper, who delivered it to the German emissaries. They didn't quite understand it, but Harper was able to explain it to them at greater length with some vigorous American language."

The 101st Airborne Division is holding out, but not without danger. It has withstood a series of armored attacks by the simple tactic of wiping the tanks clean of infantry, letting the tanks run on, and then destroying them at close quarters in the narrow streets of the town. Still, the General has his worries: "On the evening of December 22, I had become very concerned about a shortage of supplies, particularly of ammunition. We were also short, of course, of food and medical supplies. But it was serious when it became necessary to ration the artillery ammunition, and to tell the infantrymen when they called for artillery support that we were not able to provide it. The continued heavy fog made it impossible for the Air Force to parachute ammunition and other supplies in to us. However, fortunately for us, the morning of December 23 broke bright, clear and sunny, and before noon on that day a great group of C-47 airplanes came in and parachuted tons of ammunition and supplies to us with a very accurate drop right inside our perimeter."

Relief is already in sight. General Patton's Third Army is pounding up from the southeast and divisions from Field Marshal Montgomery's 21st Army Group are coming down from the north. The precipitous Patton is delighted. "This time," he rumbles joyfully, "the Kraut has stuck his head in a meat grinder and we've got hold of the handle!" On Christmas Day, tanks of his spearpoint roll into the lines circling Bastogne, and McAuliffe's paratroopers make ready for the offensive. The German armies in the Ardennes are doomed.

It is the end of the last German offensive of the war, a brain child of Hitler's, the final effort of the Wehrmacht to justify their cause and save their country from disaster. It is a daring plan, employing all Germany's remaining power in the West. Its objects are the capture of Brussels and Antwerp, the severance of the Allied forces in the center and isolation of U.S. First Army and 21st Army Group from their sources of supply, the acquisition of great stocks of matériel, and the destruction of twenty-five to thirty Allied divisions. In order to carry it out Hitler assembles three armies. On 11 and 12 December 1944 he calls his commanders to his headquarters, the "Eagle's Nest" near Ziegenberg in Hesse. They are shocked by his appearance. His shoulders are bent, his face deathly pale and puffy. One arm—his left—twitches violently, so that he has to seize it with his other hand. That too trembles involuntarily. One leg drags when he walks. When he sits he hunches in his chair like a rag doll. Irritably he outlines his plans.

There will be three armies: two will be armored and the third infantry. Colonel General of the SS Sepp Dietrich, commanding Sixth Panzer Army, will cross the Meuse and strike out for Antwerp. General Hasso-Eccard von Manteuffel's Fifth Panzer Army will head for Brussels. Seventh Army, re-created under General Brandenberger after its mauling in Normandy, will cover the southern flank. The force comprises nine panzer divisions and fourteen of infantry, with three more of each in reserve. In great secret they move into position in the thick forests of the Ardennes. On 16 December they are ready, and the Battle of the Bulge begins with a searing barrage on three battle-weary American divisions lying innocently in snow-covered trenches spread across far too wide a front.

It lasts for almost a month, by which time Bastogne has sucked in all the German reserves as well as some of the divisions intended for Antwerp. Now the Allied pincers begin inexorably to close. Seeing themselves trapped in a salient they cannot hope to hold, the Germans begin to retreat, leaving behind them evidence of their ruthlessness.

Pressing on their heels one day early in January, men of the 30th U.S. Infantry Division come upon an infamous field. Where all others are flat and even plains of white, this is oddly humped with unnatural drifts of snow. Curious, the men investigate the nearest little hillock. They find a body, stiff as iron in the zero cold, its arms frozen pitifully above its head in the gesture of surrender, its face a black mask of blood. This field at Malmédy contains one hundred and twenty-seven bodies, the complement of B Battery, 283 Field Artillery Observation Battalion. Each one has been lacerated by machine-gun fire, each has been given the quietus with a pistol at the back of the head. They are prisoners of war, thus massacred by a unit of the SS. No crash of gunfire would be loud enough to sound their requiem.

The fighting in the fog and snow of the Ardennes is harsh and bloody. But not without its more human moments. One day General Matthew B. Ridgway, an ardent commander, is walking about looking for action when he comes across a veteran who has seen many battles, and learned much. "He was a mortar man, down in a hole, with his weapon," the General records. "He wasn't firing.

" 'Here,' I said, 'get going with that mortar. Those people are right over there. Pour some fire on 'em. Let's blast 'em out of there.' He looked at me glumly. 'General,' he said, 'every time we shoot, them SOBs shoot right back.'

" 'The hell with that,' I said. 'Get that mortar working.'

"He took a sight on the opposite ridge top, dropped a shell down the tube, and the mortar belched with a bang and a smoke. Hardly had our shell exploded on the ridge opposite than there was a tremendous explosion a few yards to our left, and shell fragments screeched through the trees. Deafened by the explosion and shaken by the blast, I picked myself up off the ground. The mortar man peered warily out of his hole. 'See whadda mean?' he said."

By the end of the month the Germans are back where they started. They have inflicted some seventy-seven thousand casualties on the Americans. They themselves have lost a hundred and twenty thousand. Their last serviceable units have melted away.

Churchill tells the House of Commons: *I have seen it suggested that the terrific battle which has been proceeding since December 16 on the American front is an Anglo-American battle. In fact, however, the United States troops have done almost all the fighting, and have suffered almost all the losses. . . . I never hesitate . . . to stand up for our own soldiers when their achievements have been cold-shouldered or neglected or overshadowed, as they sometimes are, but we must not forget that it is to American homes that the telegrams of personal losses and anxiety have been going during the past month.*

Later he sums up the outcome of this desperate attempt by Hitler to buy time. *This was the enemy's final offensive of the war. At the time it caused us no little anxiety. Our own advance had to be postponed, but we benefited in the end. The Germans could not replace their losses, and our subsequent battles on the Rhine, though severe, were undoubtedly eased. The German High Command, and even Hitler, must have been disillusioned. Taken by surprise, Eisenhower and his commanders acted swiftly, but they will agree that the major credit lies elsewhere. In Montgomery's words,*

"The Battle of the Ardennes was won primarily by the staunch fighting qualities of the American soldier."

Hitler's attention is now forced elsewhere. The Russians have launched a new offensive from their bridgehead at Baronov and are cutting towards Germany's vitals with frightening speed. Sixth SS Panzer Army is hastily switched from the west in an effort to delay what is now obvious to all but the fanatics as the end.

Churchill, too, has become preoccupied with another matter. By 1 November the last German garrisons have quit Greece. What authority will replace them? At the Moscow Conference Churchill persuaded Stalin—at some cost—to recognize Greece as a British sphere of influence. Churchill is therefore pledged to support the Royal Hellenic Government controlled by Prime Minister Papandreou.

But Greece was in ruins, Churchill points out. *The Germans destroyed roads and railroads as they withdrew northward. Our Air Force harassed them as they went, but on land we could do little to interfere. E.L.A.S. armed bands filled the gap left by the departing invaders, and their central command made little effort to enforce the solemn promises which had been given. Everywhere was want and dissention. Finances were disordered and food exhausted. Our own military resources were stretched to the limit.* He fears that into this vacuum will step the Communist forces of E.L.A.S. and E.A.M. He is not far wrong. Civil war breaks out in Athens and the Piraeus on 3 December 1944. Churchill sends an urgent message to the British commander in Greece that ends, *We have to hold and dominate Athens. It would be a great thing for you to succeed in this without bloodshed if possible, but also with bloodshed if necessary.*

At once Churchill is attacked as a reactionary by the

British and American press and by some of his colleagues. He is forced to explain his reasons and expound his philosophy. He does so in a speech in the House on 8 December: *Democracy is not based on violence or terrorism, but on reason, on fair play, on freedom, on respecting the rights of other people. Democracy is no harlot to be picked up in the street by a man with a Tommy gun. I trust the people, the mass of the people, in almost any country, but I like to make sure that it is the people and not a gang of bandits who think that by violence they can overturn constituted authority, in some cases ancient Parliaments, Governments and States . . . We are told that because we do not allow gangs of heavily armed guerrillas to descend from the mountains and install themselves, with all the bloody terror and vigor of which they are capable, in power in great capitals, we are traitors to democracy . . . I shall call upon the House as a matter of confidence in His Majesty's Government, and of confidence in the spirit with which we have marched from one peril to another till victory is in sight, to reject such pretensions with the scorn that they deserve.*

During the latter part of December the entanglement in Greece becomes so obscure and so threatening that at last Churchill decides he must go there himself. It is Christmas Eve and his family are already gathered round the Christmas tree, a gift from President Roosevelt, and ready to start a party for the children. In spite of their protests Churchill boards a Skymaster that night and awakes the next morning in Naples.

In the early afternoon his party sets down safely on Kalamaki airfield and drives off with an escort of armored cars for Piraeus harbor, where the cruiser *Ajax*, their temporary home, is lying at anchor. They are welcomed by her commander, Captain Cuthbert, who recalls, "That evening Churchill, Anthony Eden, Harold Macmillan, Field Marshal Alexander and others arrived on board. There were conferences that night. The next morning, Mr. Churchill said he wished to see the fighting. A good deal of shelling was going on. Spitfires were diving down, firing rockets. After a few minutes I said to Mr. Churchill, 'Would you like me to fire my guns, sir?' He said, 'Oh, no, Captain . . . No, I'm on a mission of peace. I'm a cooing dove with a sprig of mistletoe in my beak. But, Captain, far be it from me to stand in the way of military necessity.'"

Shells falling in the harbor are raising brief spouts of water as Churchill and his colleagues leave for their conference that morning. Their escorts are awaiting them on the jetty. Churchill hears the noise of battle and clambers quickly into his armored car. He glances round like a good leader to make sure his party is fully prepared for any chance of war. His glance falls on his companion in all perils. *I said to my private secretary, Jock Colville, "Where is your pistol?" and when he said that he had not got one I scolded him, for I certainly had my own. In a few moments, while we were crowding into our steel box, he said, "I have got a Tommy gun."*

"Where did you get it from?" I asked.

"I borrowed it from the driver," he replied.

"What is he going to do?" I asked.

"He will be busy driving."

"But there will be no trouble unless we are stopped," I answered, "and what is he going to do then?" Jock had no reply. A black mark!

Colville himself continues the story. "When we reached the Ministry of Foreign Affairs the Greeks were there already. There was no electricity, and we had to go in and sit by the light of hurricane lamps. We waited and waited for the rebels to come. It was a long time and nothing happened, so eventually the proceedings started without them. Several speeches had been made, and the Prime Minister was half-way through his when it was announced that the rebels had arrived. However, they could not be let into the conference hall because they had come with arms in their hands and bandoliers across their shoulders. It was thought that if they could get in like that and there was trouble, they might well shoot up the Greek Government. They, on their part, were not willing to leave their guns in the hands of the British military authorities. However, after a long wait, a compromise was reached. The rebels took off their arms and locked them in the lavatory. They themselves took the key and a British sentry was posted outside to see that nobody tried to break the door down."

At the conference it becomes clear to everyone that the most powerful political figure in Greece at this moment is Archbishop Damaskinos, a former champion wrestler. At first Churchill is wary of him, doubtful whether if appointed Regent he will be able to withstand Communist pressure. At one point he remarks, exquisitely enough, *It would distress me to think that any new task Your Beatitude assumes as Regent might in any way interfere with your spiritual functions.* But by the end of the talks Churchill has grown confident that with British support the Archbishop will be able to restore order to Greece.

Back in London on 29 December, Churchill and Eden begin the second part of their task. They present the issues to the King of Greece, and by 4:30 in the morning have finally persuaded him to delegate all his royal powers to the Archbishop as Regent. The King makes an announcement. He will remain in exile until recalled by his people, and charges the Archbishop to restore order to his unhappy country.

Gradually the Communist irregulars are driven clear of Athens, Salonika and Patras. A truce is signed on 11 January: all prisoners are released, and the rebels are given safe-conduct to return to their homes. *Thus ended the six weeks' struggle for Athens,* Churchill sums up, *and, as it ultimately proved, for the freedom of Greece from Communist subjugation. When three million men were fighting on either side on the Western Front and vast American forces were deployed against Japan in the Pacific the spasms of Greece may seem petty, but nevertheless they stood at the nerve center of power, law, and freedom in the Western world.*

EPISODE **22**

YALTA: FATEFUL RENDEZVOUS

First Witch: *When shall we three meet again?*
In thunder, lightning, or in rain?
Second Witch: *When the hurly-burly's done,*
When the battle's lost and won.
WILLIAM SHAKESPEARE: *Macbeth*

PUSHING through the still, aquamarine water the black boat leaves no wake, its high, curving prow scarcely disturbing the smooth surface and behind it trailing only a faint rippling. Standing upright in the ancient fashion, the boatman leans forward onto his oars with the ease of years of labor, twists his wrists and brings the gleaming blades out of the water without a sound. Starkly limned between blue sea and bluer sky, he might be a fisherman coming home from a secret reef with his catch of octopus and squid and fat golden dory, riding in from some far century toward a Roman wharf.

Lazily, silently, the sharp prows skirt a cable and head for the earth-brown walls of the harbor. They stretch in an arc, above them in tiers the dusty houses of the town. There are gaps in the lines of dwellings and tall warehouses, voids through which the sun strikes on piles of crumbled stone and pounded mortar. Along the quays a morning bustle is awakening. Water sellers stride over the cobbles rattling their brass utensils. Urchins dash round bollards and in and out of dark alleys looking for mischief and high adventure. More sober citizens stroll towards their offices and shops, pausing now and then to greet a friend or glance over the harbor.

Now the boat must twist and turn through a field of buoys and hawsers. The long steel sides of warships tower gray above it. For this is one of the bases of the Mediterranean Fleet, the brave harbor of Valletta, on Malta, now bathing in this equable sunshine her wounds sustained when gallant Malta stood alone against the most savage onslaught of the *Luftwaffe*'s best squadrons. Lying out towards the roads is the cruiser *Orion*.

Sailors move about her spotless decks, but with decorum. She carries an important guest, recovering from a fever. But this is an important day. By mid-morning the guest declares himself well, and prepares for the arrival of a friend. He appears shortly on the quarterdeck, noting with approval the smartness of the ship's dress, from the hooded muzzles of her great guns to the immaculate coils of cable at her stern. He finds the weather warm, with a faint breeze coming in from the sea and the sky above clear of the smallest cloud.

Southward there is a speck in the sky, and almost at once there comes a faint high-pitched snarl of engines. The speck heads in, resolving itself into an arrowhead of Spitfires. They stoop towards the harbor, keeping formation, then soar deliriously in a tight, precise arc and flash away again to sea. When they return, their charge is steaming below them, rounding the harbor bluff. She is the U.S.S. *Quincy*, bearing the President of the United States to his last rendezvous of the Grand Alliance.

At the sight of her striped ensign the bands of the ships' companies in the harbor begin "The Star-Spangled Banner." Churchill catches sight of the President sitting on her bridge and waves a welcome. Slowly *Quincy* glides to her berth alongside the venerable quay wall.

Churchill feels well enough to lunch aboard her. The two leaders review the war situation, and that evening consider the political attitudes they must adopt at the fateful conference they are about to join. Its subject is the Allies' plans for world peace, and Churchill is already uneasy. President Roosevelt feels that he cannot stay at Yalta for more than five or six days. Though Churchill must accept this limitation he warns his old friend that there must be preliminary conferences between Americans and British, concluding, *I do not see any other way of realizing our hopes about World Organization in five or six days. Even the Almighty took seven.* . . . Churchill is particularly apprehensive lest the Russians occupy more of Western Europe than is necessary. Though agreement is reached on many points, he still feels a sense of foreboding as he leaves Malta for his fourteen hundred mile flight to the Crimea.

It would have been difficult to choose a worse site for a conference. Fighting of the bitterest kind has characterized the Russian struggle in the Crimea. The Germans have been driven out ten months before, but in retreating they have destroyed whatever they had the power to blow up or burn. Even now the area is not completely cleared of their mines, except for the grounds of the Yusupov and Livadia

Palaces and the villas in which the delegations will live.

Parties of British and Americans have been at Yalta for weeks, helping the Russians prepare for the conference. Their staffs alone number some seven hundred people. Among these early arrivals is Mrs. Joan Bright Astley, who encounters problems at once. "I was a sort of housekeeper who went ahead to get things ready for the various important people who came to the conferences. For Yalta, in the far-off Crimea, as usual I went on ahead and found myself in a nightmare of snow, ice and bad communications. There was not enough room for the people who were already on their way. When I was over at the American headquarters I saw that the President and Mr. Stettinius each had a large double bed to themselves. My Prime Minister had a single one. I knew he would hate this and I didn't wish to see him in a temper. I had seen it once, and I didn't want it to happen again. I went to the Russians and said, 'Please can I have Mr. Stettinius's bed? It's for Mr. Churchill.' Dead silence. Days passed, and then, just before the conference was due to open, a bed came from Moscow, a large double bed . . ."

Churchill's plane touches down first on Saki airfield, and he waits in deep snow for the "Sacred Cow" to arrive. The President is carried down from it on an elevator and lifted into an open car to inspect the guard of honor. Churchill is sickened by his frail appearance. The journey to Yalta by car takes almost eight hours. In places the roads are lined with impassive troops, some of them women, standing shoulder to shoulder under the iron skies. Then, as they cross the mountains, and begin to drop down to the Black Sea, they pass suddenly from dank cold into warm sunshine and see in the distance the white glimmer of Yalta beside the dark but gentle sea.

The British are quartered, appropriately enough, in a

villa built by an English architect for Prince Vorontzov, once the Czar's Ambassador to the Court of St. James. The villa is half Gothic, half Moorish, and surrounded by luxuriant shrubberies and funereally dark cypresses. Two white lions guard its entrance.

The Russians are at pains to be hospitable. *Every effort was made by our hosts to ensure our comfort,* Churchill remembers, *and every chance remark noted with kindly attention. On one occasion Portal had admired a large glass tank with plants growing in it, and remarked that it contained no fish. Two days later a consignment of goldfish arrived. Another time somebody said casually that there was no lemon peel in the cocktails. The next day a lemon tree loaded with fruit was growing in the hall. All must have come by air from far away.*

But some of Churchill's staff encounter minor difficulties at first. Sir Alexander Cadogan, permanent head of the Foreign Office, notes, "The Russians had done everything they possibly could for our comfort and entertainment, but of course they had not been trained in the matter of an English breakfast. Caviar and mince pies are all very well once in a while, but they begin to pall after a bit. However, we soon managed to initiate them into the mysteries of some of the simpler egg dishes. When it got into its stride, the conference routine was more or less like this: Every morning at half past eleven, a meeting of the three Foreign Secretaries with their delegations at one of the delegation headquarters, followed by lunch, then at three o'clock in the afternoon a meeting of the Big Three."

The first plenary meeting starts at a quarter after four o'clock on 5 February 1945 in Livadia Palace, where the Americans are quartered. The first topic is the future of

Germany. Stalin broaches it by asking how Germany is to be dismembered, recalling that at Teheran the President suggested cutting Germany into five parts, with which he (Stalin) had agreed. Churchill, however, had then favored splitting Germany in two, with Prussia and Austria-Bavaria as one unit, and Westphalia and the Ruhr as the other, under international control. They must now agree, Stalin says, as to what shall be done.

Sir Alexander Cadogan has been watching Stalin closely during this résumé. He records, "I had seen a good deal of Stalin in Moscow on various occasions in negotiation with different British leaders, and I was particularly interested on this occasion to watch him conducting this triangular duel . . . On the first day Stalin sat an hour and a half or so without saying a word. There was in fact no call for him to do so, as both the President and the Prime Minister had much to say. He just sat there taking it all in and being apparently rather amused. When he did chip in, he never used a superfluous word and spoke very much to the point. He had obviously got a good sense of humor, and rather a quick temper."

Churchill is hesitant during this opening session. He believes that no specific methods can be agreed on before the whole question has been under discussion for a considerable time. Certainly nothing can be settled in five or six days. The President suggests that the Foreign Ministers be asked to produce a study plan by the following day, and a detailed plan within a month. The subject is then shelved.

The next day is devoted to an even more formidable problem, the implementation of proposals made at the Dumbarton Oaks Conference, which has produced plans for a future world organization, but which ended without being able to formulate a workable design for the Security Council. The difficulty here rests on what the voting rights should be, and it is the most vital consideration of all. The safety of the entire world organization depends upon finding a viable solution.

President Roosevelt has offered one system. It suggests that each member of the Security Council shall have one vote; seven of the members must vote their approval of any measure before it can be carried out. Major matters must have the approval of all four permanent members—the United States, the Soviet Union, Great Britain and China—before action can be taken. Dissent by any one of these four will defeat a proposal. Thus is born the veto, which in coming years the Soviet Union will employ no fewer than eighty-eight times.

Next day the Russians agree to this proposal, and the discussion turns to membership of the General Assembly and to arrangements for convening the first conference of the world organization. The details are settled quickly and the date is set—Wednesday, 25 April 1945.

On 8 February the Russians throw open the Yusupov Palace for a banquet. Stalin pays eloquent tribute to Churchill in proposing his health. "I propose a toast for the leader of the British Empire," he proclaims, "the most courageous of all Prime Ministers in the world, embodying political experience with military leadership, who when all Europe was ready to fall flat before Hitler said that Britain would stand and fight alone against Germany even without any allies. Even if the existing and possible allies deserted her he said she would continue to fight. To the health of the man who is born once in a hundred years, and who bravely held up the banner of Great Britain. I have said what I feel, what I have at heart, and of what I am conscious."

In reply Churchill gives some hint of his premonitions. No amount of elegance or suavity can dispel his mortal gloom. *I must say that never in this war have I felt the responsibility weigh so heavily on me, even in the darkest hours, as now during this Conference. But now . . . we see that we are on the crest of the hill and there is before us the prospect of open country. Do not let us underestimate the difficulties. Nations, comrades in arms, have in the past drifted apart within five or ten years of war. Thus toiling, millions have followed a vicious circle, falling into the pit, and then by their sacrifices raising themselves up again. We now have a chance of avoiding the errors of previous generations and of making a sure peace. People cry out for peace and joy. Will the families be reunited? Will the warrior come home? Will the shattered dwellings be rebuilt? Will the toiler see his home? To defend one's country is glorious, but there are greater conquests before us. Before us lies the realization of the dream of the poor—that they shall live in peace, protected by our invincible power from aggression and evil . . . The Marshal spoke of the future. This is the most important of all. Otherwise the oceans of bloodshed will have been useless and outrageous. I propose the toast to the broad sunlight of victorious peace.*

What remains for formal discussion is the future of Poland, and this is a thorny subject indeed. This unhappy country, now liberated—and occupied—by the might of the Red Army, is claimed by two quite separate governments. One, exiled in London, will not resume relations with the Soviet Union. The other has been nurtured and protected by the Russians throughout the war.

At last it is decided that a Polish Provisional Government of National Unity shall be formed by means of a free ballot to be held as soon as possible. At the same time Poland's frontiers shall be delineated. In the East they will follow in the main the Curzon Line (the demarcation arranged in 1919) with small alterations in Poland's favor. In the West they will benefit by the accession of parts of

Eastern Germany. There is no substantial disagreement among the Allies on these proposals.

The remaining issue of the Yalta Conference is not discussed formally. This is the conditions under which Russia will enter the war against Japan. The American military chiefs reckon that it will take eighteen months from the collapse of Germany before Japan can be humbled. Russia has already announced her price, and now the Americans are prepared to discuss it in order to shorten the war in the Pacific and reduce the number of their casualties. Churchill plays no real part in these informal talks, but when Americans and Russians have reached agreement he is asked to approve it. This he does, stifling his misgivings.

The bargain is that Russia will enter the war in the East within two or three months of Germany's surrender. In return for this service she will recover, after the defeat of Japan, certain territories and rights lost by Imperial Russia in 1904. These are the southern part of Sakhalin and its nearby islands, a major interest in the port of Dairen and the lease of the naval base at Port Arthur, and the joint operation with the Chinese of the railroad leading to Dairen. The status quo in Outer Mongolia will be preserved. The Kurile Islands will pass to the Soviet Union.

The final dinner of the Conference is held in the Vorontzov villa, with the British as hosts. The atmosphere is friendly, as well it might be, with every party believing that on the whole it has got what it came for. Towards the end of the evening Churchill finds himself chatting with Stalin. He mentions that when Hitler has been beaten there will be a General Election in England. The Marshal seeks to comfort his host. *Stalin thought my position was assured, "since the people would understand that they needed a leader, and who could be a better leader than he who had won the victory?" I explained that we had two parties in*

Britain, and I belonged to only one of them. "One party is much better," said Stalin, with deep conviction.

So with this pleasant evening the momentous meeting comes to an end. It is to prove one of the most controversial events of modern times. It has its champions and its detractors. One viewpoint infrequently encountered in discussions about its outcome is that outlined by Sir Ian Jacob, one of Churchill's military aides at the time. "The Yalta Conference was held at a time when the war with Germany was very near its end. And so political matters were coming very much to the fore. It struck me at the time that whereas conferences of the type we held during the war—Casablanca, Quebec, Teheran—all on military matters, had been admirably suited to the settlement of strategy and tactics for the next six months with clear-cut conclusions, this method was quite unsuitable for political questions which involved the whole future of countries and for which little preparation had been made beforehand. To expect to settle vast questions properly in a week is, I think, asking a great deal. I believe that that is why everybody looks back upon the Yalta Conference as one in which the Russians really got away with it."

Before leaving the Crimea Churchill is anxious to make a pilgrimage. He drives to Sevastopol, where the liner *Franconia* is moored, acting as a headquarters ship. There he instructs one of the War Office Intelligence Staff, Brigadier Peake, to familiarize himself with all the details of the Battle of Balaklava and equip himself to act as a guide. The party visits that heroic field, where once the Light Brigade rode forward under a misapprehension and installed itself forever in the annals of glory and the anthologies of lyric poetry. They are accompanied by the Russian Admiral commanding the Black Sea Fleet. This worthy begins a commentary on a more recent encounter, in which the German armor was smashed by the Red Army. Simultaneously Brigadier Peake unfolds his dissertation on that far-off charge of cavalry. Happily the military dispositions on both occasions correspond quite closely, and the dual recitation comes to an end without embarrassment.

At Saki airfield, where Churchill's plane is waiting, he finds an impressive guard of honor of troops of the NKVD. *I inspected them in my usual manner,* Churchill records, *looking each man straight in the eye. This took some time, as there were at least two hundred of them.* He flies off to Athens, and thence to Egypt, where the President has been conferring with a number of political leaders of the Middle East.

The President's cruiser is lying in Alexandria harbor. Churchill arrives aboard in time for lunch. He is struck by the frailness of his friend's appearance, and his unusual silence. With dread he concludes that the end is near. When *Quincy* has sailed Churchill holds a reception for King Ibn Saud at the oasis of Fayum.

Difficulties in arranging for suitable hospitality are soon encountered. *A number of social problems arose. I had been told that neither smoking nor alcoholic beverages were allowed in the Royal Presence. As I was the host at luncheon I raised the matter at once, and said to the interpreter that if it was the religion of His Majesty to deprive himself of smoking and alcohol I must point out that my rule of life prescribed as an absolutely sacred rite smoking cigars and also the drinking of alcohol before, after, and if need be during all meals and in the intervals between them. The King graciously accepted the position. His own cupbearer from Mecca offered me a glass of water from its sacred well, the most delicious that I had ever tasted.*

Reporting immediately to the House of Commons on his return, Churchill announces his confidence in the good faith of the Soviets, which has so earnestly been pledged by Stalin. It is no time to make public his secret fears. *Somber indeed would be the fortunes of mankind,* he points out, *if some awful schism arose between the Western democracies and the Russian Soviet Union.* He continues, *We are now entering a world of imponderables, and at every stage occasions for self-questioning arise. It is a mistake to look too far ahead. Only one link in the chain of destiny can be handled at a time. I trust the House will feel that hope has been powerfully strengthened by our meeting in the Crimea. The ties that bind the three Great Powers together and their mutual comprehension of each other have grown. The United States has entered deeply and constructively into the life and salvation of Europe. We have all three set our hands to far-reaching engagements at once practical and solemn.* But even as he is speaking to the optimistic Members crowding the benches of the House, the Russians are violating their agreements.

Vyshinsky is in Bucharest. He orders the young King Michael to dismiss the all-party government, and Soviet tanks deploy in the city's streets to make sure he is obeyed. Within a few days there is a new government in Rumania. Its members are nominated by the Soviet authorities and their policies are directed from Moscow. It is the first indication that Churchill's fears for the future are not without foundation.

As the Allied armies roll in toward the heart of the Reich from east, west and south, as the once vaunted Wehrmacht begins to crumble before them, Churchill's apprehension grows. The borders between the occupation zones have long since been decided. If the Western Allies in their final lunge penetrate beyond them eastward they will be morally bound to withdraw the moment the fighting stops. Will the Russians, with their new-found might and confidence, observe the same niceties of conduct? Churchill makes a suggestion to the ailing President on 1 April. *The Russian armies will no doubt overrun all Austria and enter Vienna. If they also take Berlin will not their impression that they have been the overwhelming contributor to our common victory be unduly imprinted in their minds, and may this not lead them into a mood which will raise grave and formidable difficulties in the future? I therefore consider that from a political standpoint we should march as far east into Germany as possible, and that should Berlin be in our grasp we should certainly take it. This also appears sound on military grounds.*

A month later his theme is still the same. He writes to Eden, busy at the first meeting of the United Nations in San Francisco: *We have several powerful bargaining counters on our side, the use of which might make for a peaceful agreement. First, the Allies ought not to retreat from their present positions to the occupational line until we are satisfied about Poland, and also about the temporary character of the Russian occupation of Germany, and the conditions to be established in the Russianized or Russian-controlled countries in the Danube valley, particularly Austria and Czechoslovakia, and the Balkans. Secondly, we may be able to please them about the exits from the Black Sea and the Baltic as part of a general settlement. All these matters can only be settled before the United States armies in Europe are weakened. If they are not settled before the United States armies withdraw from Europe and the Western world folds up its war machines, there are no prospects of a satisfactory solution and very little of preventing a third world war.*

Many thought Churchill overly pessimistic. Yet subsequent events show him to have been the only Western leader to sense the new era of stress and conflict into which Europe, and later the rest of the world, is to move. One of his personal secretaries remembers his mood at the time. He is less boisterous than formerly; he will pause in the middle of dictation and stare gloomily out of the window. She considers this period the most melancholy of all she has gone through with the Prime Minister. No single catastrophe of the whole war has ever cast him into such black depths of depression and frustration as those in which he must now live out the hours. For he is watching the march of events which only he and the enigmatic Stalin, alone among the statesmen of the world, have the percipience to measure. It is as though, isolated on the pinnacle of leadership, he finds that the promised land which has been bought by blood and sweat and tears is after all an ominous landscape of desert and chasms and lowering clouds.

THE
ULTIMATE
BARRIER

Where now are the Hebrew children,
Where now are the Hebrew children,
Where now are the Hebrew children?
Safe in the Promised Land.
                    Traditional Song

THE BLACK trunks of the trees seem made of stone. From the crevices and corrugations of their rough bark gleam drops and runnels of water. There is an intermittent drip of moisture from the dark green branches high above, and all about between the trees eddy thin wraiths of mist. Underfoot the ground is hard with winter, and here and there little patches of snow and ice glisten gray and soiled. Gloomy bridle paths strike through the forest and occasional tracks lead to the hut of a woodcutter, but elsewhere there are only the somber lines of trees, clogged clumps of bracken, and the cathedral silence of thick, tall woods. The Reichswald is a dark and dreary place.

Ten miles long and six miles wide, it is shaped like a lozenge. Its western edge forms the German frontier. Through it from north to south runs the Siegfried Line and in front of that every approach is sown with mines and scarred with anti-tank ditches. The Germans have realized that the final drive for the Rhine will come from the north; they have reinforced this sector with every available reserve. This is some of the worst fighting terrain in Europe. Between the Maas and the Rhine stretch acres of featureless, water-logged fields that offer no cover to the attacker and no firm ground over which his supply columns might pass. Beyond them toward Germany looms the ominous line of the Reichs-wald's pines. For three weeks Montgomery's men struggle through the Forest in some of the bitterest and most costly fighting of the war.

The days are short, and for the fighting men deep in the dripping woods there seems to be neither dawn nor dusk, but only twilight and night. The enemy is the best that is left of the German Army—two divisions of paratroops, one of Panzer Grenadiers, and one of armor. The roads leading into the Forest are under two feet of water, and all else is a morass. The nights are icy and the days wringing wet. As the fate of their race hangs over them, the Germans defend this last patch of the Fatherland west of the Rhine with ferocity and resolution. Despairing, fanatic, they exact a deadly price from their assailants.

After a time it seems to the men locked in this dark combat that nothing exists outside this universe of trees. They grow accustomed to the cold. The whine and crack of bullets through the gray glades becomes familiar. Rewards are measured in yards gained, in single machine-gun posts oblit-erated. The crackle of automatics and the dull boom of grenades are incidental punctuation to timeless routine days. Men survive by the sharpness of their animal instincts, by

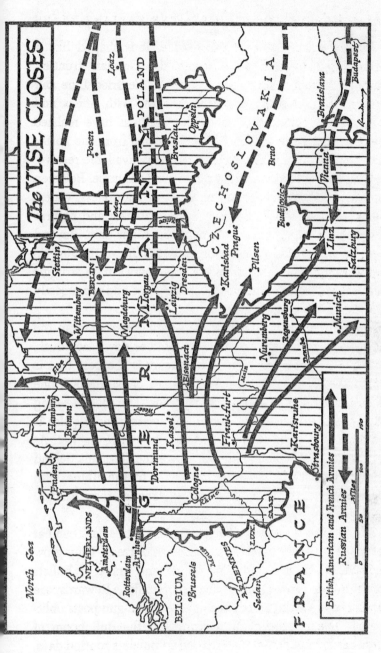

The VISE CLOSES

German resistance on both fronts collapses in the spring of 1945. The Allies from the west and the Russians from the east close the vise on the armies of the Third Reich. On April 25, Russian and Allied forces meet at Torgau on the Elbe and the two fronts are joined. On May 7, 1945, Germany surrenders.

brute cunning and quickness of reaction; their sensibilities atrophy.

Lieutenant Colonel Martin Lindsay, commanding a battalion of the Gordon Highlanders, notes in his diary, "I went for a walk in the woods today and came upon Sergeant B lighting a wood fire underneath a dead and frozen Hun strung up to the branch of a tree. He was trying to thaw him out, in order to take off his boots. Personally, I have found the Army boots quite adequate, but most people seem to think that the type which goes almost up to the knee is warmer."

While the British in the north are clawing towards the Rhine the Americans further south have encountered better luck. In typical fashion they exploit it to the full. On 7 March the armored spearhead of U.S. 9th Armored Division is pressing towards the river, the U.S. First Army following. The leading tanks cautiously climb the last hill before the river bank, expecting to find on the other side an uninterrupted view of Remagen, but not of its railway bridge that spans the Rhine.

Nosing over the crest, they halt in astonishment. The bridge is intact! They charge downhill at top speed, hurtle through the town, and within minutes are at the approaches to the bridge. As the tanks roll up towards the ramp two detonations shake the easternmost span. But the roadway is undamaged. The infantry leap after the tanks and storm across.

As their commander describes it, somewhat laconically, "We went right on down the bridge. It was manned by German engineers in the tower. There were lots of snipers and machine guns. The tanks covered the towers and fired on them. The Germans jumped from the tops of the towers onto the bridge. They ran back across the bridge and our infantry pursued them." Engineers quickly cut the wires leading to the nearest charges, then discover that all the wires run through a main conduit all along the bridge. They sever it by rifle fire. By four o'clock in the afternoon a powerful force of U.S. First Army is across the Rhine. As the American flood is being funnelled over the bridge the German officers originally charged with its defense and destruction are being swiftly tried, and shortly they are shot.

Further south still, the Americans have already breached the Siegfried Line. The intricate fortifications, long hailed by Hitler as impregnable, cannot even slow them down. Even the confident General Patton is rather surprised at the ease with which the supposedly formidable West Wall can be reduced.

"There were quite a number of pillboxes on the far side of the river," he says. "One, I remember, was camouflaged like a barn, and a wooden barn at that. When you opened the door through which the hay was supposed to be put, you came to a concrete wall nine feet thick with an 88mm gun sticking out. Another was completely built inside an old house, the outer walls of which were knocked down when it became necessary for the pillbox to go into action. The amazing thing about all these defenses is that they produced no results. During the course of these operations, 90th Division alone put out one hundred and twenty pillboxes in about forty-eight hours, with the loss of less than one hundred and twenty men. This feat was accomplished by careful reconnaissance, then smothering the embrasures with machine-gun and rifle fire, and using dynamite charges against the back door, or else by using self-propelled 155mm guns at short range. At three hundred yards the 155 shell will remove a pillbox for every round fired." The moral is clear: "Pacifists would do well to study the Siegfried and Maginot Lines, remembering that these defenses were forced; that Troy fell; that the walls of Hadrian succumbed; that the

Great Wall of China was futile; and that, by the same token, the mighty seas which are alleged to defend us can also be circumvented by a resolute and ingenious opponent. In war, the only sure defense is offense, and the efficiency of offense depends on the warlike souls of those conducting it."

One such is decorated by the General with the Medal of Honor. He is Private Harold A. Garman of 5th Infantry Division. During the crossing of the Sauer River a small boat containing four wounded men is caught on its way back from the enemy shore by a storm of machine-gun fire. The two men paddling it swim for the bank, along with one of the wounded. Two others of the wounded roll into the water but are too weak to swim and so clutch feebly at the side of the boat, where their remaining comrade lies immobile. Slowly the craft drifts back towards the enemy shore. Private Garman swims out to it through the bullet-lashed water and pushes it painfully to safety. When General Patton asks why he did it, Private Garman looks surprised. "Well, someone had to," he explains.

With the Siegfried Line overcome, a bridgehead established at Remagen, and the Reichswald cleared, the moment has come for the Allies to force the Rhine in the north. It is a joint operation by British Second Army and U.S. Ninth Army, with British 6th Airborne Division and U.S. 17th Airborne Division dropping on the far bank after the initial assault by water.

Churchill is most anxious to be among those present, but meets with some opposition. "He was staying with me at my headquarters in Holland, actually near Nijmegen," Field Marshal Montgomery recalls, "and he knew that I was going to cross the Rhine with my group of armies in March. And he was determined to be there. I knew this. I told my Chief of Staff he mustn't come. We must keep him away." Back in London, Churchill is not ready to accept defeat thus easily, and enlists to his cause the very man who is charged with preventing him from watching the crossing, General de Guingand, Montgomery's Chief of Staff. Finding honeyed words of no avail, Churchill announces bluntly that he expects to attend. Unhappily de Guingand declares, "My chief won't let you come, sir." The Prime Minister's reaction, predictably enough, is an explosion. A signal is hurriedly sent off to Holland. "I was tipped the wink from London," Montgomery says, "that I had better watch my step. I wrote the old man a letter in which I said, 'We're going to cross the Rhine, and the one person we want there is you!' That did it."

The preparation has been vast. Huge convoys have deposited acres of equipment and supplies on the Allied bank, carefully shrouded by batteries of smoke-generators fuming day and night. In the two weeks preceding the assault heavy bombers have unloaded fifty thousand tons of bombs on the German positions. Three thousand fighter aircraft stand ready in support of the ground forces. Two thousand guns line the bank, zeroed in for the opening barrage.

It is a night attack. The first waves of a force of eighty thousand men board their amphibious armored carriers as dust falls on 23 March 1945. The solemn thunder of artillery swells out and splits the sky; the air reverberates with the shock of their charges, shrieks and wails with the passing of their shells. The far bank flickers livid with incessant shellbursts. Sliding and waddling, the carriers lumber through the mud, splash down into the black water and churn sturdily across the current. Behind them come engineers with their pontoons. By dawn the bridgeheads are firmly established.

It is time for the second phase of the operation, the airborne drop. This involves an air armada of 1,572 heavy planes towing 1,326 gliders, covered by 900 fighters and preceded by 1,253 fighters directed at ground targets that might interfere with the safe arrival of the air-borne troops. It begins in full daylight, by which time Churchill has been established on a vantage point slightly above a group of war correspondents. One of them, Alan Moorehead, describes the scene: "At the last moment Churchill arrived to see the show. It was said that he was very angry because Montgomery had refused to allow him to go over on one of the assault barges. So there he stood on the hilltop. At the appointed time the bombers came over from England, a host of them, flying very low down. This was too much, I remember, for Churchill. He threw his hat into the air and ran downhill in the same direction as the bombers, towards the river, shouting 'Here they come! Here they come!' It was a schoolboy gesture, but it was so genuine, so moving, that I think all of us that day went on across the river feeling much better than we imagined we would feel."

Churchill himself is anxious to follow suit, but is denied that pleasure for the time being. Jock Colville, his private secretary, succeeds in doing so without his master's consent, having avoided the possibility of Churchill's veto by the simple expedient of not mentioning his intentions. During Colville's return, however, a bursting shell wounds a soldier standing beside him and Colville is drenched in blood. Back at Montgomery's headquarters his escapade can no longer be kept secret and he is subjected to the Field Marshal's wrath. Nothing loath, Churchill joins Montgomery in rebuke, and thus also takes his revenge.

Next day Prime Minister, the Commander-in-Chief and a contrite Colville motor to General Eisenhower's headquarters. The Supreme Commander leads them to a sandbagged observation post commanding a view of the river and an expanse of flat fields on the other side, believed to be unoccupied by the enemy. Churchill gazes longingly at the battlefield spread so quietly before him. General Eisenhower leaves on urgent business. The Prime Minister lingers for a moment, then just as he is about to follow suit he observes a launch drawing in to moor close by. His chubby face lights up. He turns to Montgomery: *So I said . . . "Why don't we go across and have a look at the other side?" Somewhat to my surprise he answered, "Why not?" . . . We landed in brilliant sunshine and perfect peace on the German shore, and walked about for half an hour or so unmolested.*

It is something of an anticlimax, really, and serves only to whet their appetites. Foiled in an attempt to take the launch downriver towards the sounds of battle, Montgomery seeks an alternative. *As we landed he said to me, "Let's go down to the railway bridge at Wesel, where we can see what is going on on the spot." So we got into his car, and, accompanied by the Americans, who were delighted at the prospect, we went to the big iron-girder railway bridge, which was broken in the middle but whose twisted ironwork offered good perches. The Germans were replying to our fire, and their shells fell in salvos of four about a mile away. Presently they came nearer. Then one salvo came overhead and plunged in the water on our side of the bridge. The shells seemed to explode on impact with the bottom, and raised great fountains of spray about a hundred yards away. Several other shells fell among the motorcars which were concealed not far behind us, and it was decided we ought to depart. I clambered down and joined my adventurous host for our two hours' drive back to headquarters.*

By the end of March the Allies are established across the Rhine in great force. A dozen bridges span the river, shaking day and night with the weight of trucks bearing the ammunition and supplies that will be needed for the final advance. The Ruhr is encircled, its garrison of 325,000 men cut off. The Western Front is smashed. Americans, Canadians, French and British group for the *coup de grâce*.

In the East the Russian juggernaut is rolling ponderously towards its goal. Militarily the Allies are close to triumph. But politically the situation between them is dissolving into mistrust, accusation, suspicion. On 21 March the British Ambassador in Moscow reports to the Russians that a series of conferences has been going on in secret in Berne between Mr. Allen Dulles, the OSS representative there, and General Karl Wolff, commander of the SS troops in Italy. The Russian reaction is bitter. They suspect that Americans and British are preparing an agreement with the Nazis, suggesting even that the design will be to transfer any German troops who surrender to fight the Red Army on the Eastern Front.

On 7 April Stalin writes to President Roosevelt, "It is difficult to admit that the lack of resistance by the Germans on the Western Front is due solely to the fact that they have been defeated. The Germans have 147 divisions on the Eastern Front. They could without prejudicing their own position detach fifteen to twenty divisions from the Eastern Front and transfer them to reinforce their troops on the Western Front. Yet the Germans have not done and are not doing this. They are continuing to wage a crazy struggle with the Russians for an insignificant railway station like Zemlyanitsa in Czechoslovakia, which is as much use to them as hot poultices to a corpse, and yet they yield without the slightest resistance such important towns in the center of Germany as Osnabrück, Mannheim and Kassel. You will agree that such behavior on the part of the Germans is more than curious and unintelligible . . ."

This is the first real breach in the tripartite alliance, but Churchill already sees that it will be followed by even deeper

rifts. For the one unifying bond between the three is about
to disappear. While there is a common foe, America, Russia
and Britain must remain close, united by the same urgent
need for self-preservation. With Germany destroyed, the fear
is banished and the unity dissolves.

It is tragic that just in these critical days the President's
life should be ebbing from him. *We can now see,* says
Churchill, *the deadly hiatus which existed between the fading of President Roosevelt's strength and the growth of President Truman's grip of the vast world problem . . . The United
States stood on the scene of victory, master of world fortunes, but without a true and coherent design. Britain,
though still very powerful, could not act decisively alone.
I could at this stage only warn and plead. Thus this climax of
apparently measureless success was to me a most unhappy
time. I moved amid cheering crowds, or sat at a table,
adorned with congratulations and blessings from every part
of the Grand Alliance, with an aching heart and a mind oppressed by forebodings.*

Churchill sees that it is vital to peace to settle the major
issues in Europe before any part of Germany conquered by
the Western Allies is relinquished to the Russians, and certainly before the Anglo-American armies are reduced in
strength. But Churchill's will is no longer paramount.

None of this percolates to the battle line, where in spite of
the superiority of their adversaries, the Germans are contest-
ing every foot of ground. Many of their units are bolstered
by old men and boys of the *Volksturm,* clerks, walking
wounding, men ill-trained and ill-equipped but still so informed with desperation that they will fight. The savagery
of the battle is not diminished.

Colonel John Hines, whose combat command of armor is
engaged in the swamp and woodland outside Frankfurt, describes his attack on an airfield. He drives straight into the

teeth of the anti-aircraft artillery massed there, including high-velocity 88s firing solid shot. "I remember we flushed some German infantry in foxholes who came past us to surrender. I was standing in the turret of my tank talking on the radio telephone . . . I was either talking to or trying to contact Colonel Britton and looking over the rear of my tank towards Frankfurt when a shell which I did not hear coming hit the deck of my tank and the side of the turret. I had my left hand on the hatch and was facing the shell. I remember seeing the explosion and trying to pull down the hatch with my left hand, only to find that I had lost the fingers of it. I remember dropping down into the tank and finding that I was choking from bone and shrapnel fragments in my throat and scooping them out with the fingers of my right hand." The shell has taken out both the Colonel's eyes.

Stubbornly, at road blocks, in woods and villages, behind hedgerows and in the streets of shuttered towns, little isolated groups of Germans still fight against impossible odds. Disorganized, useless and bloody, these scattered engagements cost lives on both sides. Private Lester Atwell is with an American infantry division beyond Eisenach. "We were advancing down a road in convoy when a German tank drove out of a grove of trees, fired point-blank, killed two of our men, and then retreated from sight again. The convoy halted and two of our rifle companies went forward and surrounded the little grove that contained, they discovered, a platoon of German soldiers in deep foxholes. The German tank kept swivelling and firing, and after a while four of our own tanks came up. Each from a different direction sprayed the tiny stretch of woods with long streams of flaming gasoline. Within a few seconds the place became an inferno, and the shrieks and screams of the Germans could be heard through the high curtains of fire. A few, in flames, tried to crawl through, but they were mowed down by our machine guns. Within half an hour we went on, and all that was left of the little wood was a deep bed of glowing coals, hideous to see and to think about in the spring sunlight."

On 12 April 1945 Lieutenant General William H. Simpson's U.S. Ninth Army reaches the Elbe, its 2nd Armored Division having thrust forward fifty miles in a single day. The Americans are sixty miles from Berlin and within days of linking up with the Russians. That night they survey the broad waters of the river knowing that this is their last barrier.

In the morning, however, comes black news that wipes the joy from their conquest. A pale sun is climbing above the ground mist as the troops begin to stir from their cold bivouacs. In the chill morning air the men stretch and yawn, walking slowly into line. They talk quietly, laconically, as they wait for the cooks to serve breakfast, some smoking, some rubbing tired eyes, all quiet and patient. About them the trees are veiled and wreathed with silver gray; the road glistens with dew. Trucks and tents are pearled with moisture. There is a smell of canvas and gasoline and frying bacon. The landscape is dim, the sound subdued and murmurous.

Suddenly a brisk voice echoes down the line. An officer, pale faced and serious, shouts for attention. He makes a bald and terrible announcement. "Men," he calls, "I'd like your attention. President Roosevelt died last night." He stands there, saying nothing more, looking at the faces of his men. They are blank. There is nothing more to be spoken. He turns about. Behind him in the gray silence each man considers this appalling change, feeling himself touched personally by fate, each examining his destiny that was so wrapped up in the deeds and thoughts of this great man. Each, in his different way, asks of himself, "The President is dead. What is to become of me?"

To Churchill no news could be more cruel. *I felt as if I had been struck a physical blow. My relations with this shining personality had played so large a part in the long, terrible years we had worked together. Now they had come to an end, and I was overpowered by a sense of deep and irreparable loss.* At eleven o'clock he goes sorrowfully down to the House of Commons. There he suggests an adjournment as a token of respect, and for the first time in its history the House thus honors the head of a foreign state.

When the House meets again, Churchill is ready to deliver his valediction. Reviewing their long, intimate relationship, the Prime Minister says of his friend, *His love of his own country, his respect for its Constitution, his power of gauging the tides and currents of its mobile public opinion, were always evident, but added to these were the beatings of that generous heart which was always stirred to anger and to action by spectacles of aggression and oppression by the strong against the weak. It is indeed a loss, a bitter loss to humanity, that those heartbeats are stilled forever.*

President Roosevelt's physical affliction lay heavily upon him. It was a marvel that he bore up against it through all the many years of tumult and storm. Not one man in ten millions, stricken and crippled as he was, would have attempted to plunge into a life of physical and mental exertion and of hard, ceaseless political controversy. Not one in ten millions would have tried, not one in a generation would have succeeded, not only in entering this sphere, not only in acting vehemently in it, but in becoming indisputable master of the scene . . .

In the days of peace he had broadened and stabilized the foundations of American life and union. In war he had raised the strength, might and glory of the great Republic to a

*height never attained by any nation in history. With her left
hand she was leading the advance of the conquering Allied
Armies into the heart of Germany, and with her right, on the
other side of the globe, she was irresistibly and swiftly breaking up the power of Japan. And all the time ships, munitions,
supplies, and food of every kind were aiding on a gigantic
scale her Allies, great and small . . .*

*For us it remains only to say that in Franklin Roosevelt
there died the greatest American friend we have ever known,
and the greatest champion of freedom who has ever brought
help and comfort from the New World to the Old.*

When the news of Roosevelt's death reaches the troops on
this April day, the men of two armies have already been
sickened by a great shock. The U.S. Ninth Army has reached
Buchenwald, and the British Second Army Belsen. The Allies
are at last face to face with the New Order in Nazi Germany.
It consists of broken minds, emaciated bodies, degraded spirits. It is like nothing ever seen before in civilization, or in
barbarism either for that matter. For when the first troops
cautiously pass the tall gates of the concentration camps they
enter the confines of hell.

Since Nietzsche's conception of the Superman, the German philosophy of racial superiority has been clear for all
to see. But only since the coming of the Nazis to unques-
tioned power have they been able to practice it. At first their
concentration camps contain only "enemies of the Reich"—
political prisoners, certain types of criminals, a few clergy-
men, prostitutes, liberals and, of course, Jews. But then the
borders of the Reich begin to expand eastward, enveloping
huge territories that can be incorporated into the Fatherland,
once their inferior populations have been annihilated. The
era of slave labor begins and the motive becomes clearer.

Erich Koch, swaggering Reich Commissar for the Ukraine, brags to the people of Kiev, "We are a master race, which must remember that the lowliest German worker is racially and biologically a thousand times more valuable than the population here."

The Germans start the systematic depopulation of whole provinces in Poland, along the Baltic, and in central and southern Russia. Their aim is more than plunder, stretches beyond enslavement. It is the creation of an enormous void in the East into which may flood the masters, the new generations of the *Herrenvolk*. Millions of civilians are shipped westward in cattle trucks to work for Germany in her munitions plants and mines, on her farms, and as servants in her private homes. A small number retain some joy in life, but most are penned like animals to work and die. The slightest infraction of the harsh rules is to be met with what the Germans describe, in a sickening euphemism, as "special treatment." Himmler himself defines the term: "Special treatment is hanging. It should not take place in the immediate vicinity of the camp. A certain number should attend the special treatment." The treatment is to be accorded to any prisoner caught loafing at his (or her) work. It is Hitler who finally makes everything clear. "As for the ridiculous hundred million Slavs," he tells his generals, "we will mold the best of them to the shape that suits us, and we will isolate the rest of them in their own pigsties; and anyone who talks about cherishing the local inhabitant and civilizing him, goes straight off to a concentration camp!"

Against the conventions of Geneva and The Hague, which moderate the usages of war, though it seems ridiculous even to mention them in this context, the Germans set Russian prisoners of war to work, as well as civilians. Hundreds of thousands die of exhaustion, exposure and malnutrition, and many more under the whips and clubs of their SS guards.

Some are so weak when they arrive at the camps for execution that they cannot even walk through the gates, much to the disgust of the SS, who like to be efficient.

Not all the murdered prisoners of war are Russians, either. At the Mauthausen camp forty-seven air force officers, American, British and Dutch, are killed in ingenious fashion. They are taken barefoot to the bottom of a stone quarry, loaded down with sixty-pound boulders and driven up the steps to the top, beaten all the way with clubs. On the next journey the boulders are heavier, the blows more intense. By evening twenty-one of them lie dead on the steps; the rest die next morning.

The clearance of Germany's eastern conquests requires a special organization. The task is given to the Security Service of the SS, the *Sicherheitsdienst*. Four special units are formed and with its usual delicacy the SD christens them Special Action Groups *(Einsatzgruppen)*. They are Extermination Squads A, B, C, and D. Gas vans are issued to them, into which they can cram their victims for asphyxiation. But the vans cannot accommodate the vast numbers awaiting execution, and the Extermination Squads are forced back on older methods, already tried and true. They take recourse to the machine gun and the pistol.

A German engineer, one Hermann Graebe, watches one of these units going about its duties near Dubno in the Ukraine. Great pits have been gouged in the sour earth, but are hidden at first from Graebe by mounds of excavated soil. Under the banks huddle a crowd of people, part of Dubno's population of five thousand Jews. There are men, women and children. All are stark naked.

Graebe gives his account. "An old woman with snow-white hair was holding a one-year-old child in her arms and singing to it and tickling it. The child was cooing with delight. The parents were looking on with tears in their eyes. The father was holding the hand of a boy about ten years old and speaking to him softly; the boy was fighting his tears. The father pointed to the sky, stroked his head and seemed to explain something to him . . . I walked around the mound and found myself confronted by a tremendous grave. People were closely wedged together and lying on top of each other so that only their heads were visible. Nearly all had blood running over their shoulders from their heads. Some of the people were still moving. Some were lifting their arms and turning their heads to show that they were still alive. The pit was already two-thirds full. I estimated that it contained about a thousand people. I looked for the man who did the shooting. He was an SS man, who sat at the edge of the narrow end of the pit, his feet dangling into the pit. He had a tommy gun on his knees and was smoking a cigarette."

On 4 October 1943 Heinrich Himmler tells his SS leaders assembled at Posen "Most of *you* must know what it means when a hundred corpses are lying side by side, or five hundred, or a thousand. To have stuck it out and at the same time—apart from exceptions caused by human weakness—to have remained decent fellows, that is what has made us hard. This is a page of glory in our history which has never been written and is never to be written."

But eventually, in spite of Himmler's prophecy, the page is written. Its statistics alone affright the imagination. Every one of the thirty concentration camps is a death camp. But some are specially designed as extermination camps through which will be achieved what is referred to as "the final solution of the Jewish question."

The outstanding of these is Auschwitz, with its cynical inscription arching over its gate, ARBEIT MACHT FREI. The only road to freedom from Auschwitz runs through poison gas and flame. This is the most successful of all the camps, its four enormous gas chambers and two crematoria are eventually "processing" six thousand Jews a day. Night and day the tall chimneys of the incinerators belch flame and smoke. A fine gray dust floats perpetually over the entire camp and the surrounding countryside.

In Poland four other camps use the same methods as Auschwitz, but on a smaller scale. There are also minor camps in the east, but these rely on shooting, not being equipped with gas chambers, and therefore their labors are less fruitful.

Not only the SD are involved in this nightmare. Rudolf Hoess, infamous commander of Auschwitz, points out, "We were required to carry out these exterminations in secrecy, but of course the foul and nauseating stench from the continuous burning of bodies permeated the entire area and all of the people living in the surrounding communities knew that exterminations were going on at Auschwitz."

So do many German businessmen. The competition for contracts to build the crematoria or furnish the lethal crystals of Zyklon B is in the very best traditions of free enterprise. One ingenious firm in Danzig even boasts a tank designed to make soap out of human fat. The Reichsbank too is involved, for its vaults are soon brimming with banknotes taken from the Jews and bars of gold made from the fillings extracted from their teeth, as well as watches, diamond rings and other valuables. The bank is so embarrassed by this massive deposit that as early as 15 September 1942 it tries to sell a long list of articles to the municipal pawnshop in Berlin. It becomes clear at the Nuremberg Trials that this vast conspiracy to annihilate a race is far from a secret held only by the SS. The entire German nation cannot have helped being aware of the monstrous depravities being practiced in its name; though perhaps it could not publicly protest. It is noteworthy that some of the war criminals handed over to the Germans for justice were never brought to trial, and in fact a few were appointed to positions in the Bonn Government.

In April 1945, with Buchenwald liberated, Lieutenant Colonel Martin Lindsay hears a story from one of his officers. "Bruce tells me that quite a nice young German hospital nurse came to see him in his Company H.Q. He showed her the pictures of the Buchenwald concentration camp. She looked horrified, then suddenly her face cleared. 'But it's only the Jews,' she said."

Everywhere in Germany the Allied troops prepare grimly for the final act. At last they have witnessed with their own eyes the true nature of the enemy. No words of propaganda or explanation could expunge the burning memory of walking skeletons, of corpses ripped open so that the liver can be cut out and eaten, of children with the faces of aged idiots, of butcher's hooks in rows in the blood-stained torture chambers, of naked women dead in their own excrement and vomit. Here is the reality behind the myth, here the true face of the Master Race. Americans and British drive for Berlin with holy anger in their hearts. The Thousand Year Reich bursts open in decay and rottenness.

THE LAST
JUDGMENT

'Tis the Last Judgment's fire must cure this place,
Calcine its clods and set my people free.
ROBERT BROWNING: *Childe Roland to the Dark*
Tower Came

UNDER THE blazing whiteness of the single enormous light
the surgeon's eyes are strained and hooded. His forehead is
beaded with sweat, and his cheek beneath the mask twitches
occasionally. The faces round him are intent, frozen with
concentration on the white-shrouded shape stretched along
the operating table. There is a faint hiss of gas, a quiet
rhythmic intake and expulsion of breath. Now and then the
surgeon calls for an instrument or comments briefly to his
assistant in German. His brow wrinkles with anxiety, partly
for his patient, but more for himself.

His patient is squat, bulky with muscle. His peasant face
has a flat oriental cast, with slanted eyes and snub nose. It
is not a cruel face, though it is utterly alien. He is a Siberian
cavalryman, one of the troops who stormed Vienna. In his
stomach gapes a deep knife wound which now the surgeon is

struggling to suture. How he suffered it is a mystery; all the surgeon can hope for is that he will recover. For Vienna is now gripped in the full rigor of Soviet Military Law, and the death of a soldier of the Red Army is a shooting matter.

The last bandage is secured. The operating robe is removed from the stocky patient, and the theatre is filled with a tiny babel of ticking. On each of his forearms are securely strapped six watches which, before succumbing to the anaesthetic, he forbade the nurse to remove on pain of death.

Vienna falls to the Red Army on 13 April 1945. The same day they have advanced to within 35 miles of Berlin, and stand along the last defended line in the entire Reich, the River Oder. They prepare for the assault for three days, and on 16 April flood across it. As their forward units fan out on the far bank, Hitler issues his last Order of the Day. It reads:

> Soldiers of the German front in the east!
> The hordes of our Judeo-Bolshevist foe have rallied for the last assault. They want to destroy Germany and to extinguish our people. You, soldiers of the east, have seen with your own eyes what fate awaits German women and children: the aged, the men, the infants, are murdered, the German women and girls defiled and made into barrack whores. The rest are marched to Siberia.
> We have been waiting for this assault. Since January every step has been taken to raise a strong eastern front. Colossal artillery forces are welcoming the enemy. Countless new units are replacing our losses. Troops of every kind hold our front.
> Once again, Bolshevism will suffer Asia's old fate—it will founder on the capital of the German Reich.
> He who at this moment does not do his duty is a traitor to the German nation. The regiments or divisions that relinquish their posts are acting so disgracefully that they must hang their heads in shame before the women and children who here in our cities are braving the terror bombing.
> ... If during these next days and weeks every soldier in the east does his duty, Asia's final onslaught will come to nought—just as the invasion of our Western enemies will in the end fail.
> Berlin stays German. Vienna will be German again. And Europe will never be Russian!
> Rise up to defend your homes, your women, your children—rise up to defend your own future!

At this hour the eyes of the German nation are upon you, you, my fighters in the east, hoping that your steadfastness, your ardor, and your arms will smother the Bolshevist attack in a sea of blood!

This moment, which has removed from the face of the earth the greatest war criminal of all ages [President Roosevelt], will decide the turn in the fortunes of war!

Adolf Hitler

Nine days later the Russians have surrounded Berlin. Seventy-five miles south of that ruined city the Americans too are advancing. Just as the steel pincers of Russian armor close mercilessly round the city, patrols of the U.S. 69th Division are warily approaching Torgau on the Elbe. In the distance they see green-clad figures coming from the east. They are the forward units of Marshal Konev's crack 58th Soviet Guards Division. Soldiers of both forces rush forward to embrace one another. The Allies are joined at last in the very heart of Germany.

Hitler's minions are beginning to desert him. Himmler and Goering are already attempting to make peace. General William B. Quinn, who later interrogates Goering, describes the manner of his defection: "On approximately 22 April, Hermann Goering, who was in Berchtesgaden at that time, telegraphed Adolf Hitler and indicated to him that although the war was not yet over, if anything happened to Hitler he, Goering, would take over as Fuehrer. He suggested to Hitler that he, Goering, negotiate with the Americans for the surrender of the German forces. This made Hitler furious. Finally he ordered the SS people to look into Berchtesgaden and arrest Goering, which they did. The SS took Goering to a villa near Berchtesgaden, but Martin Bormann, Hitler's deputy, ordered Goering assassinated. It so happened that Goering had some friends, too. His *Luftwaffe* people replaced the SS, whereupon Goering was saved for a short while. After

GERMANY OCCUPIED

Occupation Zones as Agreed Upon at Quebec

Occupation Zones as Finally Adopted

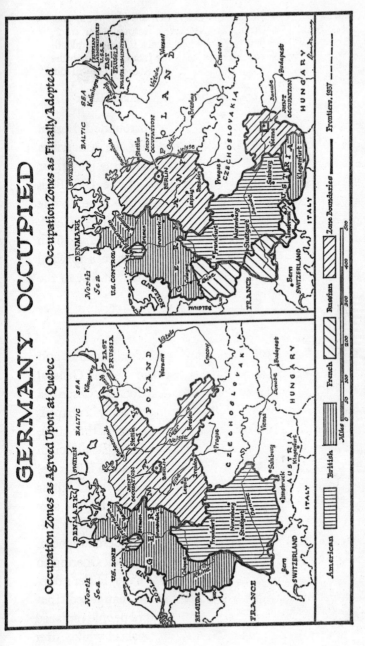

American ▦ British ▥ French ▨ Russian ▨ Zone Boundaries —— Frontiers, 1937 ——

Though the actual occupation zones differ from those envisaged at the Quebec Conference, the Allies find that their aims have been realized. A major difference is the inclusion of France as an occupying power. Britain, the United States and France are to share the occupation of the western part of Germany. In the east, Russia begins to build her iron curtain.

the *Luftwaffe* had rescued Goering he sent a message to General Eisenhower through an agent. It was read by General Patch, and General Patch said, 'He is not going to see Eisenhower. If he wants to surrender he can surrender like any other person.' Whereupon Goering decided to do exactly that. A few days later he drove in in a beautiful sports limousine and gave himself up. He then became the two hundred and forty-ninth distinguished guest in my prisoner of war camp."

Himmler is more subtle. He is already in touch with Count Folke Bernadotte, vice-chairman of the Swedish Red Cross and nephew of King Gustavus V of Sweden. Bernadotte has been arranging the repatriation of British and German prisoners of war, and is thus in communication with both London and Berlin. When Hitler decides to stay in Berlin to the last, Himmler dispatches an aide to Bernadotte with a message reporting that Hitler is dying of a cerebral hemorrhage, announcing that he has assumed all powers, and suggesting a meeting with Bernadotte at Lübeck on the Baltic. At one o'clock on the morning of 24 April Himmler makes his offer. He will surrender all German forces in the west at once. But only in the west. Count Bernadotte relays this message to the Allies.

Churchill's response is to forward the news at once to President Truman and Marshal Stalin. The latter's reply surprises him. It is "the most cordial message I ever had from him" and contains an unusual sentiment: "I consider your proposal to present to Himmler a demand for unconditional surrender on all fronts, including the Soviet front, the only correct one. Knowing you, I had no doubt you would act in this way . . ."

Thereupon the Allies return to Himmler through Count Folke Bernadotte a formal demand for unconditional surrender on all fronts. No more is heard from the master of the

SS until after the cease-fire has sounded. On 22 May a non-descript figure in civilian clothes, flat-chested and stoop-shouldered, is being put through a routine check at a British control post. His papers are not in order. Questioned further, the man reveals he is Heinrich Himmler. Doctors are called at once to examine him, but as they search him they hear a faint crunch. There is a whiff of almonds. The pale pig eyes behind the spectacles glaze, the back arches in an agonized spasm. After twelve minutes, in spite of stomach pumps and emetics, the most barbarous individual of modern times is dead. He has bitten on a tiny phial of cyanide hidden in a false tooth. The gallows have been cheated.

One by one the lords of Fascism sink down into the abyss. Benito Mussolini, already forgotten, has come to the last days of his pitiful Republic of Salo. With the Allies advancing north of the River Po and Italian partisans swarming over northern Italy, he cowers with the remnants of his government on the bank of Lake Garda. On the evening of 25 April a convoy of trucks and cars leaves his headquarters for Como. There the Duce joins a column of German transport heading for the Swiss frontier. He is made to wear a German helmet and an ill-fitting greatcoat as disguise in case of an encounter with partisans. But the ruse is ineffectual.

With his mistress Clara Petacci beside him, he waits for deliverance or death. At 6:50 A.M. on 27 April the German column is halted by a roadblock in a little place called Musso. There is a brief skirmish with the partisans, but the convoy moves on. It is stopped again further down the road, and there Mussolini is finally recognized. He and his mistress are taken to a white farmhouse and held captive that night. Next afternoon their executioner arrives, introducing himself as Colonel Valerian.

His real name is Walter Audisio; he is an officer of the Committee of National Liberation and a Communist party member. He drives his wretched prisoners to a villa not far away and there makes them stand against a rough stone wall. He pronounces sentence: "By order of the general command of the *Corpo Voluntari della Liberta*, I am charged with rendering justice to the Italian people." He raises his submachine gun. There is an ineffectual click. He draws a heavy pistol. It too jams. Reaching behind him, Audisio snatches another submachine gun from one of the partisans. Its barrel is decorated with a neat red ribbon. It cracks out in a long burst.

The bodies are carried by night in a truck to Milan with a group of partisans standing on them. When the sun comes up they are hoisted head down on meat hooks fastened to a girder in a gas station on the Piazzale Loreto. The sometime ruler of an empire is reduced to carrion.

For Hitler, too, the eternal night is drawing near. Germany is in the dark grasp of a Twilight of the Gods, the Götterdämmerung celebrated by Wagner, whose thunderous compositions provide Hitler's favorite music. As Mussolini's bloated corps swing ignominiously in Milan, Russian troops are skirmishing in the streets of Berlin. They burn or blast with high explosives everything in their path. Flamethrowers, tanks, light artillery, scorch and shatter house after house, street after street. Their patrols infiltrate the subway system, reappearing suddenly with grenades and Tommy guns behind the German defenses. Systematically, inexorably, they take the proud city into their clutch. Though the remnants of the Wehrmacht fight on dourly in scattered detachments without panic, the terror of the civilians grows into hysteria.

Else Wendel, a housewife, is trying to calm her two small sons when the Russians come. Sitting in the cellar reading to

370] WINSTON CHURCHILL: THE VALIANT YEARS

the boys by candlelight, she hears suddenly a thunder of blows on the door. She lets in two Russian soldiers, who begin to search the house, one of them covering her all the time with his rifle. "Now they wished to see the cellar," Mrs. Wendel says. "The staircase was dark as the electricity was cut off. I could sense the Russian behind me becoming nervous. Then I felt the gun pressed against my neck. It was a clear warning that if I was leading them into a trap, I should fall first! I opened the door into the cellar. A candle was burning there, and the two small boys were standing with their mouths wide open and staring at me and the soldiers. They looked so thin and pale and frightened they might have been carved out of stone. Immediately the Russian saw them, he took the gun off my neck and broke into loud laughter. 'Oh, children!' he shouted. The other Russian smiled and let his rifle drop to his side. Then he turned to me and indicated that the search was off, and I was to return upstairs with them. Actually I was more nervous on the way upstairs than on the way down. In reaction, my legs shook so much I nearly fell twice on the steps. They took me outside the house and stood me up against the door post, aimed and shot —not *at* me, but to each side of me. Then they turned and left me standing there, turned to stone now, in relief and astonishment."

Russian shells are already falling in the garden of the Reich Chancellery, where Hitler awaits the end in his massive bunker. Late at night on 28 April the Fuehrer learns of Himmler's defection, rather circuitously, from a BBC radio report. He utters a single animal cry of anger and frustration. Next day the Russians reach the Potsdammerplatz, a block from the Chancellery. Their next attack will bring them to the doors of the bunker itself. Hitler begins to settle his affairs.

•   •   •

Between midnight and three o'clock on the morning of 29 April he marries Eva Braun, his docile, devoted and apparently rather stupid mistress. After the ceremony, conducted hurriedly, but with such formality as the bureaucratic observance provides, a wedding breakfast is laid out. It will also serve as a funeral feast. No amount of fond recollection of the good old days in Nuremberg and Munich can obscure the fact that Berlin has become a purgatory in which all present are caught and must suffer. Hitler quietly leaves, calls a secretary, and begins to dictate his last will and his testament, to the German people.

The latter begins with a typical perversion of the truth. "It is untrue that I or anybody else in Germany wanted war in 1939. It was wanted and provoked exclusively by those international statesmen who either were of Jewish origin or worked for Jewish interests. I have made too many offers for the limitation and control of armaments, which posterity will not for all time be able to disregard, for responsibility for the outbreak of this war to be placed on me. Further, I have never wished that after the appalling First World War there should be a second one against either England or America. Centuries will go by, but from the ruins of our towns and monuments the hatred of those ultimately responsible will always grow anew. They are the people whom we have to thank for all this: international Jewry and its helpers."

Hitler then explains why he has chosen to stay in Berlin. "After six years of war, which in spite of all setbacks will one day go down in history as the most glorious and heroic manifestation of the struggle for the existence of a nation, I cannot forsake the city that is the capital of this state . . . I wish to share my fate with that which millions of others have taken upon themselves by staying in this town. Further, I shall not fall in the hands of the enemy, who requires a new spectacle, presented by the Jews, to divert their hysterical masses." His last instruction to those who will succeed him as rulers of Germany is, "Above all, I enjoin the government and the people to uphold the racial laws to the limit and to resist mercilessly the poisoner of all nations, international Jewry."

The Fuehrer's will is a simpler document. After a brief review of his obscure origins and subsequent rise to supreme power, it gives his reasons for marrying thus belatedly, and explains why he and his one-day bride are about to kill themselves. As to his personal fortune, which is not large—"My possessions, insofar as they are worth anything, belong to the party, or, if this no longer exists, to the State. If the State too is destroyed, there is no need for any further instructions on my part. The paintings in the collections bought by me during the years were never assembled for private purposes but solely for the establishment of a picture gallery in my home town of Linz on the Danube."

Dawn is breaking as Hitler finishes these two valedictory messages. It is a red dawn, harsh with fire from the blazing streets of Berlin. Overhead dense black clouds of smoke billow and drift between the ravaged earth and the sullen sky. It is Sunday.

By noon the Russians have reached the Wilhelmstrasse and the approaches to the Chancellery. Here, Teutonically methodical, Hitler and the bizarre survivors of his staff are holding a council of war in accordance with their usual custom. There is really very little to discuss, and nothing at all to decide. The initiative in every decision but one has been taken away. However, Hitler is able to issue one final message, which places the blame for this defeat on the Army and the General Staff. It ends, "The efforts and sacrifices of the German people in this war have been so great that I cannot believe that they have been in vain. The aim must still be to win territory in the East for the German people."

The last act of the melodrama opens. Hitler's pet Alsatian, Blondi, is poisoned by injection, a macabre gesture. At 2:30 A.M. the Fuehrer leaves his private suite to bid farewell to his personal staff. At noon there is another lunatic military conference. After it Hitler lunches alone, while his chauffeur is carrying a hundred and eighty liters of gasoline to an emergency exit leading to the garden fifty feet above.

In mid-afternoon on Monday, 30 April, Hitler and his new wife take their own lives, she by means of a poison capsule, he with a pistol shot in the mouth. He has been twelve years and three months in power. He was fifty-six years and ten days old.

The two bodies, hidden by blankets (one of them bloody), are carried into the garden, now under regular bombardment by Russian artillery. They are dumped in a shellhole, flooded with gasoline, and ignited. A few mourners, black silhouettes against the gouts of flame, stand stiffly at the salute, Nazi fashion. But these obsequies are brief indeed, for almost at once a new deluge of shellfire screams into the garden from the Russian lines now drawn tight about the bunker.

Hitler's nominee as ruler of the Third Reich at this moment of its departure into history is Grand Admiral Doenitz. His appointment is a final insult to the German Army. On the very day he succeeds to such powers as are left, Doenitz receives news of the unconditional surrender of all German forces in Italy. A million men have laid down their arms. He knows that resistance is at an end. On 3 May he sends his emissaries to seek terms.

Field Marshal Montgomery's headquarters have been set up on Luneburg Heath. The bulky caravans are neatly drawn up and camouflaged, and there is the usual orderly bustle of a nerve center. In the middle of the caravans there is an open space, like a lawn, where a flagpole has been set up. A fresh breeze is making the Union Jack flutter bravely. Shortly before lunch a party, led by General-Admiral von Friedeburg (Commander-in-Chief of the German Navy), arrives and asks for the Field Marshal.

Montgomery recalls, "They were brought to my caravan site and were drawn up under the Union Jack . . . I kept them waiting for a few minutes and then came out of my caravan and walked towards them. They all saluted, under the Union Jack. It was a great moment; I knew the Germans had come to surrender and that the war was over. Few of those in the signals and operations caravans at my Tac head-quarters will forget the thrill experienced when they heard the faint 'tapping' of the Germans trying to pick us up on the wireless command link—to receive the surrender instructions from their delegation. I said to my interpreter, 'Who are these men?' He told me. I then said, 'What do they want?'"

What they want is to surrender to the British the three German armies now retreating before the Russian armies of the north. Montgomery refuses to accept the offer. "Von Friedeburg said it was unthinkable to surrender to the Russians as they were savages, and the German soldiers would be sent straight off to Russia. I said the Germans should have thought of all these things before they began the war, and particularly before they attacked the Russians in June, 1941." Montgomery suggests an alternative. He will accept the surrender of all German troops on his western and northern flanks as a tactical surrender on the battlefield; this will give him control of Denmark. Von Friedeburg and his staff leave to consult their superiors.

Next day, 4 May, they are back again. They meet Montgomery's demands and sign the Instrument of Surrender. "The document was in English," Montgomery writes, "and the delegation could not understand it; but I gave them copies in German . . . The original is typed on an ordinary sheet of army foolscap. I was asked to forward it to Supreme Headquarters. Instead I sent photostat copies. The original is in my possession and I will never part with it; it is a historic document. I do not know what happened to the pen we all used; I suppose someone pinched it."

From Luneburg, von Friedeburg proceeds humbly to Rheims. There, in a little red schoolhouse, General Walter Bedell Smith, General Eisenhower's Chief of Staff, awaits him. He says, "Our preparations for the forthcoming negotiations included preparation of a fictitious map on a small scale such as you would find in a high school geography book. But it showed the whole front and the correct location of all our divisions, and all of the German divisions as we knew them. It was fictitious, however, in that it included a large striking force with a line indicating an attack to join up with the Russians. When Admiral von Friedeburg told me that he was without authority to sign, but was simply there in the guise of a negotiator, I noticed that at the same time his eyes wandered to this map. So I picked it up and handed it to him. He looked at it for a moment or two and tears began to run down his cheeks. He went into the room where our communication facilities were available for him, and of course we monitored the conversation. The principal part of this was the statement that what they (the Germans) had hoped to accomplish was no longer possible, and that the only alternative to a debacle was immediate surrender."

At this Supreme Headquarters, on 7 May 1945, the Germans bow their heads and at last accept what they cannot avoid. General Eisenhower sends a signal to the Combined Chiefs of Staff, reporting, "The mission of this Allied Force was fulfilled at 3 A.M., local time, 7 May 1945. Eisenhower."

All hostilities cease at 2301 hours on 8 May 1945, and a few hours later the surrender terms are formally ratified in Berlin.

In England the word passes on 8 May that the Prime Minister will be making a broadcast to the nation. The evening is warm and light as people gather and wait, knowing what the news will be, but holding back their excitement until Churchill announces it. Not a soul is stirring in the entire island when the BBC announcer introduces the Prime Minister. It is a simple statement, without oratory. *Hostilities will end officially at one minute after midnight tonight, Tuesday the 8th of May,* Churchill tells the people, . . . *but in the interest of saving lives the first cease-fire began yesterday and was sounded along all the fronts. The German War is therefore at an end. We may allow ourselves a brief period of rejoicing.*

The unconditional surrender of our enemies was the signal for the greatest outburst of joy in the history of mankind, Churchill later writes. *The Second World War had indeed been fought to the bitter end in Europe. The vanquished as well as the victors felt inexpressible relief. But for us in Britain and the British Empire, who had alone been in the struggle from the first day to the last and staked our existence on the result, there was a meaning beyond what even our most powerful and most valiant Allies could feel. Weary and worn, impoverished but undaunted and now triumphant, we had a moment that was sublime. We gave thanks to God for the noblest of all His blessings, the sense that we had done our duty.*

In this joyous moment of victory President Truman sends Churchill a message of congratulation. As part of his reply the Prime Minister pays tribute to the Supreme Commander. *Let me tell you what General Eisenhower has meant to us.*

In him we have had a man who set the unity of the Allied Armies above all nationalistic thoughts. In his headquarters unity and strategy were the only reigning spirits. The unity reached such a point that British and American troops could be mixed in the line of battle and large masses could be transferred from one command to the other without the slightest difficulty. At no time has the principle of alliance between noble races been carried and maintained at so high a pitch. In the name of the British Empire and Commonwealth I express to you our admiration of the firm, farsighted, and illuminating character and qualities of General of the Army Eisenhower.

But when the first hours of delirium have begun to fade, Churchill speaks at length to the British of what is in his heart, in a solemn broadcast. He recounts the course of his five years' Ministry, retracing the long road from the disasters of 1940 to this triumphant summer of 1945. He celebrates the victory over Germany, yet feels bound to warn of difficulties yet to be overcome.

I wish, he says, I could tell you tonight that all our toils and our troubles were over. Then indeed I could end my five years' service happily, and if you thought that you had had enough of me and that I ought to be put out to grass I would take it with the best of grace. But, on the contrary, I must warn you, as I did when I began this five years' task . . . that there is still a lot to do, and that you must be prepared for further efforts of mind and body and further sacrifices to great causes if you are not to fall back into the rut of inertia, the confusion of aim, and the craven fear of being great. You must not weaken in any way in your alert and vigilant frame of mind.

On the continent of Europe we have yet to make sure that the simple and honorable purposes for which we entered the war are not brushed aside or overlooked in the

months following our success, and that the words "freedom,"
"democracy," and "liberation" are not distorted from their true
meaning as we have understood them. There would be little
use in punishing the Hitlerites for their crimes if law and
justice did not rule, and if totalitarian or police governments
were to take the place of the German invaders. We seek
nothing for ourselves. But we must make sure that those
causes which we fought for find recognition at the peace
table in facts as well as words, and above all we must labor
to insure that the world organization which the United
Nations are creating at San Francisco does not become an
idle name, does not become a shield for the strong and a
mockery for the weak. It is the victors who must search their
hearts in their glowing hours, and be worthy by their nobility
of the immense forces that they wield.

We must never forget that beyond all lurks Japan, harassed and falling, but still a people of a hundred millions,
for whose warriors death has few terrors . . . We are bound
by the ties of honor and fraternal loyalty to the United
States to fight this great war at the other end of the world
at their side without flagging or failing. We must remember
that Australia and New Zealand and Canada were and are
all directly menaced by this evil power. These Dominions
came to our aid in our dark times, and we must not leave
unfinished any task which concerns their safety and their
future. I told you hard things at the beginning of these last
five years; you did not shrink, and I should be unworthy of
your confidence and generosity if I did not still cry: Forward,
unflinching, unswerving, indomitable, till the whole task is
done and the whole world is safe and clean.

EPISODE **25**

FAREWELL, MR. CHURCHILL

The genius of a good leader is to leave behind him a situation which common sense, without the grace of genius, can deal with successfully.
WALTER LIPPMANN

WHEN THE WAR in Europe ends, a significant percentage of the population of England has never exercised its right to vote. There has been no opportunity. The Conservative Government formed after the General Election of 1935 survives the outbreak of war, then in the crisis of 1940 becomes a national coalition of all parties under Winston Churchill. In 1945, ten years after that Election, the British are beginning to feel it is time to have another. Particularly so if they happen to be young men who have risked their lives for their country without ever having been able to have some say in the constitution of its government.

In the jungles of Malaya and the burning plain towns of

379

the Deccan, in ships cleaving the green waters off Zanzibar, on airfields from Iceland to Kano, in barracks and tents and trenches scattered across three continents, the young men of Britain are impatient for their democratic rights. The politicians are quick to recognize the mood. Nor is it confined to the Services. Millions of workers have toiled unquestioning throughout the war; now they must have a voice in the future of their country. The years of fighting are over, or nearly so: the years of postwar reconstruction are about to begin. Party politics are reborn the moment the lights are switched on again in Piccadilly Circus.

It is yet another burden for the tired shoulders of the Prime Minister. At the German surrender he is concerned about three things: Russian imperialism in Europe, the defeat of Japan, and the growing partisanship of his colleagues in the House of Commons. Of these, the attitude of the Soviet Union is to Churchill the most pressing and the one most fraught with future dangers. Even in his victory address to the nation on 10 May he sounds a warning. The same day he cables his fears to President Truman, coining, to express them, a phrase immortal in its aptness and its ominous imagery. Speaking of the Russian forces in Europe he says, *An iron curtain is drawn down upon their front. We do not know what is going on behind . . . Meanwhile the attention of our peoples will be occupied in inflicting severities upon Germany, which is ruined and prostrate, and it would be open to the Russians in a very short time to advance if they chose to the waters of the North Sea and the Atlantic. Surely it is vital now to come to an understanding with Russia, or see where we are with her, before we weaken our armies mortally or retire to the zones of occupation. This can only be done by a personal meeting. I should be most grateful for your opinion and advice. Of course we may take the view that Russia will behave impeccably, and no doubt that*

offers the most convenient solution. To sum up, this issue
of a settlement with Russia before our strength has gone
seems to me to dwarf all others.

Arrangements are set in train for a conference of the three
major powers in Berlin. Meanwhile, in England what Churchill calls "the odor of dissolution" is growing stronger. He himself has publicly suggested an election at the end of the war
with Germany. Conservative, Labor and Liberal members,
and the handful of independents too, are anxious to dissolve
the present Parliament and start an election campaign for the
new government that will have the people's mandate to
undertake the building of postwar Britain.

The tide of party loyalties and differences of political
opinion swells into a flood. The right to recommend the
dissolution of Parliament rests with the Prime Minister. In
the two weeks following V-E Day, Churchill becomes more
and more certain that this is what he must do. On 23 May
he seeks audience of the King and tenders his resignation,
an act that marks the end of an era.

Churchill is asked to form a "Caretaker Government,"
which he does with Conservative members and their allies.
It will continue the government until the results of the
election are known. Polling day is set for 5 July, but since
the Forces' vote must be sent home for counting from places
as far away as Mandalay, the declaration of the results cannot be made until 26 July, twenty-one days later. *In several*
Continental countries, when it was known that the ballot
boxes would be in charge of the British Government for
three weeks, astonishment was expressed that there could be
any doubt about the result, Churchill comments. *However,*
in our country these matters are treated exactly as if they
were a cricket match, or other sporting event. Long may it
so continue.

"Mr. Churchill was always basically and fundamentally

a House of Commons man," observes Sir Leslie Rowan, the Prime Minister's private secretary. "He took the view that no government could carry out its policies effectively unless it could show that it had the full support of the House of Commons. Now this, of course, involved a fairly rigid discipline, and he was prepared, because he believed in the House of Commons and in the way it worked, to accept that discipline whether in war or in peace." Churchill plunges into the turmoil of an election battle, stumping the country with as many as four major speeches a day, and in the end near exhaustion with the double duty of leading his country and his party as well.

Two days after polling day he leaves with his wife and daughter for a brief holiday in France. For too short a time he spends the mornings reading in bed and the afternoons with his paintbox and easel. But from time to time as he searches for a color that will express the vivid panorama of the Bay of St. Jean de Luz spreading before him, his hand hesitates and his mind wanders uncomfortably back to the secrets lying in the ballot boxes. What will be the outcome when the boxes are opened and the tally is made? To what fate will those pieces of anonymous paper consign him and all he has worked and suffered for?

Rested, but by no means recovered, Churchill flies from Bordeaux to Berlin on 15 July. His first day there is spent threading the chaos of her shattered streets and visiting the ruins of the Chancellery and the Fuehrer's bunker. He is shown the room in which Hitler shot himself, and the crater in which his corpse was roughly cremated. He then goes off to a lighter duty, the ceremonial opening of a club for the Desert Rats, the men of the famous armored division that has fought all the way from Alamein. *Some three or four hundred of them were gathered in the club,* Churchill records. *They all sang "For He's a Jolly Good Fellow," and were*

entirely friendly. I thought I detected a certain air of sheep-
ishness, which might be due to most of them having voted
adversely.

The Potsdam Conference opens. Stalin arrives escorted
by a score of dark-uniformed NKVD guards carrying Tommy
guns at the ready. President Truman's car is watched over by
half a dozen Secret Service men in civilian clothes cut generously enough to disguise—or almost to disguise—the bulges
of automatics in shoulder holsters. The Prime Minister's
bodyguard rides beside the chauffeur. He is a lance corporal
of the Royal Marines, and he is armed with an antique bayonet eighteen inches long.

The principal business of the Conference is to discuss the
political and economic problems of Germany under Allied
occupation, and to try finally to settle the delineation of
Poland's frontiers. It has scarcely begun when there comes
news that is to change the face of the earth. Churchill receives it in the form of a slip of paper from the Americans.
On it is the cryptic message, "Babies satisfactorily born."
Henry Stimson, the dependable American Secretary of War,
quickly explains. The experiment in the desert of New
Mexico is a success. The atom bomb has been born.

To this moment, no one has known what might happen at
this first nuclear test. Sir Geoffrey Taylor, one of the British
scientists working on the project, describes it. "Our uncertainty was reflected in the bets which were made at Los
Alamos on the amount of energy to be released. These
ranged from zero to the equivalent of eighty thousand tons
of T.N.T. . . . We arrived about three o'clock in the morning
at a spot twenty miles from the hundred-foot tower on which
the bomb was mounted . . . We were provided with a strip
of very dark glass to protect our eyes. This glass is so dark
that at midday it makes the sun look like a little undeveloped
dull green potato . . . At exactly the expected moment, I saw

through the dark glass a brilliant ball of fire which was far brighter than the sun. In a second or two it died down to a brightness which seemed to be about that of the sun, so, realizing that it must be lighting up the countryside, I looked behind me and saw the scrub-covered hills, twenty-two miles from the bomb, lighted up as though by a midday sun. Then I turned around and looked directly at the ball of fire. I saw it expand slowly, and begin to rise, growing fainter as it rose. Later it developed into a huge mushroom-shaped cloud, and soon reached a height of forty thousand feet . . . the whole effect was so staggering that I found it difficult to believe my eyes."

Here, obviously, is the means to end the Japanese war at once, decisively, and at little cost to the Allies. Churchill has been expecting the casualty list in the eighteen-month final struggle with Japan to reach a million Americans and at least half that number of British. Now the carnage can be avoided, at least on the Allied side. In such circumstances the decision whether to use the atom bomb is never raised as an issue. In fact, there is no real decision made (in the sense that one of several possible courses of action is chosen). The bomb exists as fact; it is tacitly accepted that it will be used. The explosions at Hiroshima and Nagasaki will usher civilization overnight into a new age. Henceforth when tension arises between nations the question will be not so much whether an issue warrants a declaration of war, as whether or not humanity shall commit suicide.

Towards the end of the first week of the Conference it falls to the British delegation to entertain at a banquet. Stalin is in high spirits. Suddenly he seizes a menu and to everyone's astonishment begins to walk round the table inviting all the guests to sign it. When the Prime Minister's turn comes he signs happily, then decides to offer a challenge . . . *I have mentioned before how the toasts at these*

banquets were always drunk by the Soviet representatives
out of tiny glasses, and Stalin had never varied from this
practice. But now I thought I would take him on a step. So
I filled a small-sized claret glass with brandy for him and
another for myself. I looked at him significantly. We both
drained our glasses at a stroke and gazed approvingly at one
another.

On the afternoon of 25 July Churchill flies home to await
the outcome of the Election, and so does Attlee, who has
been sitting beside him and who will, if all goes well for
the Labor Party, succeed him in office. The Conservative
Central Office is certain of victory. Comforted, Churchill
goes to sleep reasonably confident of a mandate from the
people to carry on his leadership. *However,* he writes, *just*
before dawn I woke suddenly with a sharp stab of almost
physical pain. A hitherto subconscious conviction that we
were beaten broke forth and dominated my mind . . . The
power to shape the future would be denied me. The knowl-
edge and experience I had gathered, the authority and good-
will I had gained in so many countries would vanish. I was
discontented at the prospect, and turned over at once to
sleep again. I did not wake till nine o'clock, and when I went
into the Map Room the first results had begun to come in.
They were, as I now expected, unfavorable. By noon it was
clear that the Socialists would have a majority. At luncheon
my wife said to me, "It will be a blessing in disguise." I re-
plied, "At the moment it seems quite effectively disguised."

Sir Robert Boothby, himself a Conservative member, is
present during this scene. Afterwards he seeks an explanation of this apparent disinheritance of Churchill by the
people: "It should not be forgotten that in the 1945 election
Churchill had to bear . . . the whole brunt of the misdeeds
of the Government before the war, presided over successively
by Mr. Baldwin and Mr. Neville Chamberlain. That was a

Government that reduced a great country and a great Empire from a position of absolute security and world power to the brink of total destruction within a decade. It took the Roman Empire two hundred years of quite enjoyable decadence to achieve the same result."

J. B. Priestley, a member of the opposite faction, also presents a view of the reasons for Churchill's fall. "Many people all over the world were surprised and disappointed when Churchill lost the election in 1945. But they had the wrong view. They were thinking of it as a contest between personalities, as if Winston Churchill were fighting Clement Attlee. But of course it wasn't like that at all. It was two great political parties who were fighting this contest. And the fact was that the majority of the British electorate didn't want the Tories back again. They had been there for many years before the war. Now there was a new spirit, and people felt the Labor Party better embodied that spirit."

That very afternoon Churchill once more craves audience of the King, tenders his resignation and advises His Majesty, as is the custom, to send for Mr. Attlee. After five years of unparalleled service he is once more a private citizen. At the moment of total triumph he has been denied the fruits. He issues a last message to the nation he has served with such love and such genius.

The decision of the British people has been recorded in the votes counted today. I have therefore laid down the charge which was placed upon me in darker times. I regret that I have not been permitted to finish the work against Japan. For this however all plans and preparations have been made, and the results may come much quicker than we have hitherto been entitled to expect. Immense responsibilities abroad and at home fall upon the new Government, and we must all hope that they will be successful in bearing them.

It only remains for me to express to the British people, for

whom I have acted in these perilous years, my profound
gratitude for the unflinching, unswerving support which they
have given me during my task, and for the many expressions
of kindness which they have shown towards their servant.

Next day Churchill completes his preparations for a holiday abroad. He entertains his personal staff and a few close
friends for lunch. There is champagne. The glasses are filled.
At the head of the table Churchill rises. Once more the formidable jaw thrusts out. His level eyes sweep round the
room. He raises his glass, the bubbles dancing golden and
joyful in it, and offers a toast: *To the future!*

INDEX

INDEX